True Nordic

How Scandinavia Influenced Design in Canada

black dog publishing
london uk

Published on the occasion of the exhibition
True Nordic: How Scandinavia Influenced Design in Canada

Gardiner Museum
111 Queen's Park, Toronto, Ontario M5S 2C7
October 13, 2016 to January 8, 2017

New Brunswick Museum
1 Market Square, Saint John, New Brunswick E2L 4Z6
March 3 to September 5, 2017

Vancouver Art Gallery
750 Hornby Street, Vancouver, British Columbia V6Z 2H7
October 21, 2017 to January 21, 2018

Curated by Rachel Gotlieb and Michael Prokopow
Exhibition and publication organized by the Gardiner Museum, Toronto

Copy editor: Paula Sarson

Contents

Preface

Kelvin Browne

Director & CEO Gardiner Museum

Growing up in the 1960s in the interior of British Columbia, the latest trends in design were rather distant to an aspiring architect like me, except for one, Scandinavian modern. Prior to its arrival, modern design was not popular when it infrequently surfaced as the chrome and leather seating in office lobbies; no one I knew then would dream of having this kind of modern in their home. However, the arrival of a sleek, contemporary *Danish* dining-room set, made of *solid* teak at a house a few doors away provoked much talk—it was new but not the disparaged functional modern—and soon the style began to appear everywhere in town. When I subsequently went to high school in Winnipeg and then university in Toronto, I realized that the Scandinavian trend had this kind of impact across the country.

I'm sure the new dining room of our neighbours while teak was likely made in Canada, but for my parents the point was it was Scandinavian. That it was contemporary and unlike any of the aspirational English furniture they owned didn't seem to faze them. The wood was so beautiful, the craftsmanship so obvious, and the fabric on the seats so practical that it seemed impossible for them not to want it. In some ways, modernism packaged by Scandinavia was the Trojan Horse of contemporary—my parents were never conscious that they were inadvertently avant-garde by embracing it.

I don't know if our neighbours knew much about Scandinavia, I doubt it, and I don't believe there was a desire to travel there or otherwise understand where this new style came from. Scandinavia was northern like Canada, some speculated even colder than Canada in winter, and they were probably very sincere people given their love of wood, ceramics, and things made by hand. I recall the sense that we thought Danes or Finns or whomever, even if we didn't know them, were sort of like us albeit they cross-country skied to work and were far more fit, or so we imagined, with the emphasis on *imagined*. Maybe this sense of kinship, however illusory, gave a friendly connection to the design style that didn't come with American-inspired modern furnishings, for instance. Did we believe our values were more aligned with those of Scandinavia than our much more proximate US neighbours?

I recently bought a Danish dining-room set, made in Denmark circa 1950. Its relatively modest scale is ideal for a small dining room, and its calm, unfussy lines at ease with a simple, old house where it now resides. That said, I can't help but look at it and relive my thrill when I first saw examples of the style, and how subversive it was bringing the *new* to my hometown. This is certainly part of the excitement I personally find with *True Nordic: How Scandinavia Influenced Design in Canada*, and the extraordinary story it tells of our fascination with Scandinavia and its impact on Canadian design.

Acknowledgements

The Gardiner Museum would like to acknowledge the generous support provided by the Department of Canadian Heritage's Museum Assistance Program, The Jack Weinbaum Family Foundation, The McLean Foundation, the Raphael Yu Centre of Canadian Ceramics, and Diana Reitberger. We also thank all the institutional and private lenders, and artists across Canada who have contributed to this exhibition; Dr. Robert Buckingham, Lee Jacobson and Michael Prokopow (in honour of Wendy Russell and Rosemary Wells) for their financial contributions to the exhibition; as well as Ian Turner and Kaitlin Chamberlain for their invaluable help on this publication. Finally, we are especially grateful to guest curators Rachel Gotlieb and Michael Prokopow for their work on the exhibition and as co-editors of this book; the intellectual rigour and originality with which they have approached the subject will make *True Nordic* a lasting contribution to the study of design in Canada.

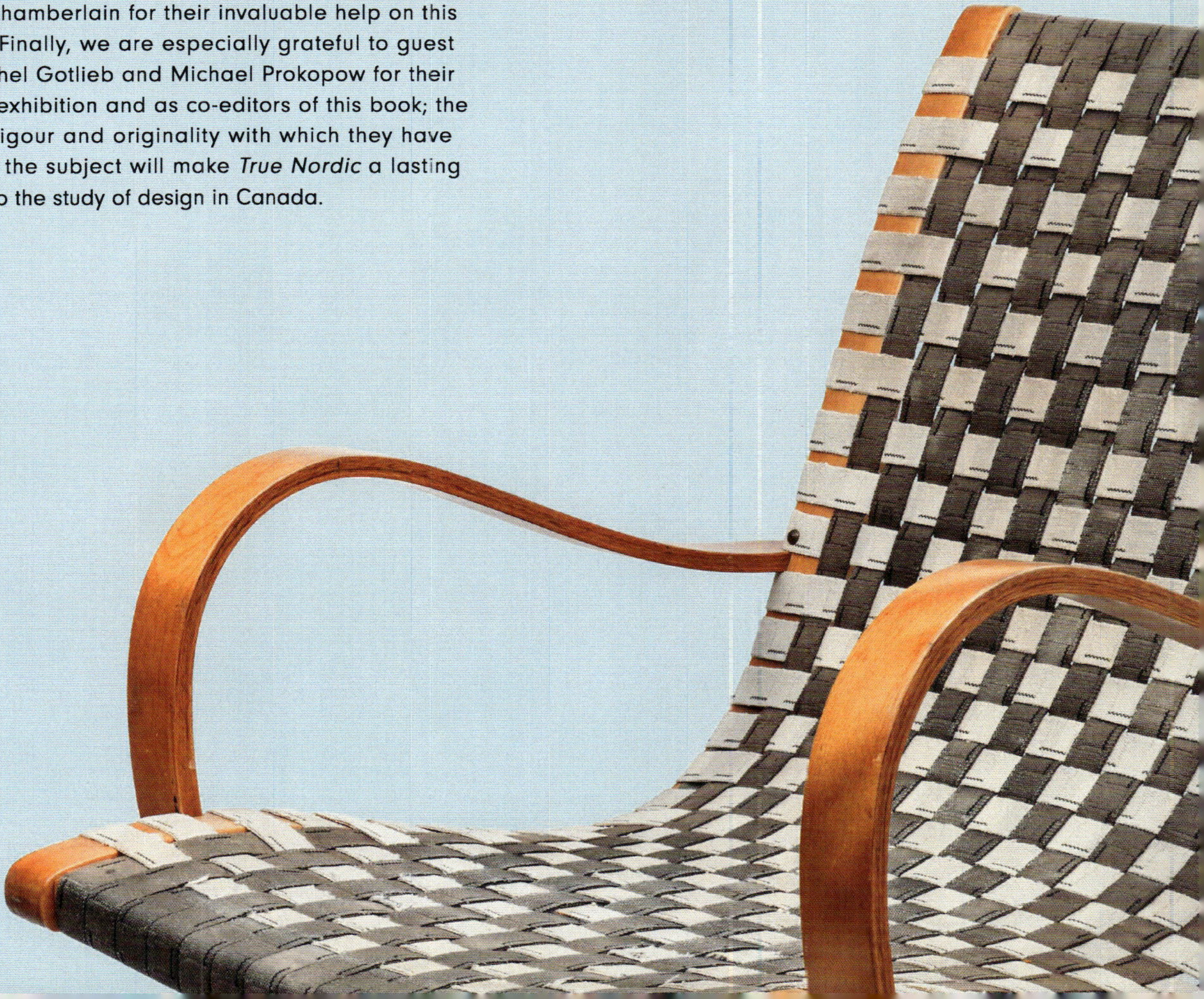

Introduction

Rachel Gotlieb and Michael Prokopow

True Nordic: How Scandinavia Influenced Design in Canada has been many years in the making and represents the first exhibition and publication devoted to the subject. This project reflects our ongoing engagement with the design history of Canada and, in particular, the stimuli the design cultures of Denmark, Finland, Norway, and Sweden exerted on the country after the end of the First World War. We have long been asking questions about the material and cultural consequences in Canada of the emigration of Scandinavian peoples and about the movement of Scandinavian ideas and objects to this country.

Practical, humane in orientation, and perceived as aesthetically refined and socially progressive, Scandinavian design and its vernacular interpretations had wide appeal in Canada. Admired equally by social and economic elites and enjoying enormous appeal amongst the growing middle classes with their suburban dreams, the modern look of Scandinavian design reflected the optimistic spirit of the nation. With its broad and distinctive stylistic character, Scandinavian design replaced in public affection any number of popular styles. The genial and modest aesthetics of Nordic forms challenged the streamlined and pyramidic massing that characterized art moderne (or what was eventually named "art deco") and offered a viable alternative to historicist European forms: the ornate styling, for example, of Louis Quatorze and conventional safety of faux Chippendale. Likewise, it presented something promisingly different to the traditional pioneer aesthetics of rustic Canadiana and the contemporaneous Bauhaus-informed International Style, defined, as it was, by geometric and rectilinear shapes and narrow materiality.

As a geographically and culturally amalgamating rubric in use since the 1930s by critics and design commentators on both sides of the Atlantic, "Scandinavian design," is often discussed and understood as homogeneous. However, while popular thinking about Nordic design might focus on the prevalence of blond wood, the frequent presence of curvilinear forms, and the inclination towards gentle, often earthy palettes, in truth, design from Scandinavia is marked by strikingly varied stylistic and material expression and is more nuanced and complex than might be thought. Far from monolithic, the differences of the individual countries that make up Scandinavia are significant. For many people—whether or not from Nordic Europe—the stereotypes that attend the idea of Scandinavian design are reductive and frequently considered yokes on design creativity. This said, it is our contention, however, that in Canada what was understood as Scandinavian design—a category and container promoted in the postwar era by national governments, curators, exhibition-makers, marketers, and other interested parties who aided in the cultivation of an idea of Nordic design's humane character and preferences for certain types of shapes and materials—was, for the most part, experienced and consumed as a harmonized entity.

The four essays presented here provide varying viewpoints about the meaning Scandinavia held for Canadians. That Canada shared close affinities with its Nordic counterparts' climate, geography, temperament, and democratic governance has been frequently cited. However, the national and geographic landscape of Canada is also different: its dependence on its rich natural resources, its bifurcated heritage originating in the colonial histories of Britain and France, as well as the proximate reality of the cultural dominance of the United States for a sovereign Canada. All remain factors contributing to a society in which concerns about identity were frequently raised and continue to be raised.

Rachel Gotlieb offers a detailed and thorough account of how Scandinavian design came to Canada, and how arguably, it never really left. Concerned with the cultural implications of Scandinavian aesthetics on craft and design in the country, Michael Prokopow provides a provocative assessment of the material culture from recent past to the present. Architect and *éminence grise,* George Baird considers the impact of Scandinavian principles on architecture in central Canada through the lens of personal perspective and experience. And philosopher and writer, Mark Kingwell gives an insightful and decidedly whimsical account of Canadians' Nordic and, sometimes, not so Nordic sense and sensibilities. Together, the essays constitute a thoughtfully nuanced consideration of Canadian culture and its operations.

In selecting the work for the *True Nordic* exhibition, our rationale pivoted on three concerns: to demonstrate the transposition of culture—intellectual and material—from the old world to the new; to show the effects in Canada of the dissemination and popularization of Scandinavian design (whether in the form of ideas, images, or objects); and to interrogate the persistent presence of the Nordic aesthetic sensibility in the current design culture and the noteworthy reversal of new to old world in this digitized global landscape. We believe, as do the Scandinavians, that craft and design should not be distinguished and so we have included here prototypes, limited editions, craft product, and one-offs, as well as objects that all somehow express the spirit of Scandinavian design. Omissions have been made, sometimes due to space limitations and other times oversight. For this we take full responsibility.

The objects in the exhibition represent the work of known designers, craftspeople, and artisans. Other objects are anonymous. Many objects have been borrowed from institutions or have been loaned from private collections, and some—in all honesty—were found in yard sales and thrift stores. In every instance, however, the works on exhibit demonstrate what we see as the characteristics of form and materiality marking Nordic and Scandinavian design. For whether the object was custom-made for clients, mass produced at a time when all things Nordic and modern were the rage, or fashioned by artisans for whom there existed an appreciation of Scandinavian aesthetics in the context of Canadian design practice, the objects selected constitute pieces of evidence in the argument the exhibition makes about the role Scandinavian design played in Canada. Primarily domestic in focus and sensitive to the economic hierarchies that attend the making and preservation of things, *True Nordic* offers a carefully considered narrative about Canadian society and its relationship with a complex and imported visual history across nearly ten decades of historical and social change.

We are grateful to the generous lenders of the exhibition, who include both designers and collectors, many of whom are scholars themselves and who have shared their knowledge, particularly Allan Collier, Callie Stacey, Rosalind Pepall, Diane Charbonneau, Noel Guyomarch, John David Lawrence, David Weir, David Allison, Daina Augaitis, and Ian Thom. Credit and thanks are also due to Tara Akitt and Loryssa Quattrociocchi for their assistance with the exhibition. Last, but certainly not least, we express profound gratitude to the Gardiner Museum for producing and circulating this exhibition and publication with the support from Canadian Heritage, Carol Weinbaum and the Jack Weinbaum Family Foundation, and the McLean Foundation, instilling the confidence, means, and technical expertise to accomplish *True Nordic.*

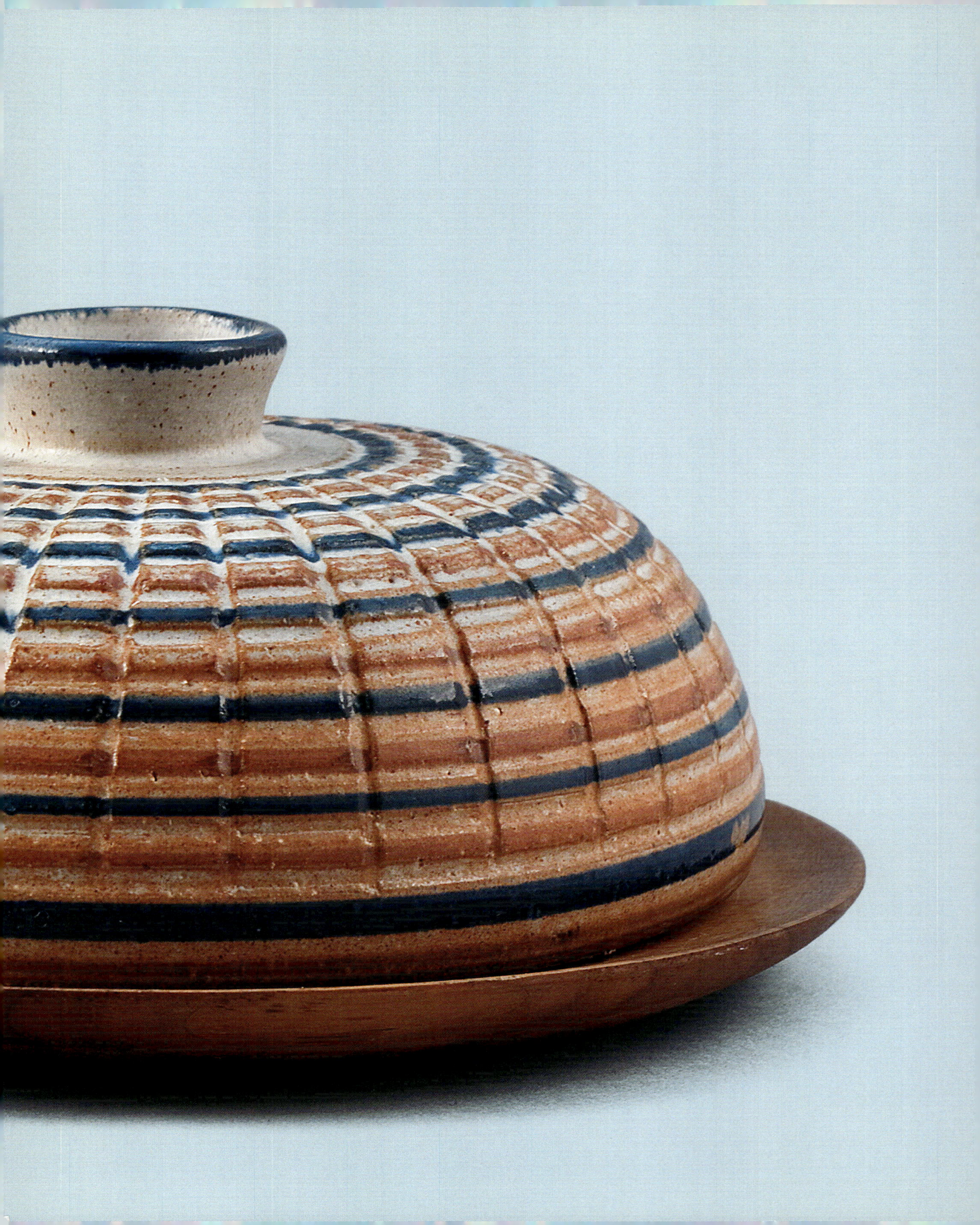

Scandinavian Design Comes to Canada

Rachel Gotlieb

Design ideas and stylistic trends have long circumnavigated the global marketplace through printed media, education, the movement of people, and the trade of actual commercial goods. Scandinavian-styled objects—generally understood as modern and functional, made in natural materials, with gentle curves, rough or smooth surfaces, and often though not always, evoking imagery from nature—arrived in Canada in the last century, reflecting these disseminating forces. Émigre artisans, public exhibitions, décor magazines, commercial importing, as well as local makers and manufacturers, each contributed to this new visual culture. As this brief overview reveals, these currents cannot be mapped in an easy chronology but reflect a more complex and nuanced history that overlaps and intersects.

Defining Scandinavian Design

The concept of what is called Scandinavian design originated in Sweden and Finland at international exhibitions in the late 1920s and 1930s, developing further after the Second World War, and expanded to include the nations of Denmark and Norway.[1] Simply put, these four countries, sharing a common northern Germanic-based dialect (apart from Finland), geography, and social democratic system of government, united to construct a generic and umbrella image to promote the commercial trade of northern Europe. As a result, the first manifestation of Scandinavian design came to embody unpretentious decorative and functional objects that illustrated some, but not necessarily all, of the inherent attributes: skilled, vernacular craftsmanship; organic imagery; stained, oiled, or hand-rubbed woods (initially cheaper and more available than tubular metal and plastic); webbed upholstery; lustrous silver and metal; nubby woven fabrics; and monochromatic pottery often articulated in biomorphic forms and shapes. (figure 1)

This focus on natural materials and expressive imagery was often referred to as a warming of modernism and offered a palatable alternative to the rational platonic abstraction of the International Style. While this look continued in the 1960s, Scandinavian styling also broadened with the application of advanced moulded plastic technology. Playful pop and space-age motifs that invaded Western visual culture also increased the scope and repertoire of Scandinavian aesthetics, especially in housewares, printed fabrics, and seating.

Scandinavian Émigrés Arrive

In 2011 Danish design historian Jørn Guldberg asked if the concept of Scandinavian design in the United States applied more to the people who made it than to the physical and functional qualities of things.[2] For Canada, the answer is people. Between the mid-1920s and early 1930s with the

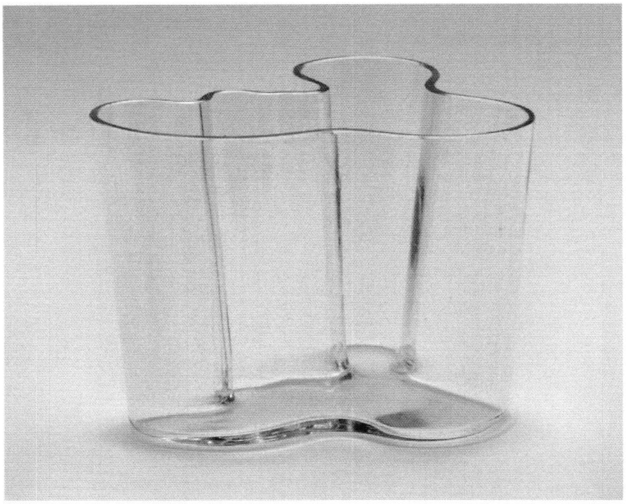

1 Alvar Aalto, vase, 1936–1956, manufactured by Karhula-littala, Finland. The Museum of Modern Art, given anonymously © The Museum of Modern Art / Licensed by SCALA / Art Resource, NY

onslaught of the Depression, Canadians witnessed the arrival of artisans from Sweden and Denmark who settled across the country to take advantage of its economic opportunities. These artisans independently shaped its craft scene for the next half century, stimulating a regional and national marketplace for handcrafted domestic goods. More importantly, they instilled in Canadians the importance of home crafts—learning by doing—a touchstone for a way of life inherited from their elementary educational training, known as Sloyd. Scandinavian design in Canada—until the 1940s perceived as Swedish or Danish and mostly artisanal—was initially mediated through the people who brought their craftsmanship, notably in ceramics, metal and textiles, to the country, many of whom both relished and cultivated their bohemian personas when they gave public interviews and demonstrations at fairs and department stores.[3]

Introducing handcrafted pottery to British Columbia, Axel Ebring from Sweden moved to the province in the late nineteenth century, during the first wave of immigration, initially to farm. (cat. 1–4) However, his contribution to Canadian craft did not occur until the mid-1920s, when, at middle age, he took up pottery (the trade of his grandfather and father), establishing one of the earliest studio potteries in the province.[4] He first worked in rural Notch Hill, north of Salmon Arm, using local materials. In 1935 he moved to nearby Vernon to access better clay to make everyday chargers, pitchers, and lamp bases.

An important teacher of metalworking who trained some of Canada's leading artisans working in this material,[5] Swedish-born, Rudolph "Rudy" Renzius came from a family of metalsmiths specializing in wrought iron, copper, and brass. He advanced his training at the Georg Jensen smithy and with pewter master Just Andersen.[6] Settling in Toronto in 1930, the six-foot blond Swede often dressed in an artist smock and bow ribbon tie, much impressing his clientele.[7] Known for his simply designed pewter hollow ware and jewellery, Renzius also taught vocational crafts at summer camps and schools and wrote instruction pamphlets on silver and wood, which emphasized the strong link between craft and culture.[8] (cat. 13)

The populist booster of handicraft among the first generation emigrants was Thor Hansen, also of Danish descent. In 1927 he moved to the prairies of Saskatchewan working as a farm labourer and then operating a fabric and needlepoint store in Regina. A decade later he was living in Toronto, supervising the arts and crafts corporate program at the British American Oil Company (B/A), a remarkable feat since his art and design skills were largely self-taught. In his public advocacy, the charismatic speaker often referenced his Danish heritage in his interviews and public lectures (the latter tallied at over a thousand), to contextualize Canada's weak craft tradition.[9] "The basement workshop," Hansen explained, "is the greatest blessing of the 20th century," or, put another way, handmade craft nurtures both culture and the soul.[10] Hansen practised what he preached, creating a series of patterns based upon the landscape of Ontario's Georgian Bay for the use of a local quilting and rug-hooking club. (cat. 25–26)

Between the mid-1920s and early 1930s with the onslaught of the Depression, Canadians witnessed the arrival of artisans from Sweden and Denmark who settled across the country to take advantage of its economic opportunities.

Karen Bulow encouraged the popular craft of professional and amateur weaving in the country. The Danish émigré arrived in Montreal with her portable loom in 1929, and by the early 1930s she had established a successful weaving studio in a converted flower shop. Aptly called Canadian Homespuns, it became well known locally and nationally for handwoven belts, scarves, ties (a mainstay), as well as upholstery and drapery for interior design firms. (cat. 14–15) Supported by the Quebec government's strategy to renew crafts in the rural communities, she trained young women from the country to

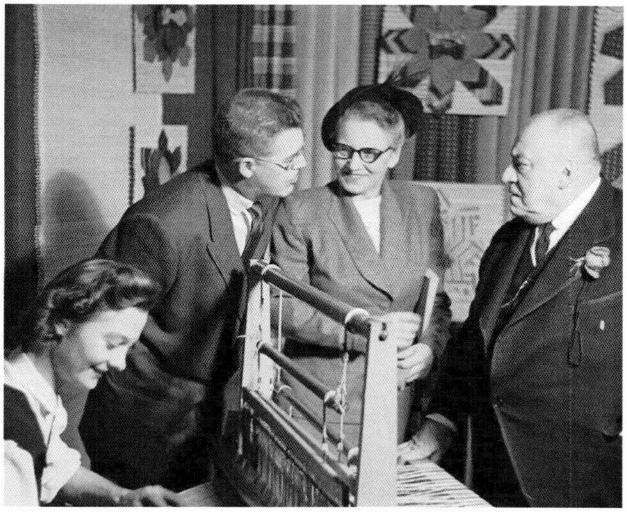

2 "Mayor Houde inspects booth of Karen Bulow, maker of woven ties, only woman exhibitor of styles. At loom is Ilga Niedre, displaced person from Latvia," *Weekend Magazine*, March 24, 1951. Photograph by Louis Jacques, Library and Archives Canada © Library and Archives Canada

weave and often paid them by the piece when they returned home to make her patterns.[11] (figure 2) Weaving in the Scandinavian tradition grew into a widespread hobby across the country, and at one time, depending upon preference and proximity, a weaver could access Finnish Rya yarns and Toika looms by mail order from Chelsea, Quebec, and Swedish-style looms from Armstrong, British Columbia.[12]

The elite tradition of Scandinavian-styled silver rests with Carl Poul Petersen, another Dane, who like many of his compatriots moved to Canada at the start of the Depression. He joined Henry Birks and Sons in Montreal, Canada's pre-eminent silver company and then opened the eponymous studio, producing jewellery, domestic hollowware, and flatware for Canada's upper-middle class. (figure 3) Flourishing in the 1950s and 1960s, his clientele included Saidye Bronfman, wife of Samuel Bronfman, founder of the famed Seagram's distillery. Petersen apprenticed with Georg Jensen and emulated his style of exquisitely wrought, shiny surfaces embellished with applied motifs of acorns, grapes, and other flora and fauna around the rim, finials, and handles.[13] (cat. 16–23) His youngest brother, Vagn Petersen, a cabinetmaker

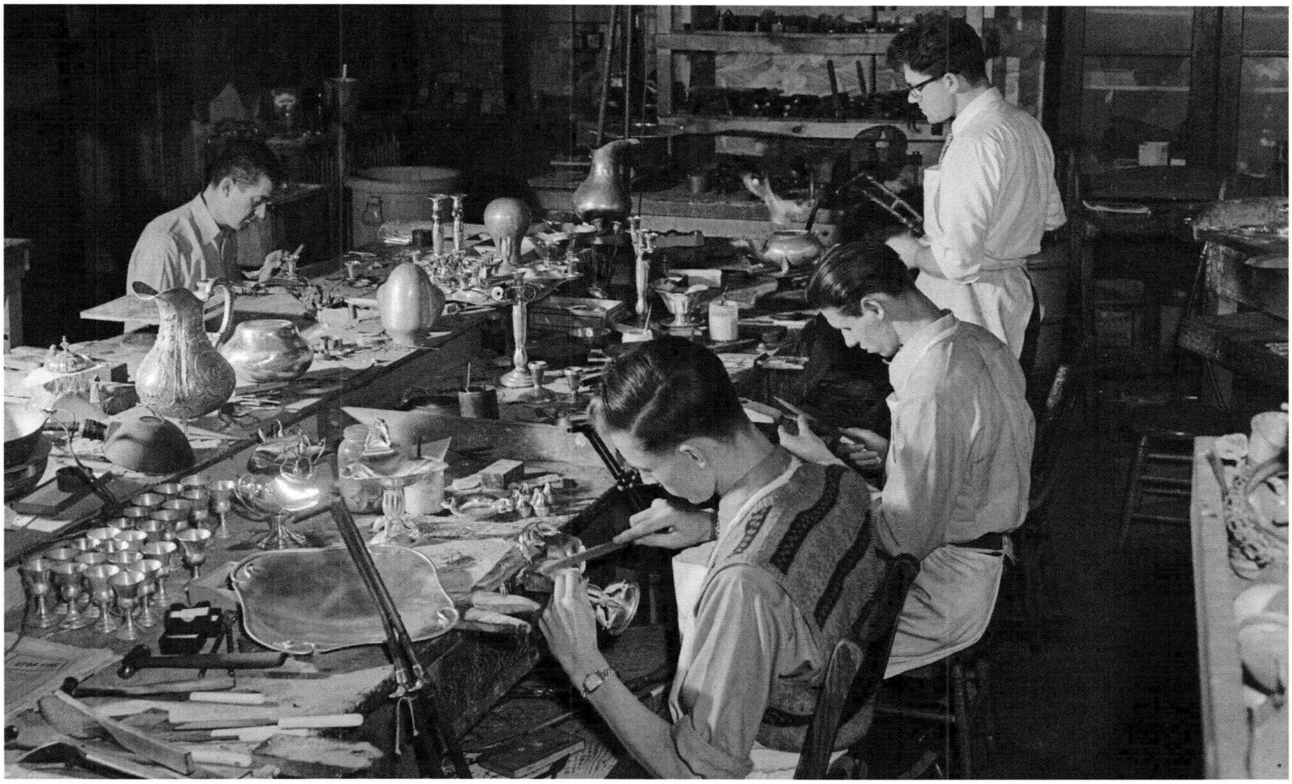

3 Main workshop at C. P. Peterson & Sons Ltd., workers doing their crafts, c. 1925–1965. National Film Board of Canada. Photothèque, Library and Archives Canada © Library and Archives Canada

trained under Otto Meyer in Copenhagen, emigrated in 1948, and sold "Danish furniture" in imported walnut and teak for Westmount patrons.[14] (cat. 34)

While Montreal was the centre for Nordic-inspired weaving and silver, Canada's Atlantic provinces led in Scandinavian studio pottery, thanks to two rival potteries operated by husband and wife partnerships Kjeld and Erica Deichmann and Ernst and Alma Lorenzen. Danish émigré Kjeld Deichmann initially resided in Saskatchewan and met his wife, Erica, daughter of a Danish Canadian Lutheran pastor. They moved to the countryside in Moss Glen, New Brunswick, but with the discovery of local clays went to Denmark, so that Kjeld could apprentice with potter Axel Brühl. Since the pottery was small, there was no place for Erica to work; instead she learned weaving—considered more appropriate at the time for a young wife—from two sisters living nearby.

When they returned in 1934, Kjeld opened Dykelands Pottery, but the work was so demanding that Erica's assistance was required. She developed and perfected the glaze recipes—reportedly in the thousands—painted and hand-modelled "goofus" figurines (a quirky hybrid creature between a horse, sheep, and giraffe) as well as mermaids in sea greens and earthy browns, which reference the Scandinavian folklore tradition. (figure 4) Kjeld threw the pots on the potter's wheel barefoot, to the delight of the media and the National Film Board, which produced several films of the Deichmann family pottery.[15] (figure 5 and cat. 5–11)

Ernst Lorenzen, a Dane, attended University of New Brunswick's forestry program and married Alma, who was of French-Acadian heritage. After the Second World War, they started the New Brunswick Pottery, and in 1949, subsidized by a patron of a major brickworks factory, moved to Lantz, Nova Scotia. Similar to the Deichmanns, Ernst sported a beret while operating the wheel, and Alma completed the surface decoration on their functional pottery. (cat. 63) The Lorenzens became known for their some two hundred hand-formed ceramic mushroom replicas, based upon the sketches they made when they went foraging. Mycologists collected them for their scientific accuracy.[16]

Cultural Agencies and Retailers Play a Role

As the first wave of Scandinavian émigrés cultivated the taste for contemporary craft in the postwar era, Canadian cultural institutions and the federal government developed new policies and programs, favouring especially exhibitions, to develop a Canadian design culture. More often than

Kjeld threw the pots on the potter's wheel barefoot, to the delight of the media and the National Film Board, which produced several films of the Deichmann family pottery.

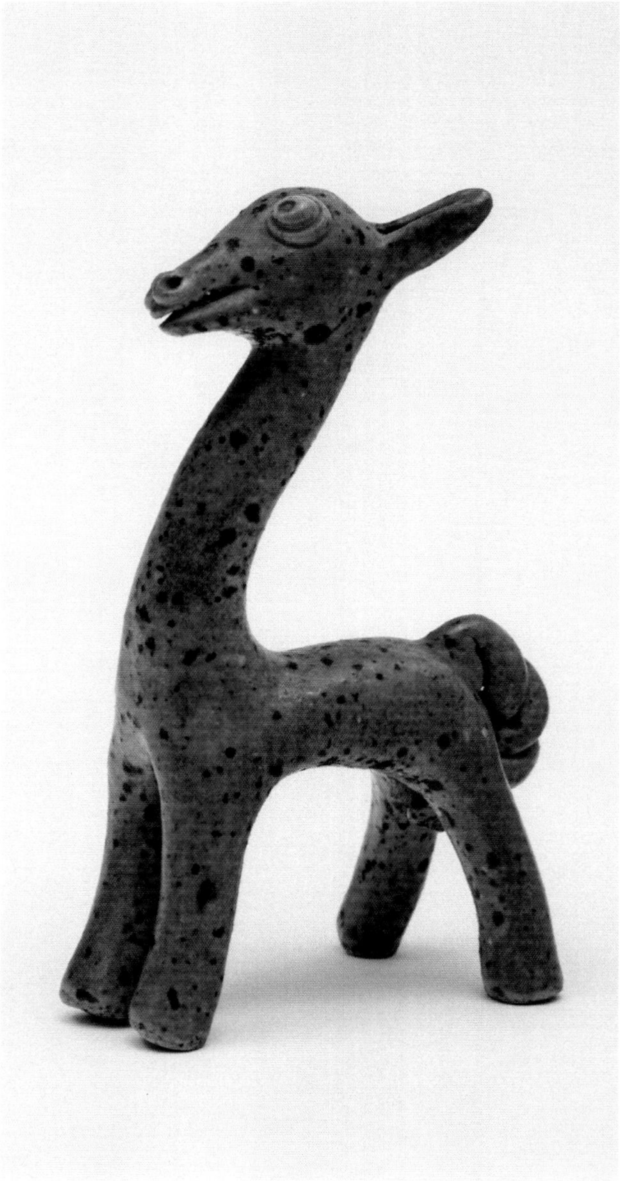

4 Kjeld Deichmann and Erica Deichmann, *Goofus*, 1950–1963
Collection of the Gardiner Museum, gift of Gail and Gerry Crawford. Photography by Toni Hafkenscheid

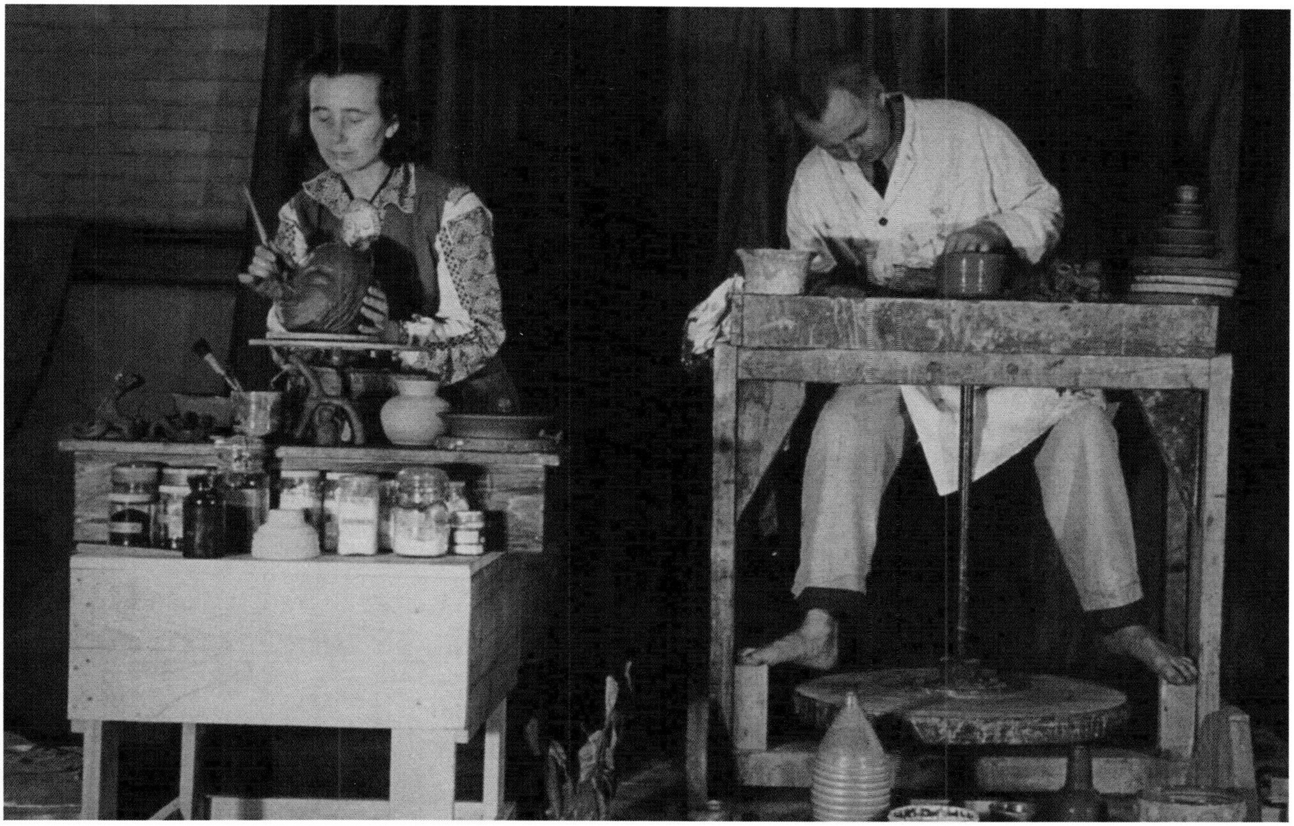

5 Erica and Kjeld Deichmann demonstrating pottery at the Art in Action show, Fredericton, New Brunswick. Photography by D. J. MacLean, 1942 Canadian Museum of History, E2007-00579

not, they turned to Scandinavian principles as a model but privileged industrial design over craft in an attempt to redirect the war industries to the domestic market.[17] In 1946 Donald Buchanan, then editor of *Canadian Art*, who, two years later, became the first director of the National Industrial Design Committee,[18] organized the proselytizing exhibition *Design for Use in Canadian Products*. Based upon the "good design" exhibitions held at the Museum of Modern Art in New York City, the show included A. J. Donahue's plywood and web-seated chair, illustrated on the cover of the exhibition's pamphlet, and moulded plywood furniture by Waclaw Czerwinski and Hilary Stykolt from Kitchener, Ontario, and Mouldcraft Plywoods from Vancouver. (cat. 28–29) As small manufacturers that adapted the steam-bent wood technology from the military aircraft industry for peacetime application, these batch-production chairs were deemed by Buchanan a suitable substitute for expensive upholstered furniture. "Good design in manufactured objects," according to Buchanan, "as we understand it today, means a combination of simplicity, fine proportions and functional utility." Significantly, he acknowledged that Sweden and Finland originated "these important modern innovations."[19]

> Canadian cultural institutions and the federal government developed new policies and programs, favouring especially exhibitions, to develop a Canadian design culture.

Design for Use in Canadian Products was just one of many didactic exhibitions in Canada in the postwar era. The Royal Ontario Museum (ROM) with the Canadian Handicrafts Guild hosted *Design in Industry* in 1949,[20] displaying metalware by Georg Jensen, and, in 1952, the Art Gallery of Ontario presented *Three Modern Styles*, showcasing contemporary furniture by Alvar Aalto.[21] A decade later, the Design Centre in Ottawa mounted, *Twelve Scandinavian Designers*, including

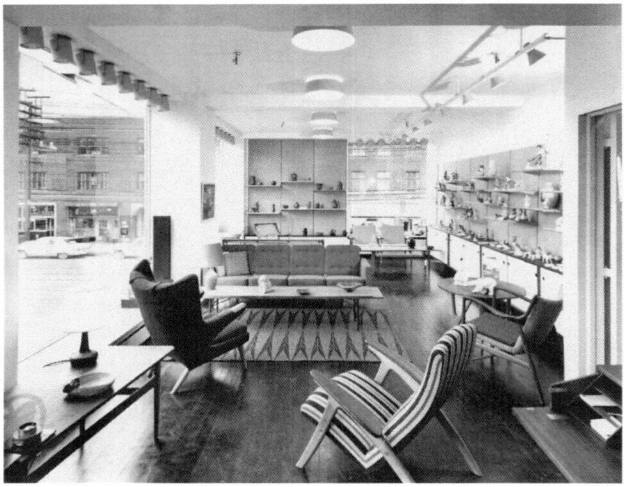

6 Georg Jensen Store, Bloor Street West, Toronto, c. 1957. Panda Associates fonds, Canadian Architectural Archives, University of Calgary, PAN 57051

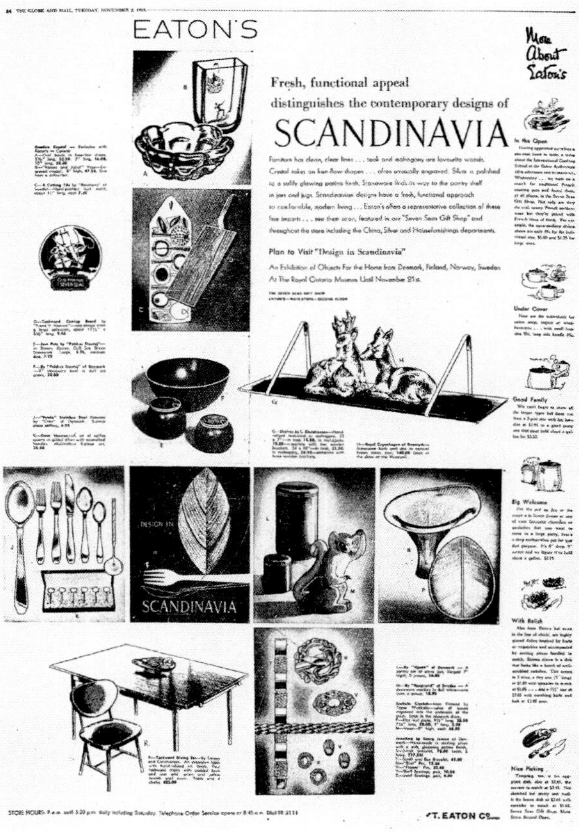

7 Eaton's advertisement promoting Scandinavian Design, *The Globe and Mail*, November 2, 1954. © Sears Canada

furnishings by Nanna and Jørgen Ditzel and domestic metalware by Henning Koppel.[22]

However, by far the most influential exhibition to fuel the appetite for Nordic housewares was *Design in Scandinavia*, which toured twenty-four institutions across North America between 1954 and 1957, including the ROM, the National Gallery with the Ottawa Design Centre, and the Vancouver Art Gallery.[23] Presenting seven hundred products from Denmark, Finland, Norway, and Sweden under four major themes—"Good Articles for Everyday Use," "Living Tradition," "Form and Material," and "Scandinavians at Home"—the missive was clear: the northern European countries of Scandinavia acted in concert to design modern, democratic, humane, and affordable household objects.[24] Various Canadian newspapers got the message and used the exhibition as a foil to compare Scandinavian and Canadian design. For the most part, the match up did not fare well. *Toronto Star* writer Gordon McCaffrey put the blame on Canadian consumers' lack of taste, observing that Scandinavian mass-produced household furniture and ornaments were of "simple design and classic beauty," while Canadian manufacturers were "churning out what our gift shop dealers agree is nothing but junk."[25] Similarly, the *Globe and Mail*'s arts reporter Pearl McCarthy questioned why Canada "with materials and talents have no comparable cultural expression in design of everyday things?"[26]

In conjunction with the exhibition the major department stores Eaton's and Simpson's organized their own special events and displays. Eaton's full-page advertisement of designs by Tapio Wirkkala and Georg Jensen pitched Scandinavian design as a "fresh, functional approach to comfortable, modern living," very much reflecting the marketing copy of the exhibition itself.[27] (figure 7) Boutique shops Shelagh's in Toronto and Pego's in Montreal also promoted the exhibition.[28] Shelagh Vansittart had direct ties to Scandinavian design through her Norwegian husband, John Stene, who made rope and oiled wood furniture.[29] Pego McNaughton was married to the rising industrial designer Jacques Guillon, giving her access to contemporary design. Following the exhibition, more niche stores opened, notably Georg Jensen in 1957 on Toronto's fashionable Bloor Street. (figure 6) Latvian-born architect Janis Kravis founded Karelia (named after a region that borders Finland and Russia), an importing business for Marimekko fabrics and housewares. He eventually set up stores in Toronto, Edmonton, and Vancouver.[30] (figure 8) Oscana Interiors in Regina, Bonli Interiors in Saskatoon, and Gunther's Mobilia in Calgary also sold Scandinavian imports.[31] The mushrooming of Scandinavian retailers in city centres paved the way for the Swedish chain Ikea to unveil its first North American store in 1976 in Vancouver.

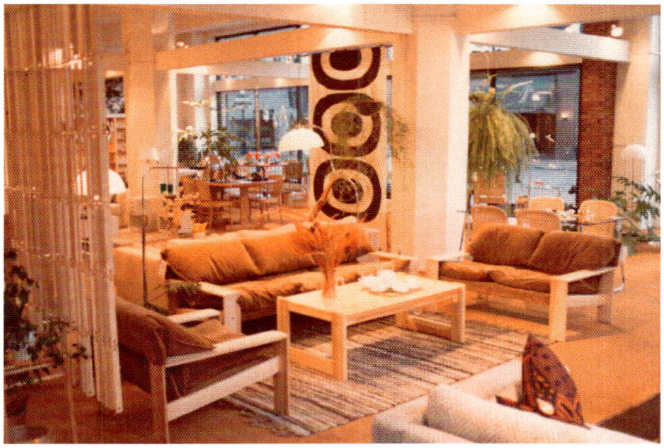

8 Karelia store interior in Vancouver, 1970s. Image courtesy of Janis Kravis

The Printed Media Have a Word

Between the 1940s and 1960s, décor magazines focused on how Scandinavian-styled objects delivered "refined" and "gracious" living, painting a picturesque view of the Scandinavian lifestyle and reflecting the rhetoric of the day.[32] According to Mandel Sprachman's florid account: "The conditions that mold Scandinavian furniture design are similar to our own. They live in a northern climate with long winters; they live in apartments or small houses (somewhat like our subdivision houses, only smaller); they raise healthy children in a relaxed family atmosphere; and they have an inherent liking for the out of doors, summer and winter."[33] By 1958 Margit Bennett from *Canadian Homes and Gardens* proclaimed: "The greatest single influence is still Scandinavian, and now it has put its light, trim look on everything."[34] Style editor Patricia Lamont was able to distinguish Scandinavian originals from Canadian reproductions "with simulated hand-rubbed finish," but she had no issue with the Canadian "versions," instead congratulating the manufacturers for being "alert" and "acknowledging their debt with such identifying tags as Scan-Mor, Danebridge, Copenhagen and Helsinki." [35]

In the 1960s, the *Telegram* and the *Star* celebrated Canadian "copy-cat" furniture manufacturers for beating Scandinavians at their own game, and "fighting fire with fire." The ten-year love affair with Danish furniture imports, which according to Len Shifrin had increased by 700 percent, was over, thanks to manufacturers like Punch in Montreal and Imperial Furniture Manufacturing in Ontario.[36] Canadian manufacturer William Baltman agreed: "We took the Scandinavian simplicity and developed our own designs to fit it."[37]

Canadian Designers and Manufacturers Adopt and Interpret

Baltman's audacious claim and the media's support are indicative of how commercial manufacturers across the country recognized the potential opportunities of Scandinavian design and branding, adding gestures of the signature curves and blond woods to their otherwise conservative repertoire of neo-colonial and faux Chippendale furniture designs. Some companies purchased the licence for them, and many more did not. For example, the German family Krug manufactured at their eponymous factory in Kitchener, Ontario, a sturdy ladder-back chair distinguished by a Nordic knot in the centre of each rail, a V-shaped stretcher, and, the best touch of all, a carved horse crowning each stile. The design originated in 1930s with the American manufacturer Romweber under the name Viking Oak, and reveals the transposition of Nordic styling, albeit folk rather than modern.[38] (figure 9)

For its "Scandinavian feeling," Canadian media praised Jan Kuypers's line of residential and household furniture manufactured by Imperial.[39] (cat. 27) Kuypers, a Dutch émigré who came to Canada to join the factory as its lead designer, deliberately referenced Scandinavian design, not only because it catered to market demand, but also he believed it was appropriate to Canada. A decade later, as partner of Toronto's leading industrial design firm Dudas Kuypers Rowan, he participated in a trade mission, visiting Europe and Scandinavian furniture plants and came to the conclusion that the Swedish use of softwood species, such as spruce and Jack pine would be suitable for Canada as well as their strategy to market exports as a co-operative.[40] Recently, Jørn Guldberg remarked to a Canadian audience, "[t]o any Scandinavian[,] Kuypers's Canadian Scandinavian furniture looks very familiar, and yet, no exact Scandinavian model or prototype does exist. Only one conspicuous detail reveals that the [Skokan] chair is not Scandinavian: the screw on the back."[41]

This is not to say, however, that Canadian manufacturers only copied. Far from it. There were many Canadian designers especially, after the 1960s, who skilfully interrogated the aesthetic only to master it as their own, including both Koen de Winter and Michel Dallaire. De Winter, a Belgian designer working in Sweden, joined the Montreal-based Danesco to run its design studio focusing on housewares, and incorporated the bold and simple shapes of brightly coloured plastics emulating the spirit of the kitchen products made by Rosti in Sweden and Dansk in Denmark. (cat. 70) Dallaire designed lighting for Sverige (Swedish for *Sweden*), a Quebec-based lighting manufacturer that was eventually purchased by Luxo of Norway (famous for its anglepoise lamp). Keith Muller and Michael Stewart (whose father-in-law, the famed Finnish architect Viljo Revell, designed Toronto City Hall) co-founded the furniture company Ambiant Systems in 1968. They excelled at moulded plywood stacking furniture, employing Paul Epp, who returned from Sweden in 1972, after apprenticing with James Krenov. (cat. 86) Ambiant also manufactured Thomas Lamb's Steamer collection made from standardized moulded plywood slats and assembled in his own distinctively organic fashion.[42]

A Second Wave of European Émigrés

It is fitting to conclude this brief overview of how Scandinavian design came to Canada by returning to the transposition of people, since the entire country is, after all, a nation of immigrants. After the Second World War, the country enjoyed a new and larger influx of Scandinavian artisans, again many were Danish, and a greater number had formal design training.[43] Among the notable were Lotte and Gunnar Bostlund, who arrived in the early 1950s and were soon producing the same slender and elegant ceramic lamp bases available in Denmark for domestic and corporate interiors. (cat. 51–55) A graduate of the Royal Danish Academy, Lotte acted as design director, while Gunnar, the engineer, supervised the slip-casting and kiln firing. Initially they operated the pottery with their six children outside of Toronto, which made for colourful editorial copy.[44] Also shaping the ceramic field was Folmer Hansen, who apprenticed and worked as a potter in his native Denmark as well as Sweden and Norway. When he arrived in 1957, he immediately joined the Deichmann Pottery, having heard about it from an immigration officer at the major port, Pier 21 in Halifax. He worked there for a year before moving out west to join David Ross in the remote Fort Qu'Appelle, Saskatchewan, where they opened the first studio pottery in the province in 1961.[45] (cat. 43, 56, 75)

Many important furniture designers arrived in the 1950s, including Sigrun Bülow-Hübe,[46] a rising star with an impeccable educational pedigree, who moved to Montreal to work as an interior designer at Eaton's. (cat. 31) A graduate of the Royal Danish Academy of Fine Arts, she studied under eminent architect and furniture designer Kaare Klint, and contributed to the Swedish pavilion at the 1947 Milan Triennale. In 1953 she co-founded AKA Works to sell, as billed in the yellow pages, "Swedish Modern Furniture" that was sometimes upholstered by her compatriot Karen Bulow.[47] Bülow-Hübe, who became the first woman to join the Association of Canadian Industrial Designers, exhibited furniture at the Canadian pavilion at the Brussels World's Fair (1958) and Habitat at Expo 67.[48] (figure 10)

Niels Bendtsen emigrated from Denmark to Vancouver in 1951, when he was a young boy, and learned traditional cabinetmaking from his father. (cat. 72) In 1972 he moved back to Denmark to further hone his furniture-making skills, and there he designed the Ribbon Chair (now in the collection of the Museum of Modern Art). Returning to Canada the following decade, he opened a store currently known as Inform Interiors to retail his softly curved upholstered furniture under the name Bensen.[49] Similarly, Christen Sørensen apprenticed as a cabinetmaker with his father and attended the School of Arts and Crafts in Copenhagen under Hans Wegner. Moving to Montreal in 1956, he formed a partnership with Jacques Guillon & Associates, collaborating on corporate interiors and later designing office furniture for

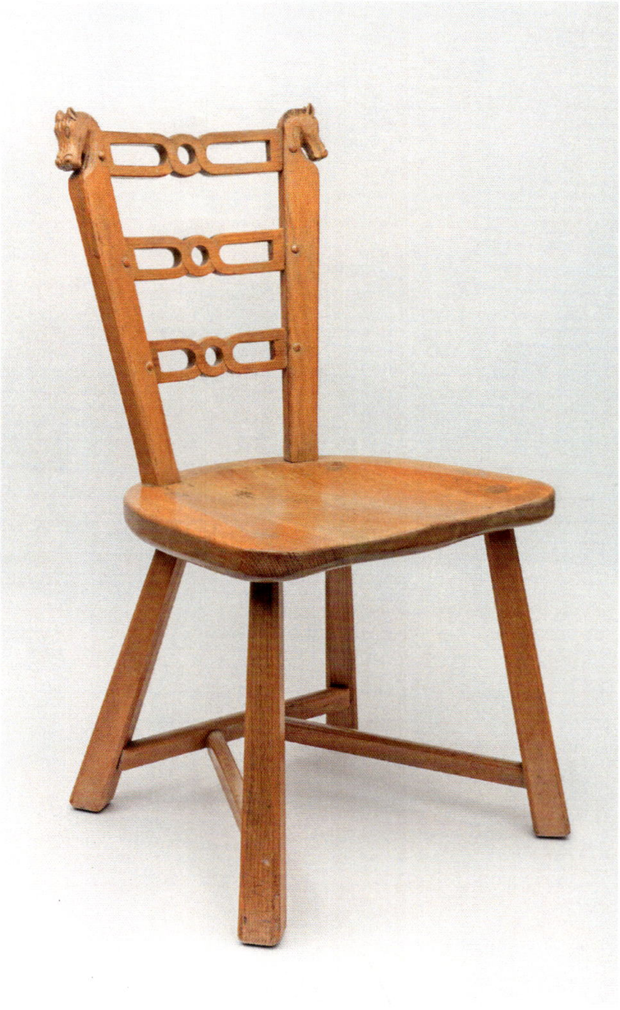

9 Viking chair, 1950s, Krug, Kitchener, Ontario. Private Collection
Photography by Toni Hafkenscheid

After the Second World War, many Canadian-born artisans and designers took advantage of the peacetime conditions to travel abroad to study with renowned Scandinavian masters and returned home with these skills, proving, yet again how Scandinavian design came to Canada through the movement of people. Some benefited from travel scholarships offered by the private Canadian-Scandinavian Foundation founded in 1950 as well as newly offered government artist grants.

leading Canadian manufacturers. Sørensen further made his mark in Canada, serving as director of Sheridan College School of Crafts and Design, outside of Toronto.[50] Danish-born Leif Jacobsen opened a custom mill shop in Toronto in 1952 and was soon subcontracting furniture for leading American furniture manufacturers Knoll and Herman Miller, as well as producing his own limited-edition furniture with fellow Dane Svend Nielsen.[51] (cat. 74) It is due to the efforts of these transposed Danes located in the major cities of Montreal, Toronto, and Vancouver that Canadian residential and corporate furniture became decidedly modern in the last century.

In the 1960s, three Scandinavian-born and -trained textiles artists gave the fledgling Canadian fibre arts—textiles as fine art rather than functional craft—a significant boost. Swedish artist Helena Hernmarck moved to Montreal in 1963 and, for the next decade, concentrated on figurative imagery drawn from photography in her loomed textiles before moving on to the United States.[52] Heralding from Finland, Kaija Sanelma Harris worked in Iceland as a textile designer and settled in Saskatoon, Saskatchewan, and was a Saidye Bronfman Award nominee.[53] In 1967 Danish weaver Suzanne Swannie accepted a position to teach hand weaving at a new adult education program in Newfoundland and Labrador. She came to reside in Nova Scotia for forty years. Swannie's Danish heritage and training—especially in the studio of John and Kirsten Becker outside of Copenhagen, who handled commissions from such important modern designers as Arne Jacobsen—clearly shaped her practice.[54] In her woven tapestries, Swannie often evokes folklore imagery or the natural landscape, which she crafts into brilliant abstracted fields of colour. (cat. 95)

Canadians Away

After the Second World War, many Canadian-born artisans and designers took advantage of the peacetime conditions to travel abroad to study with renowned Scandinavian masters and returned home with these skills, proving, yet again how Scandinavian design came to Canada through the movement of people. Some benefited from travel scholarships offered by the private Canadian-Scandinavian Foundation founded in 1950 as well as newly offered government artist grants.[55] Harold Stacey, the first president of the Metal Arts Guild of Ontario, who initially trained with Rudolph Renzius at Northern Vocational School, attended workshops under Swedish silversmith Baron Erik Fleming at Rhode Island School of Design in 1949.[56] (figure 11 and cat. 24) Quebec jeweller and goldsmith Maurice Brault learned enamelling at J. Tostrup, the pre-eminent silver firm in Norway.[57] In ceramics, Walter Dexter, a graduate of Alberta College of Art, completed postgraduate studies in 1954 at the Swedish School of Arts and Crafts in Stockholm,[58] (cat. 36) while David Ross from Winnipeg attended the State Arts and Crafts School in Gothenburg, Sweden. Ross worked in small potteries in Denmark where he met his future partner, Folmer Hansen.[59] Jean Cartier, who served as design director of Céramique de Beauce in Quebec, spent a year in the late 1950s in Stockholm, perfecting his study of glazes in the studio of Stig Lindberg.[60] (cat. 33) Similarly, Canadian potters, such as Walter Drohan and Mayta Markson, studied at Cranbrook Academy under the tutelage of Finnish artist Maija Grotell.[61]

Canadian craft and design history owes much to Donald Lloyd McKinley and Ruth Gowdy McKinley, an American couple who studied industrial design and pottery respectively at Alfred University in upstate New York. In 1963, on a Fulbright scholarship to study furniture design in Finland, Donald discovered the humanist approach of architect Alvar Aalto, and furniture designers, Yrjö Kukkapuro and Esko Pajamas,[62] while his wife, Ruth Gowdy McKinley, a functionalist potter, visited the ceramics firm Arabia and other potteries. Kyllikki Salmenhaara a long-time potter at Arabia was a close friend who had recently retired; McKinley's precise forms glazed thinly to accentuate the shape reference Salmenhaara's influential work. The McKinleys

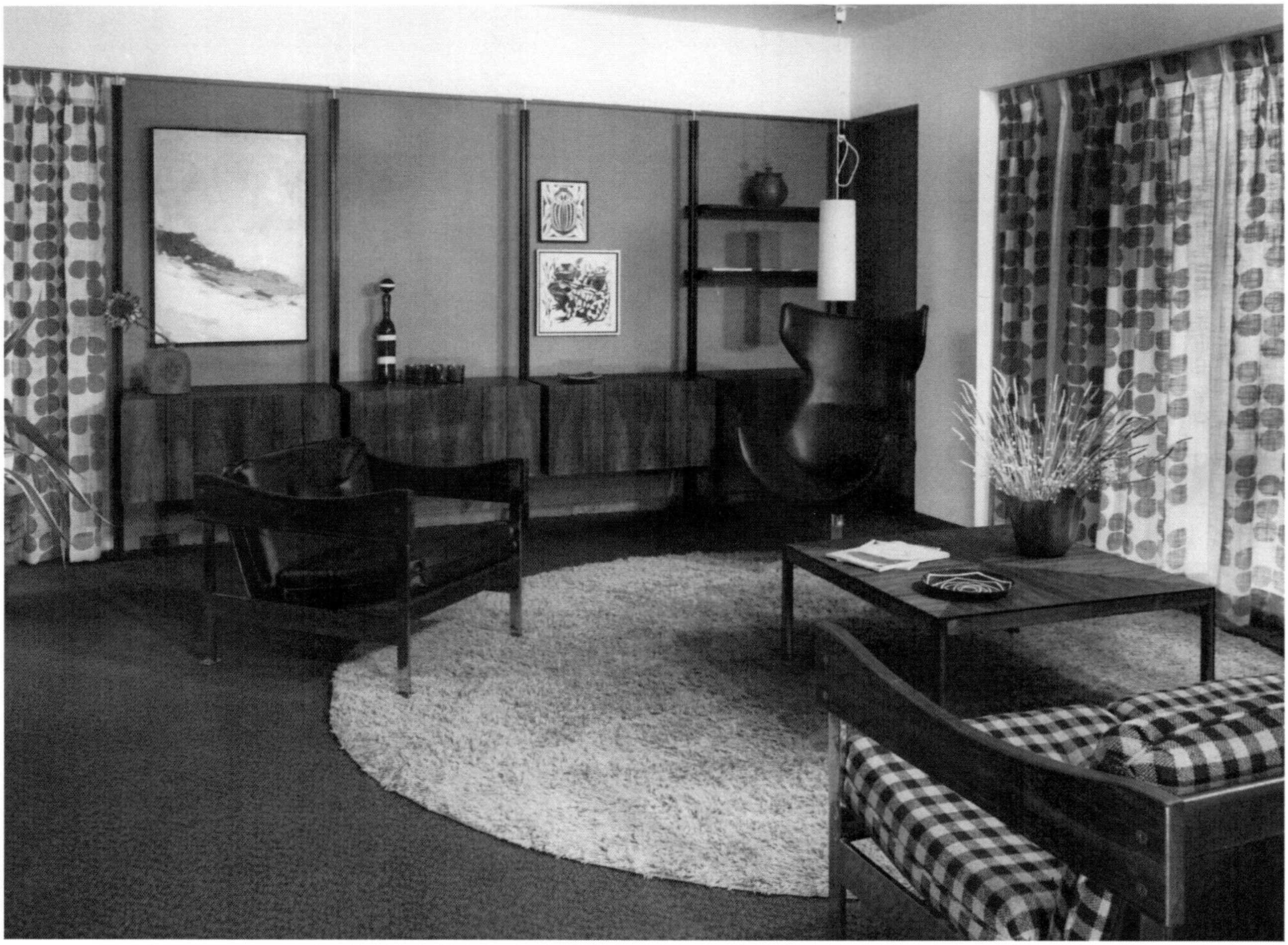

10 View of living room designed by Sigrun Bülow-Hübe for Habitat 67, 1967. Sigrun Bülow-Hübe Archive, John Bland Canadian Architecture Collection, McGill Library

brought this important experience to Sheridan College in the late 1960s, where Donald headed the furniture program for almost thirty years and Ruth reigned as residential potter on campus.[63] (cat. 61, 67, 76)

With the increasing circulation of people and exchange of ideas, it is not surprising that Canadians made their mark in Scandinavia. Notably, Roman Bartkiw, exceptional for his versatility in both studio pottery and glass, introduced Finn Lynggaard to hot glass when the Dane visited Toronto in 1970 to give an artist workshop on pottery, his original métier. (cat. 62) Bartkiw then went to Denmark, on an Ontario Arts Council grant, where he solidified his friendship with Lynggaard. "Roman put on a one-man glass show for the Danes," according to *Tactile*, the Canadian craft magazine. "People jammed the studio, eager to see and learn from Roman's instruction and demonstration, and to participate in "a happening."[64] Thanks in part to Bartkiw's influence, Lynggaard is now dubbed the father of studio glass in Denmark, and his repertoire of glass apples and bowls bear a striking resemblance to Bartkiw's artwork.[65]

With the increasing circulation of people and exchange of ideas, it is not surprising that Canadians made their mark in Scandinavia.

The cross-cultural exchanges among Scandinavian and Canadian craftmakers and industrial designers continue. For

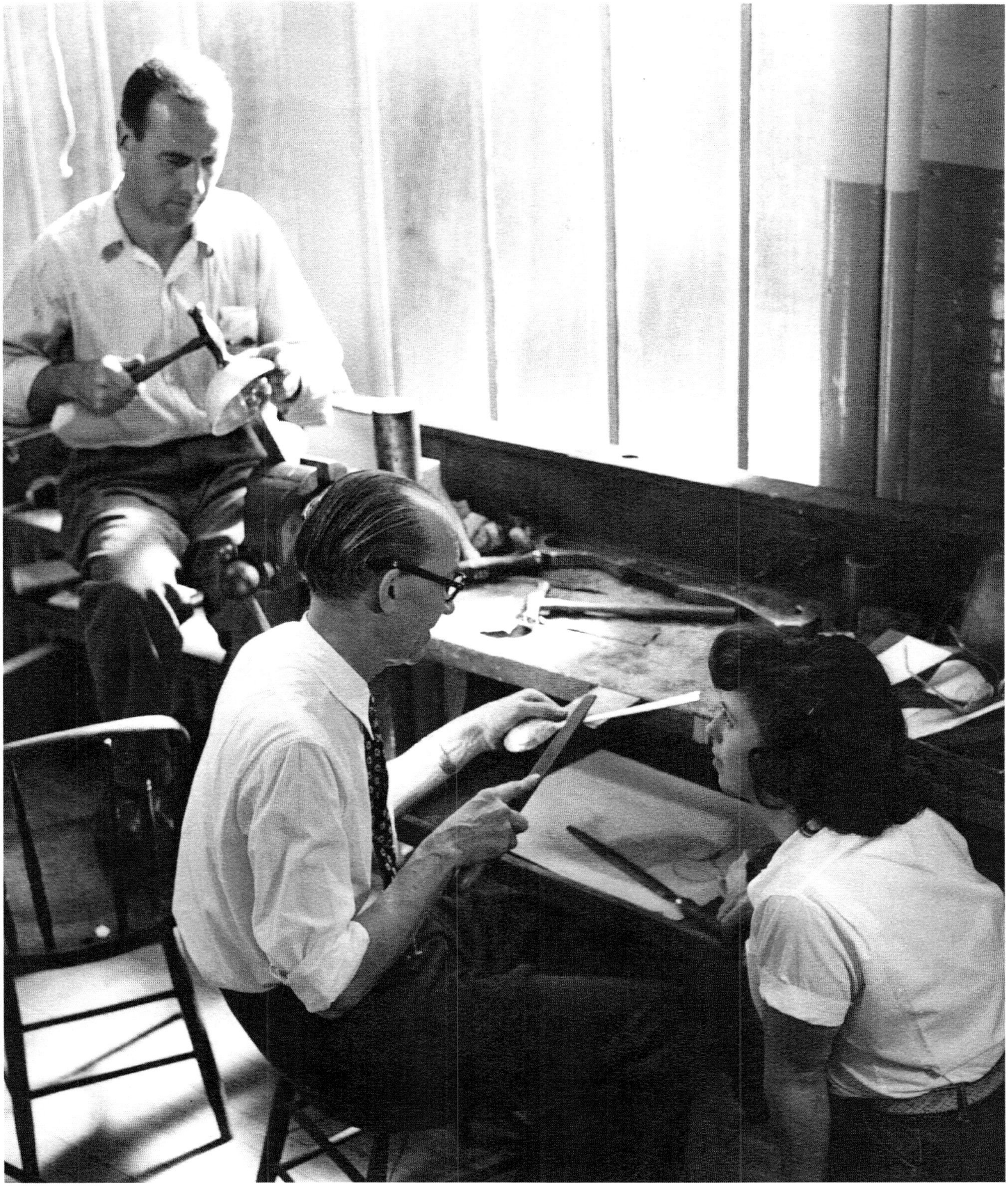

11 Harold Stacey taught by Baron Erik Fleming with Martha Brennan, August 1949
Photo collection of Callie Stacey

example, Pamela Ritchie researched traditional Norwegian coil filigree jewellery called Bunadsylv in Oslo and Telemark in the late 1970s and early 1980s and has been teaching jewellery and metalsmithing at Nova Scotia College of Art and Design (NSCAD) University in Halifax for over thirty years. She makes her own contemporary adaptation of this technique, stripping the coils (known in Norwegian as *kruser*) of their decorative beads to accentuate their own visual value.[66] (cat. 98–99) Neil Forrest, a prominent ceramic artist acclaimed for his wondrous architectonic installations, is a Professor of Ceramics at NSCAD University who, since 2011, has maintained a close teaching and research relationship with KHiO (the Oslo National Academy of Arts) in Norway.

In industrial design, Canadians are so well versed in the Scandinavian idiom that they successfully participate in the Stockholm furniture fair, garnering northern European clients. Patty Johnson has a chair produced by David Design in Sweden, a company that practices the design tenets of "understated, conscious, humane, comfortable and modern," if its website is to be believed. (cat. 96) The Danish manufacturer Woud licensed the lighting collection of Toronto-based MSDS Studio in keeping with its design mission, "simplicity anchored in our Nordic design heritage." (cat. 122)

Enduring Legacy

The strong presence of Scandinavian design in Canada in the twentieth and twenty-first centuries is culturally consequential. As a nation of immigrants with an expansive geography that contributes to regionalist impulses, a single style or a school of design dominating the nation's design and craft culture has never affected the country. The desire to emulate and consume Scandinavian design may be the closest thing to one, brought by the transposition of people who exchanged ideas and skills, bolstered by exhibitions, décor magazines, and retailers. These currents facilitated not only the distribution but also the acceptance of the Nordic-styled objects, be they industrially made, handcrafted, generic, or original, for the mass market or the elite. Scandinavian design has been and remains a beacon for Canada. Madi Cash, the marketing director of Canadian residential furniture manufacturer EQ3 in Winnipeg, gets the final word: "I see all this great Scandinavian design, and these are small countries too, but somehow they have been successful in supporting Scandinavian designers and promoting this idea to the world of what Scandinavian design is." This said in 2016, and so the myth, the style, and its legacy endure in Canada.[67]

Endnotes

1 For a recent history of Scandinavian design see *Scandinavian Design: Alternative Histories*, ed. Kjetil Fallan (London and New York: Berg Publishers, 2012); and *Scandinavian Design Beyond the Myth: Fifty Years of Scandinavian Design from the Nordic Countries*, eds. Widar Halén and Kerstin Wickman (Stockholm: Arvinius, 2003).

2 Jørn Guldberg, "'Scandinavian' Design as Discourse: The Exhibition Design in Scandinavia 1954–57," *Design Issues* 1, no. 2 (2011): 42.

3 Artisanal glass made in Canada was mainly introduced by Europeans from Czechoslovakia, Hungary and Italy in the latter half of the twentieth century.

4 Ron Candy, "Axel Ebring: the Potter of Vernon," accessed February 15, 2016, http://www.vernonmuseum.ca/cr_axel_ebring.html; and Barry White, "Axel Ebring Capsule," studioceramicscanada.com/axel-ebring/.

5 Renzius's famous students include Douglas Boyd and Andrew Fussell. See Anne Barros, *Ornament and Object* (Boston Mills, ON: Boston Mills Press, 1997), 16–17.

6 Gail Crawford, *A Fine Line: Studio Crafts in Ontario from 1930 to the Present* (Toronto: Dundurn Press, 1998), 24–25.

7 Crawford, *A Fine Line*, 25.

8 Rudy Renzius, *Hammered Silver Flatware*, ed. Ivan H. Crowell, no. 26, Macdonald College Handicraft Series (Toronto: Macmillan, 1945); and Rudy Renzius, *Built-Up Wood Carvings*, ed. Ivan H. Crowell, no. 55, Craftsmen's Library Series (Toronto: Macmillan, 1945). See Douglas Shenstone, *For the Love of Pewter: Pewterers of Canada* (Toronto: Metal Arts Guild, 1990).

9 Thor Hansen's lectures and media interviews are located in the Archives of Ontario, Fonds C 26. See Rachel Gotlieb, *Thor Hansen: Crafting a Canadian Style* (Toronto: Textile Museum of Canada, 2005).

10 "Talk 'Creative Imagination at Work' by Thor Hansen, Artist and Designer Fascinates Women's Canadian Club," *Canadian Statesman*, October 23, 1952, 7.

11 The company was also known as Canada Homespun, until it changed its name to Karen Bulow in 1960. Rachel Gotlieb, "Suzanne Swannie and Danish Modernism in Canada," in *Danish Modern: Suzanne Swannie Textil* (Halifax: MSVU Art Gallery/Mount Saint Vincent University, 2008), 15, 17; Rachel Gotlieb and Cora Golden, *Design in Canada* (Toronto: Knopf Canada, 2001), 230, 249, 138, 230; and Sandra Alfoldy, "Struggles for Recognition: Canada's Textile Pioneers," *Crafting New Traditions* (Gatineau, QC: Canadian Museum of Civilization, 2008), 77.

12 Anya Palvio from Chelsea advertised Finnish weaving products in *Ontario Handweavers and Spinners* 20, no. 1 (1976): 15. John and Teruko Low, Woolhouse, Spinners' and Weavers' Tool Catalogue," Armstrong, BC, pamphlet, nd. The Lows founded Woolhouse Tools in 1977, and the business is in the process of closing by selling-off its remaining stock.

13 Gotlieb and Golden, *Design in Canada*, 230, 249; Gloria Lesser, "Carl Poul Petersen: Master Danish-Canadian Silversmith," *Material Cultural Review* 43 (1996), accessed January 30, 2016, https://journals.lib.unb.ca/index.php/MCR/article/view/17668/22290; Gloria Lesser, *Carl Poul Petersen Silversmith* (Montreal: Montreal Museum of Fine Arts, 2002); Conrad Graham, "Notes and Comments: Silverware Crafted by Carl Poul Petersen: Recent Donation in the Decorative Arts Collection, McCord Museum of Canadian History," *Fontanus* 9 (1996): 115.

14 Unpublished notes from Rosalind Pepall interview with Vagn Petersen, September 6, 2002, provided by the Montreal Museum of Fine Art.

15 Stephen Inglis, *The Turning Point: The Deichmann Pottery, 1935–63* (Gatineau, QC: Canadian Museum of Civilization, 1991).

16 Rachel Gotlieb, "Married to Pottery: A Life of Uncertainty," in *Crafting New Traditions*, eds. Alan Elder, Melanie Egan, and Jean Johnson (Gatineau, QC: Canadian Museum of Civilization, 2008), 15–23; Gail Crawford, *Studio Ceramics in Canada* (Fredericton, NB: Goose Lanes Editions and the Gardiner Museum, 2005), 37–41. Barry White, "Alma and Ernst Lorenzen," accessed March 10, 2016, http://www.studioceramicscanada.com/ernst-alma-lorenzen.

17 Margaret Hodges, "Rethinking Scandinavian Design in Canada, 1950–1970," *Revue Art Canada/Canadian Art Review (RACAR)* 40, no. 2 (2015): 62.

18 The National Industrial Design Committee was also known as the National Industrial Design Council, National Design Council, and lastly Design Canada before it was closed in 1985. See Gotlieb and Golden, *Design in Canada*.

19 Donald Buchanan, *Design for Use in Canadian Products* (Ottawa: National Gallery of Canada, 1947), 6. Jørn Guldberg from the University of Southern Denmark referenced this statement in a conference paper, "The Promotion of Scandinavian Furniture Design in Canada in the 1950s," presented at University Art Association of Canada (UAAC) Conference, Banff, Alberta, October 19, 2013. I am grateful to him for pointing this out, and for sending me his unpublished paper. See also John B. Collins, "'Design in Industry' Exhibition, National Gallery of Canada, 1946: Turning Bombers into Lounge Chairs," *Material History Bulletin* 27 (Spring 1988): 27–36.

20 Joy Parr, *Domestic Goods, the Material, the Moral and the Economic in Postwar Years* (Toronto: University of Toronto Press, 1999), 12.

21 "Modern Design: Where Did it Come From?" *Canadian Homes and Gardens*, October 1950, 82–83.

22 The exhibition was mounted by the Smithsonian. Accessed February 26, 2016, http://www.gallery.ca/en/see/exhibitions/past/details/twelve-scandinavian-designers-1676.

23 Circulated by the Virginia Museum of Fine Arts, the Scandinavian organizing committee consisted of twelve members from the design and craft professions equally representing the four countries. The American committee was much larger with thirty-one members, mainly from the hosting museums. *Design in Scandinavia*, ed. Arne Remlov (Oslo, 1954). See also Alan Elder, "A Nordic Heritage: Scandinavian Design in Canada," *Hansen-Ross Pottery: Pioneering Fine Craft on the Prairies* (Moose Jaw, SK: Moose Jaw Museum & Art Gallery, 2011), 99.

24 For a discussion of Scandinavian design as a post-Second World War stereotypical construct, see Kjetil Fallan, ed., "Introduction," *Scandinavian Design: Alternative Histories*, 4–6.

25 Gordon McCaffrey, "Scandinavian Art vs. Canadian," *Toronto Star*, October 9, 1959.

26 Pearl McCarthy, "Scandinavia Comes to the Museum to Teach Us the Living Beauties," *Globe and Mail,* July 24, 1954.

27 Eaton's advertisement, *Globe and Mail,* November 2, 1954, 54. Eaton's also sold wood dining sets by Danish American-based designer, Jens Risom, manufactured locally by Guildhall Cabinet Shops. Simpson's placed a prominent advertisement, the day prior to the exhibit opening in *Globe and Mail,* October 18, 1954.

28 Elder, "A Nordic Heritage: Scandinavian Design in Canada," 104.

29 Gotlieb and Golden, *Design in Canada,* 252.

30 Shauna McCabe, *Marimekko, With Love* (Toronto: Textile Museum of Canada, 2013).

31 Gotlieb and Golden, *Design in Canada,* 239; Elder, "A Nordic Heritage: Scandinavian Design in Canada," 118; and Allan Collier, *The Modern Eye: Craft and Design in Canada 1940–1980* (Victoria: Art Gallery of Greater Victoria, 2011), 15.

32 "What is this Thing Called Contemporary," *Canadian Homes and Gardens,* October 1948, 30; "What's New in New York," *Canadian Homes and Gardens,* May 1950, 57.

33 Noted architect Mandel Sprachman lived in Stockholm and worked at an architectural firm after graduating from the University of Toronto. Mandel Sprachman, "Why Scandinavian 'Traditional' is Perennially Modern," *Canadian Homes and Gardens,* September 1956, 21.

34 Bennett, *Canadian Homes and Gardens,* March 1958, 1.

35 Patricia Lamont, "Scandinavian: Traditional for Today," *Canadian Homes and Gardens,* September 1956, 13.

36 Hugh Windsor, "A Team Beat Scandinavians at their Own Game," *Telegram,* April 1, 1964; Len Shifrin, "Furniture: Canada's Copy-Cat Industry," *Star,* June 13, 1968.

37 Len Shifrin, *Star,* June 13, 1968.

38 Howard Krug, *A Century of Excellence Krug Bros. & Co. Furniture Manufacturers,* ed. Ruth Cathcart (Toronto: Natural Heritage/Natural History, 2001).

39 Lamont, *Canadian Homes and Gardens,* September 1956, 20. As pointed out by Virginia Wright, in the 1940s Imperial Furniture carried a furniture line called "Imperial Saarinen" after the Finnish architects and designers Eliel and Eero Saarinen, who taught at Cranbrook Academy in Michigan. See Virginia Wright, *Modern Furniture in Canada 1920–1970* (Toronto: University of Toronto Press, 1997), 80–81.

40 *Toronto Star,* 1965.

41 Guldberg, "The Promotion of Scandinavian Furniture Design in Canada in the 1950s."

42 Gotlieb and Golden, *Design in Canada,* 103, 110–111, 229.

43 *Canadian Encyclopedia,* accessed February 19, 2015, http://www.thecanadianencyclopedia.ca/en/}article/danes/.

44 Gotlieb, "Suzanne Swannie and Danish Modernism in Canada," 20–21.

45 Heather Smith, "Fertile Ground: Hansen-Ross Pottery in Fort Qu'Appelle, Saskatchewan," in *Hansen-Ross Pottery: Pioneering Fine Craft on the Prairies,* 19.

46 Sigrun Bülow-Hübe was the older sister of renowned jewellery designer Vivianna Torun Bülow-Hübe, who remained in Denmark.

47 Margaret Hodges, "Sigrun Bülow-Hübe: Scandinavian Modernism in Canada," (master's thesis, Concordia University, 1996), 53. Bülow-Hübe archives are located at the Canadian Architecture Collection at McGill University, Montreal.

48 Hodges, "Sigrun Bülow-Hübe: Scandinavian Modernism in Canada," 96.

49 Niels Bendsten, accessed February 1, 2016, http://www.bensen.ca/about/niels-bendtsen.

50 Gotlieb and Golden, *Design in Canada,* 250–51.

51 Ibid., 243.

52 Rosalind Pepall and Diane Charbonneau, eds. *Decorative Arts and Design: The Montreal Museum Fine Arts' Collection Vol. II* (New York: Abrams, 2012), 170.

53 Michelle Heinemann, "Premier's Prize Awarded for Tapestry," *Craft Factor,* 9, no. 4. 1984 (Fall): 12.

54 Rachel Gotlieb, "Suzanne Swannie and Danish Modernism in Canada."

55 The Canadian-Scandinavian Foundation is still active and travel scholarships to Denmark, Iceland, Faroe Islands, Finland, Norway, and Sweden are available.

56 Gotlieb and Golden, *Design in Canada,* 252–53.

57 Julien Déziel, "Maurice Brault: Goldsmith and Enamellist," *Vie des Arts* 4 (1956): 18–19.

58 "Walter Dexter," accessed February 20, 2016, http://studioceramicscanada.com/walter-dexter/.

59 Heather Smith, "Fertile Ground: Hansen-Ross Pottery in Fort Qu'Appelle, Saskatchewan," 10.

60 I thank Rosalind Pepall, former curator of decorative arts from the Montreal Museum of Fine Arts for this information. Daniel Cogné, Richard Dubé and Paul Trépanier, *Beauce Pottery: The Story of Beauceware and Céramique de Beauce* (Sainte-Foy, QC: Les Editions Gid, 2004), 158.

61 Crawford, *Studio Ceramics in Canada,* 13–14.

62 Joan Murray, "Joinings: Furniture and Other Useful Objects," *American Craft* 41, no 2 (1981): 37.

63 Crawford, *A Fine Line,* 206.

64 "Glass a Canadian in Denmark," *Tactile,* March–April (1974).

65 Sandra Alfoldy, "Roman Bartkiw," accessed December 20, 2015, https://www.artgalleryofnovascotia.ca/exhibitions/roman-bartkiw.

66 Pamela Ritchie, email message to author, February 28, 2016.

67 Karen Von Hahn, "Looking for Canada's Design Style," *Toronto Star,* February 20, 2016.

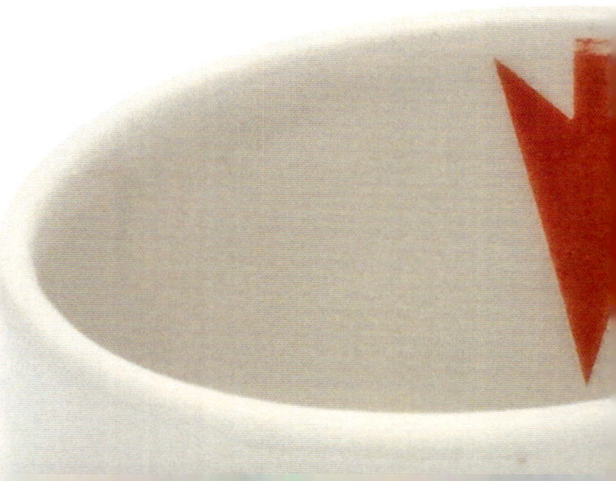

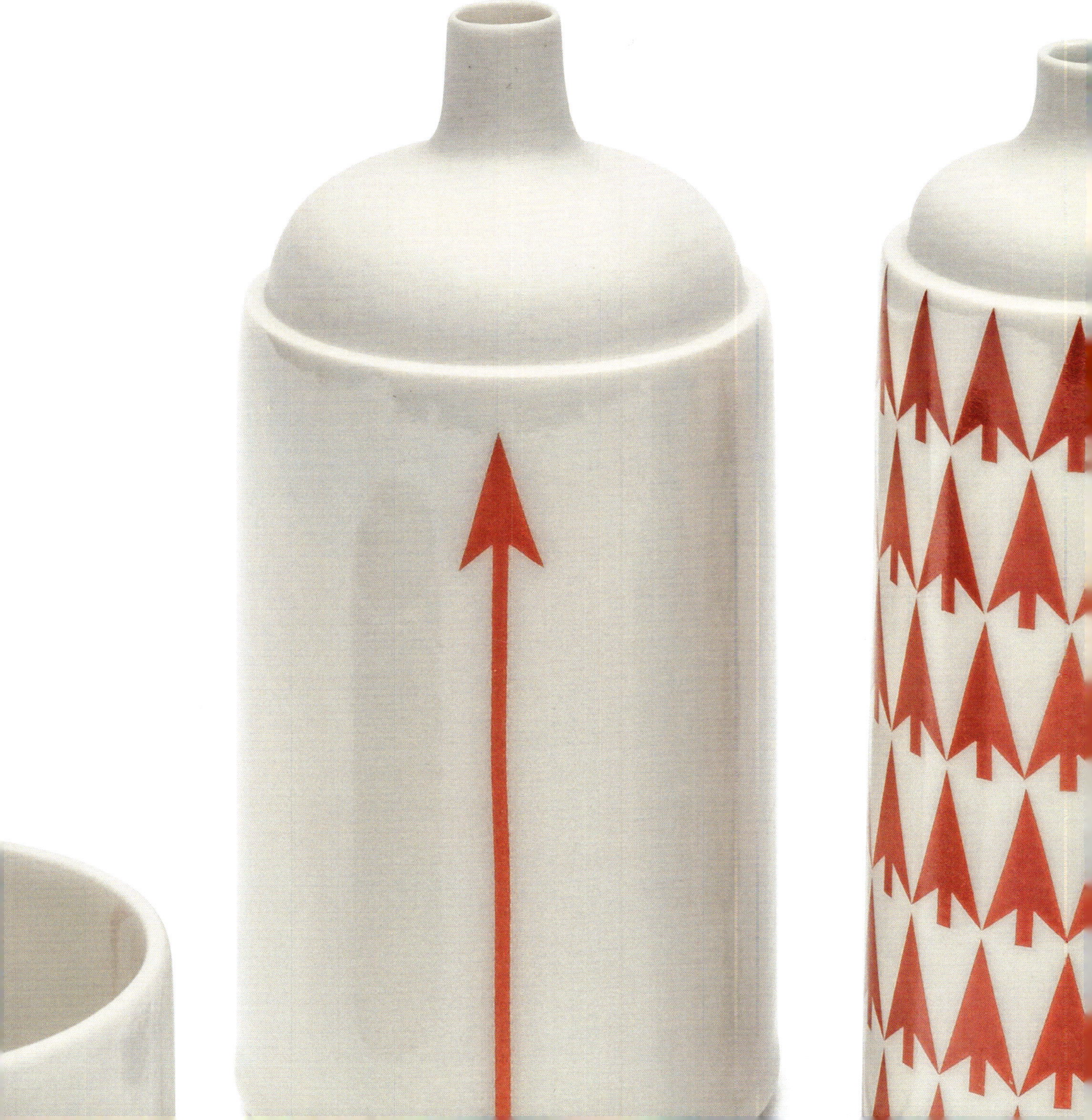

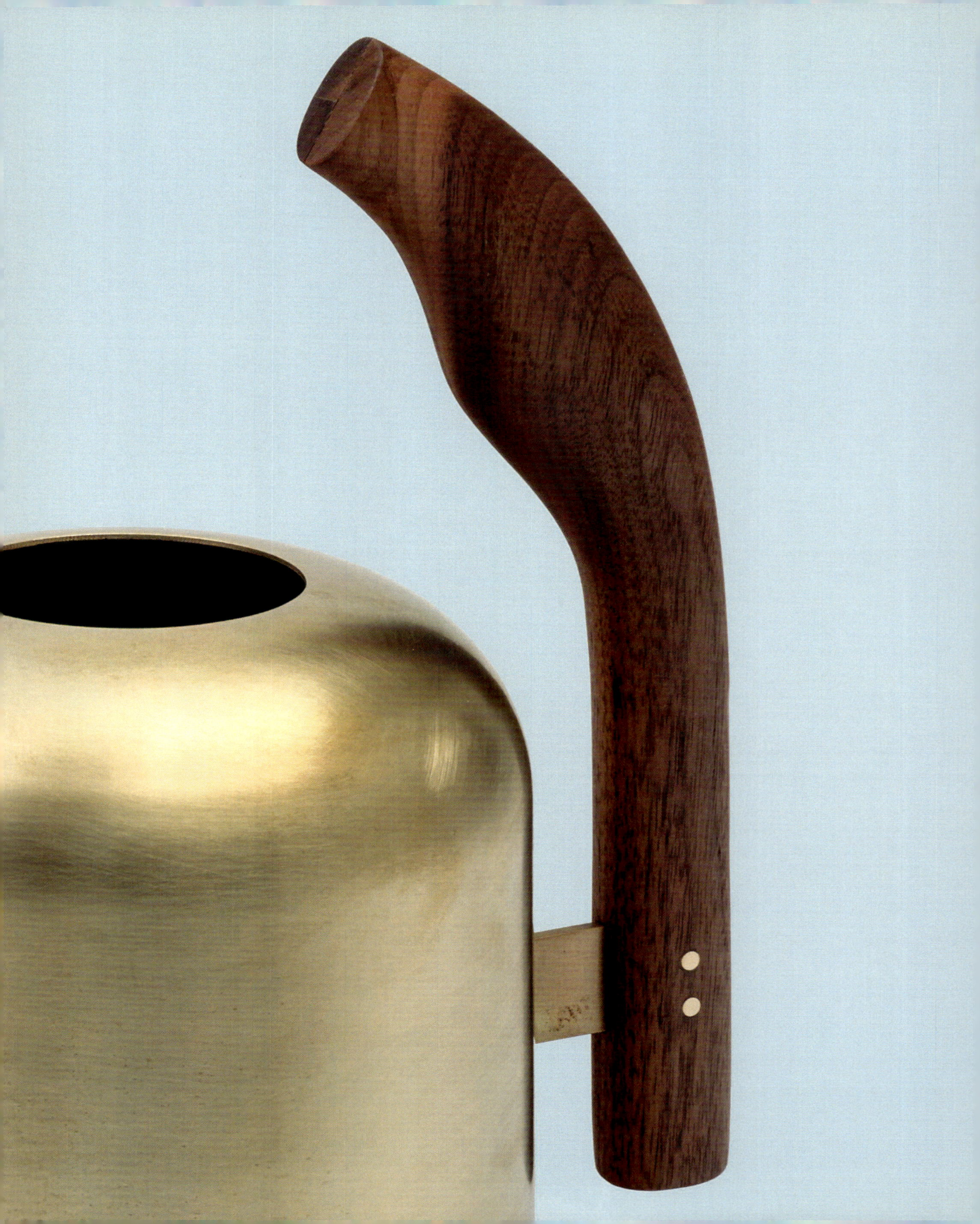

Everything Cold is New Again: Culture, the Circumpolar, and Identity in Canadian Design, 1964 to the Present

Michael Prokopow

"The history of design in Canada is a largely undocumented and undiscussed topic in design studies."[1]

Anyone browsing the August 1964 issue of *Canadian Interiors* would likely have noticed the considerable coverage of the XIII Milan Triennale and its theme of leisure. The design fair, established in 1923, was arguably the world's most important summary of current trends in industrial design and a platform for the promotion of the design cultures of participating nations. The magazine's reporting of the event took two forms: a harsh critique of the organization of the international fair—labelled a "fiasco" by reporter Madge Phillips—and a lavishly illustrated, highly complimentary photo essay about Canada's two official entries, a "northern cottage" and a formally curated display of industrial products.[2] The juxtaposition of the editor's criticism of the state of international design at the fair and enthusiastic praise of Canada's contributions was striking. Although some degree of favouritism could rightly be expected from the leading national design magazine reporting about Canadian design at an international fair, the significance of the report was that it adjudged the country's official design installation to be first rate and the aesthetic and material vocabulary of the pavillion to be a brilliant embodiment of the country.

Designed by Ottawa architects Paul Schoeler and Brian Barkham, the pavillion was unabashedly modern. A rectangular box that was completely glazed on two sides, it captured the quintessentially progressive and modest character of Canada and the important role that its northern geography played in the fashioning of the national temperament. Comprised of a large living room, a compact kitchen, a screened-in porch at the front and two bedrooms, the cabin attempted to evoke, in the densely wooded gardens of the Milan fair site, the idea of Canada. In similar ways, the interiors—the furnishings and their arrangement—presented an appealing tableau of national domesticity. The vision of Jacques St-Cyr (a designer with the Government of Canada's exhibition committee), the cabin was both stylish and comfortable. As the reviewer for *Canadian Interiors* explained, the character of the cabin was "a perfect combination of Canadiana and leisure."[3] (figure 1)

Indeed, much was made about how the cabin's architecture and its decoration captured the character of the country. Significantly, however, the furnishings in the cottage were, in large part, created by Danish emigrants to Canada, and other items, broadly modernist in form, likewise exhibited characteristics of contemporary design from Denmark, Sweden, Norway, and Finland. There was both ideological and cultural logic in the aesthetic language on display in the cottage, and the

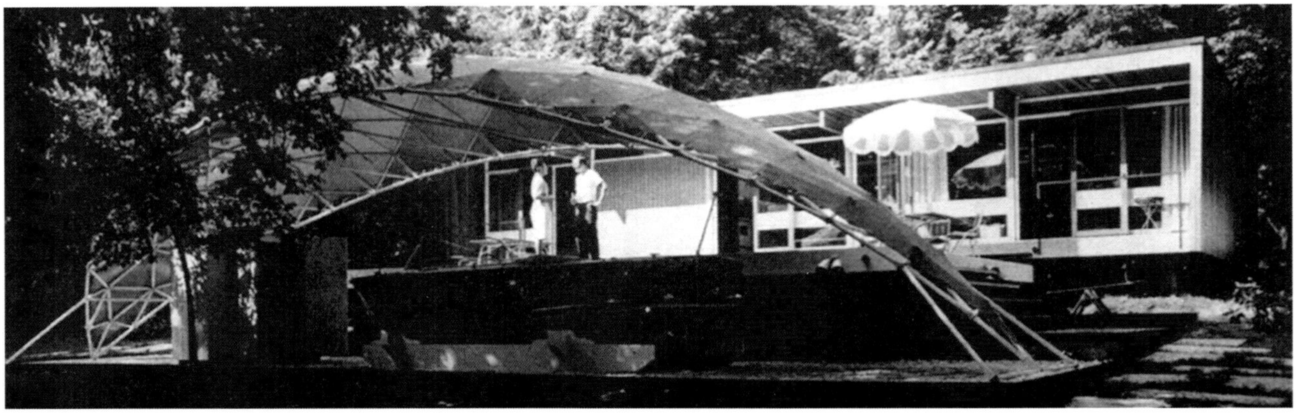

1 Canadian Cottage at the XIII Milan Triennale, exterior view, *Canadian Interiors*, August 1964
Image courtesy of *Canadian Interiors*

transposition of Nordic design sensibilities to a Canadian setting (even one staged for commercial and advertising sake) made sense. The vast popularity of what had, since the mid-1950s, been branded as "Scandinavian design," and the meanings attached to the idea of Scandinavian society and its design culture, were viewed empathetically in Canada.

In these ways, Canada's cottage in Milan represented a potent study in the semiotic operations of material culture. The objects on display—the work of skilled artisans and designers—encapsulated and exemplified the traditions of making that were closely associated with the histories and practices of Scandinavian craft and design, and at the same time, evinced a reflexively benevolent Canadian interpretation of the same. The published photographs of the furnishings in the cottage's living room reveal a tonal and material character that is referentially Nordic. (figure 2)

A pair of tall "simple modern" lamps—one light in colour and the other dark—each with tapering shades of spun nylon by ceramist Lotte Bostlund sit on tables at either end of the pair of low sofa beds against a wall of cedar panelling. Floor to ceiling "webby woven beige drapes" by Karen Bulow cover the cottage's expansive glass windows. Two upholstered adjustable teak folding deck chairs designed by Kai Stonor Poulsen and produced by the Canadian firm Scandia sit facing the sofa. Distinguished by their curvilinear armrests and small fixed neck pillows, they balance practicality with elegance. Near the window is one of two folding tables in teak by Poulsen. Designed with X bases they share certain stylistic motifs with the lounge chairs, and are reminiscent, for example, of the work of Danish furniture designers Knud Andersen and Poul Hundevad.

> It makes sense, therefore, that the conditions of Canada's northern and modest character could be understood as being Scandinavian in character, or at least owing a considerable debt to the Nordic world.

In the middle of the room on a circular floor plate filled with crushed white rocks stands Court Noxon's free-standing conical and rotating enamelled fireplace from his family firm Metalsmiths in Toronto. Against the interior window overlooking the porch sits Hugh Spencer's Clairtone Project G stereo designed in 1963. In both cases, the objects evoke a mood that hovers between the casual and the chic: the distinctive shape of Noxon's fireplace as much embodies current trends in Swedish and Danish metal fireplace design (take, for example, Stig Lindberg's remarkable enamelled stoves for Gustavsberg) as the excitement of the Apollo missions and the lure of Southern Californian living. As for Spencer's radically innovative stereo—its elegant coffin-like rosewood veneered central volume and its projecting chrome-plated arms holding fixed orb speakers—although deemed "a little citified" by the commentator for *Canadian Interiors* and "expensive for a cottage" was likewise singled out as "good Canadian design." And "as such," the reviewer noted, "belongs in a design exhibition."[4]

Thus the Canadian cottage in Milan demonstrated the confidence of the nation. The aesthetic language of the wood and glass structure and its simultaneously casual, thoughtful, and

Scandinavian-inspired contents communicated much about the nation's character and self-awareness at a particularly significant and optimistic point in its history as preparations for its centennial anniversary in 1967 were well under way. In looking to advertise Canada as a particular type of country, the organizers of the Canadian cottage purposely linked the nation to Scandinavia and its topographical, social, and cultural affinities. As much authentically earnest as idealistically staged, the presentation of contemporary Canada as a legatee of Nordic-Scandinavian design sensibilities constituted a powerful declaration of identity—aesthetic and otherwise.

It makes sense, therefore, that the conditions of Canada's northern and modest character could be understood as being Scandinavian in character, or at least owing a considerable debt to the Nordic world. Notwithstanding the fact of the dominant Danish-Canadian design presence at the Canadian cottage in Milan, it is fair to say that the tangible articulation of Canadian character as Scandinavian was much more than simply the stylistic preferences of the exhibition's organizers or a participation in prevailing trends. Rather, for reasons well considered and well understood, there existed in Canadian design culture an awareness of and affinity for the achievements and implications of Scandinavian design in the context of contemporary Canadian life and a determined, consequential exploration of Scandinavian aesthetics on the part of Canadian designers.

II

Even the most cursory examination of trends in Canadian design after 1964 would reveal that the historically bicultural nation—in ways similar to most other industrialized Western democracies—witnessed and experimented with a variety of stylistic movements and taste trajectories. These constituted challenges to the hold that modernism had, in all its focused hegemonic variation, on design culture in North America. Indeed, the 1960s saw significant changes in the design streams—architectonic, biomorphic, and rational—that had defined the modernist movement since approximately 1920.

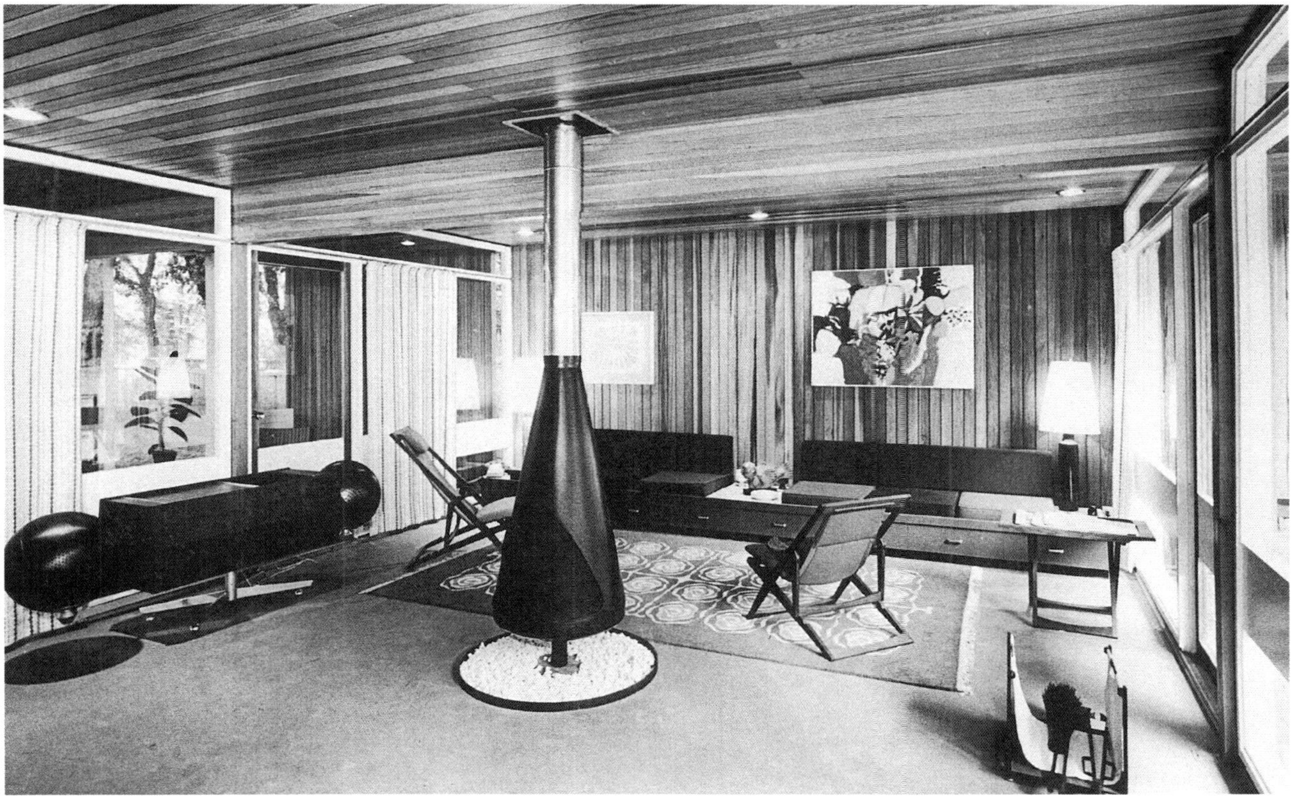

2 Canadian Cottage at the XIII Milan Triennale, main living room, *Canadian Interiors*, August 1964
Image courtesy of *Canadian Interiors*

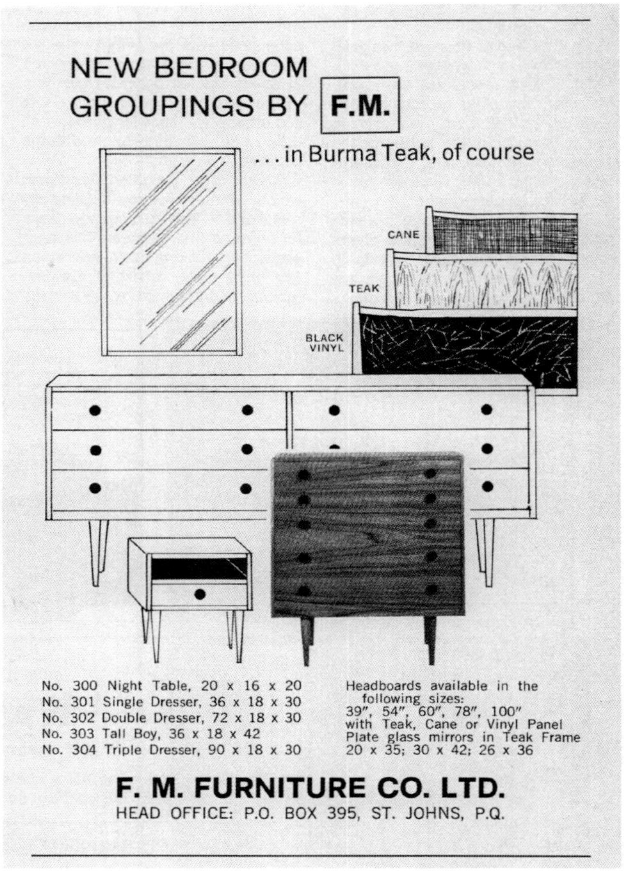

3 Advertisement, "New Bedroom Groupings by F. M.," *Canadian Interiors*, October 1965. Image courtesy of *Canadian Interiors*

The ideological and affectual visual shifts that occurred in North American design culture after 1960 meant that whatever unifying coherence that had existed, in what can be called the style culture, was diluted and eventually transformed by an eclecticism and diversity of form and content that was as dazzling and purportedly refreshing as it was confusing.

The rise of postmodern design sensibilities in Canada—limited in scope in certain ways and less ideologically contentious than in some other countries—resulted in the flattening of what had functioned as a hierarchical privileging of modernist stylistic culture. It was replaced by a visual and material landscape not only of varied forms and semiotic inferences, but also a culture of irony, pastiche, and relativity. Postmodernism resulted in a material and intellectual world defined by a suspicion of elite forms and the equal freighting of once differentiated and distinguishable objects. Suddenly the status accorded to originals and copies changed. Style was as much about forward-looking things and backward-looking things.[5]

The consequences for design in Canada were significant. Any number of designers accepted the tacit permissions granted by the condition of postmodernity to move away from the conformity of modernist form and to participate in what operated as a relativizing aesthetic movement that was as much about destabilizing norms and seeking comfort in the decorative as undermining long-held assumptions about concepts of authenticity and the status of copies and replicas. In an instant, the conventional attitudes concerning the importance of originals (and the attending concepts of the aura and the auratic) were called into question. Among the many consequences was a change in the status of things purporting to be other things.[6] While the copying of styles and forms had always been practised in Canada, the advent of postmodern thinking changed both the implications of this type of creative and economic activity and its social effects.

And such was certainly the case with Canadian furniture manufacturers producing domestic goods taking often-ubiquitous stylistic cues from contemporary Scandinavian furniture design (including affordable and abundant exported products from Denmark). This shift—tied, of course, to larger structural adjustments to the Canadian economy—meant that the long-established patterns of artisanal, craft, and small-batch production (or those specialized ateliers, workshops, studios, and factories that were responsible for the creation of significant objects tied to Scandinavian design principles) were required to adapt. The privileged popularity of Scandinavian imported and locally made objects, whether luxury wares or domestic goods, changed in status with the onslaught of both decently and indifferently made domestic interpretations and copies of Scandinavian designs.

Scandinavian-inspired Canadian design flourished in the years after 1965 because of its cultural associations and the social consequences of owning it. It was, to be sure, the style of choice for Canada's largely suburban middle class. It represented a rejection of the safe traditional styles that had defined good taste and a declaration of sorts concerning ideas about society and its character.[7] Understandably, central in the transmission of both visual information and affirmation, advertisements of all kinds—armed with images, inference, and memorable tag lines—promoted a large range of products, both commercial and domestic, that exemplified the suitability of Scandinavian design for Canadian life. Advertisements showcasing the work of Canadian firms and their active production of Nordic-inspired housewares were commonplace in the leading home décor and decorating magazines.

F. M. Furniture Co. Ltd. of St. John, Quebec, for example, actively promoted the fact that its extensive line of case goods were manufactured out of "Burma Teak" and went so far as to include the words "of course" as a way of affirming the company's serious understanding of Nordic trends and customer expectations.[8] (figure 3) While offering what were often-times generically contemporary designs—rectilinear case goods with tapered dowel legs—the company could, with confidence, make the pitch to prospective clients that "the quality and detail you associate with Danish design are achieved by specifying F. M."[9] The Toronto-based firm I. C. D.—the initials standing for the phrase "inter-continental design"—summarized the company and its services as "designers and manufacturers of Scandinavian furniture."[10] And in similar ways, for example, Toronto companies such as Reff Furniture, Deilcraft, and the R. Huber Company of Toronto and Montreal routinely referenced Denmark and Sweden in their advertisements.[11] These firms understood that genuine consumer desire existed for furniture that looked as though it was imported from Scandinavia, and responded accordingly by making furniture that copied and evoked such precedents.

Indeed, so popular was Nordic design in Canada with its myriad positive implications, that simply referencing Scandinavia had public allure and financial promise. In an effort to tie the aesthetics and sensory delights of Scandinavia to Canadian experience—domestic and otherwise—Shawinigan Chemicals Limited of Montreal and Toronto placed an advertisement in *Canadian Interiors*, praising the tactile and visual qualities of "Vinylite" plastic wall covering. Named "MALMÖ," the vibrant green, slightly textured product was intended to evoke the birch and pine forests of the Nordic world (a typical gesture of postmodernism's embrace of the simulated). "Take a good, long look at MALMÖ," the advertisement read. "It's the all-new, strikingly different wall-covering with a touch of Sweden." Supported by the exclamatory statements, "So Be Different. Look into Luxury. Look into MALMÖ," the advertisement went to considerable lengths to convince potential customers of the transporting effects of the wall covering: a sheet of the product measuring 8 by 11¼ inches accompanied the text in every issue of the magazine.[12]

For many makers, the direct translation, (possibly) copying, of Scandinavian products was simply part of the national enthusiasm for the social effects of good design in the home. In 1973 Paul Epp, who had studied in Sweden and was a junior designer at the Toronto firm of Muller+Stewart, designed a demountable seating series called Algoma. (figure 4) "The objective," Epp explained some years later "was to make a comprehensive system without requiring too many parts."[13] Defined conceptually by its ease of assembly lengths—designer Michael Stewart "contributed" the clever system for connecting the various parts—and visually by its moulded wood arms and legs (each piece being identical save for their length), the set captured the blond casual aesthetics of Swedish and Finnish domestic design in the 1970s and its effective translation to the circumstances of Canada. (figure 5)

And other makers—of varied backgrounds—actively designed and produced wares that captured the aesthetic spirit of Scandinavian design of the period. The work of Sven Sandin, the owner of "Svenstorpet Handicraft" Saint-Étienne-de-Bolton, Quebec, appeared in an advertisement for SAMO Textiles, alerting readers to Sandin's "Rya Rugs Handmade in Canada." The illustrated advertisement captured the duality of émigré makers producing work in Canada that was directly tied to regionally specific studio practice in Scandinavia.[14] Sandin's advertisements, while rare, aligned in spirit with the regular announcements that appeared in the newsletters of provincial craft organizations concerning shipments of Finnish wool and the availability of custom-made Finnish and Swedish looms.[15] Reviews were published regularly of Swedish and Finnish publications germane to Canadian weavers as were printed discussions about current studio practices and notices of lectures by prominent makers. The visit to Ottawa in October 1976 by the celebrated Finnish weaver Oili Mäki, for example, was of special significance to Canadian fibre artists, both professional and amateur. It represented the affirmation of ties between the craft practices of Scandinavia and Canada and stimulated the thinking and actions of studio practitioners across the country in the throes of a vibrant culture of craft activity.[16]

In these and other ways, the production of Scandinavian-inspired Canadian designs was part of a national, albeit commercially driven, conversation about the tangible articulation

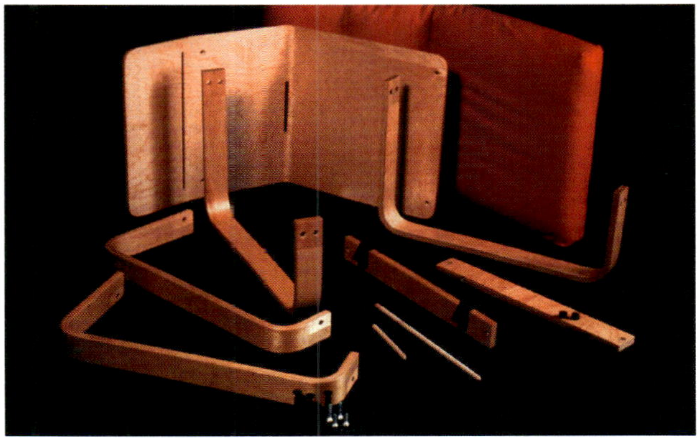

4 Paul Epp, *Algoma* seating (disassembled), for Muller + Stewart, Toronto, Ontario 1973. Image courtesy of Paul Epp

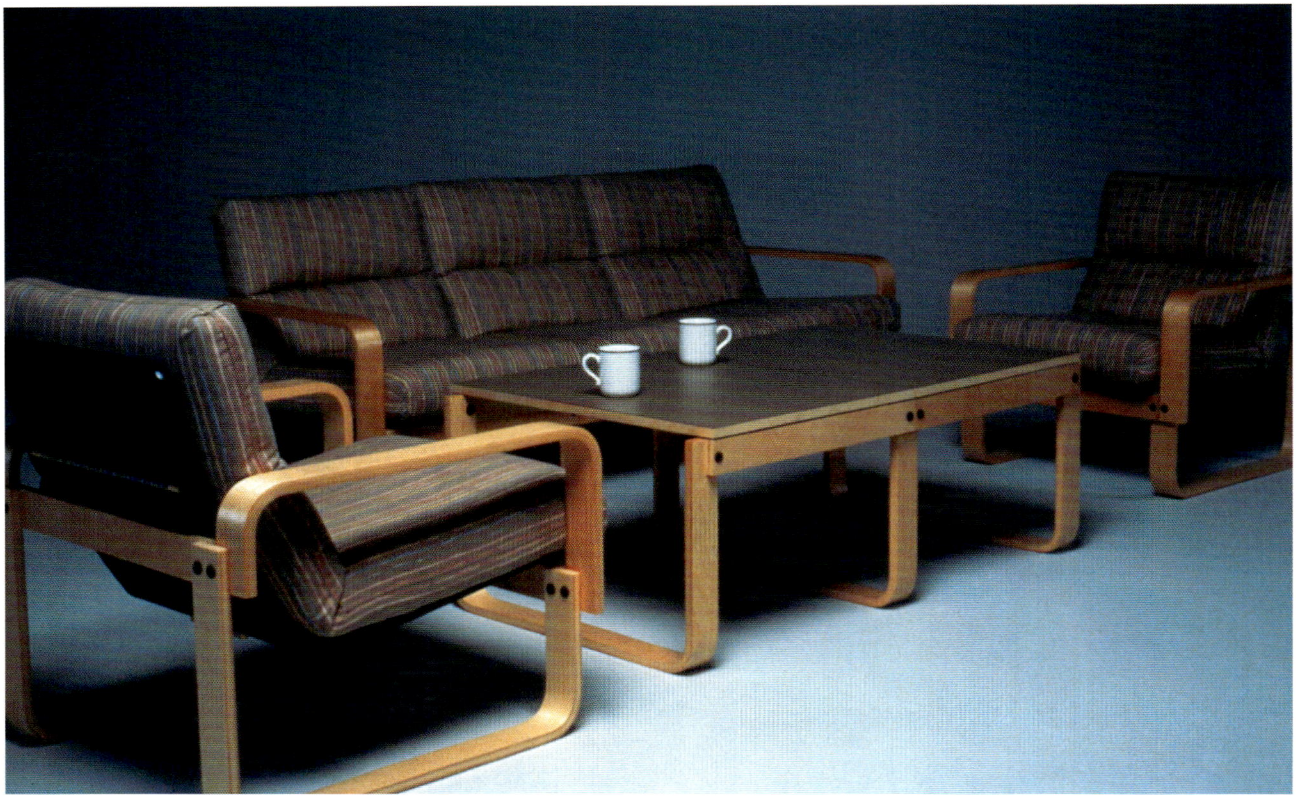

5 Paul Epp, *Algoma* seating, for Muller + Stewart, Toronto, Ontario 1973. Image courtesy of Paul Epp

of character. No wonder then that designers, artisans, and makers operating at all scales of production and across the spectrum of function and materiality actively referenced the forms of Nordic design, and participated in the popularized reinforcement of ideas about identity and character and its expression through objects. Baribocraft, for example, the woodworking firm from Lévis, Quebec, established in 1922, produced economically priced housewares that looked to Nordic and Scandinavian forms. The company's maple serving trays were dead ringers for the celebrated designs of Jens Quistgaard for Dansk, and its line of elongated and tapering candlesticks were in keeping with prevailing stylistic trends from both Denmark and Sweden. (cat. 68–69) André Morin's line of brightly coloured plastic kitchenwares (cat. 84)—from salad sets to serving trays—also evoked the product lines of Dansk and the design work of Gunnar Cyrén and others. Finnish émigré and fabric designer Esa Niemi opened a studio in Etobicoke, Ontario, (a western suburb of Toronto) and produced curtains, tea towels, and other household linens that, while reminiscent of the bold graphic traditions of Marimekko, were original and popular. (cat. 79) Niemi's tea cozy rendered

> For many makers, the direct translation, (possibly) copying, of Scandinavian products was simply part of the national enthusiasm for the social effects of good design in the home.

new a quaint British form that had residual currency in certain parts of Canada. Fashioned of a boldly block-printed cotton depicting tulips in brown, taupe, and bright orange, the reliable if somewhat mundane object embodied the reach of Scandinavian design's national popularity. Similarly, "Nordic Furniture" of Markdale, Ontario, manufactured all kinds of furniture—coffee tables, hutches, sofas, lounge chairs, and dining-room suites—that looked passably like the seemingly endless imported pieces of "Danish Modern" but which, apparently without consequence, never quite measured up to the spirit of their original and would-be progenitors. And in Burnaby, British Columbia, a small industrial firm operating under the name of Jakobsen Industries offered plastic versions of a famous two-piece planter by the Finnish ceramics firm Arabia.[17] Moulded in polystyrene, coming in different sizes, and modified slightly from Finnish designer Richard Lindh's 1964 porcelain original, the Jakobsen planters were produced in a range of colours, including chocolate brown. (cat. 80)

From the early 1970s onwards and arguably into the early 1990s, a popularized Scandinavian style was favoured by middle-class Canada (not to mention many other places as well, but for different reasons).[18] Canadian furniture and household product companies manufactured Scandinavian-looking goods because of consumer desire. The Toronto firm of A. Jensen & Son, operating under the trademark "Danish Custom Furniture", produced high-quality teak dining-room furniture in forms typical of the period. The flat-spindled chairs were slightly organic in form with their high tapered back and curvaceous legs. The woven upholstery was bright, striped, and nubby, typical of Canadian translations of Scandinavian styles of the 1970s. Overall, this largely earnest culture of interpretation represented a vernacularized world of mass-produced objects that conveyed the style and tenor of objects made on the other side of the world, but which did so on Canadian terms.

Craftspeople also looked to Nordic precedent for inspiration. Lidded, wheel-thrown casseroles with autumnal palettes were all the rage, as were graduated pottery canisters and small cork-topped containers for spices. Woven shaggy carpets were crafted in brightly coloured yarns and see-through abstract wall hangings in all shades of beige, grey, and brown became favoured decorative accessories. Weaver Marion Smith of Vancouver, British Columbia, expertly made Rya-like wall hangings and rugs in her West Vancouver studio designed by Arthur Erickson. (cat. 47–48) Ontario potter Jack Herman fashioned carefully incised bowls and small jars with handmade wooden lids in palettes of soft turquoise and grey and monochromatic tapered bottles—in pale blue-greens and sand brown and beige—with teak stoppers, likewise, handmade. (cat. 49) Jewellers such as Gilles Vidal and Robert Larin of Montreal, for example, were thoroughly familiar with studio trends in Scandinavia. (cat. 60) Larin's practice in particular was heavily influenced by the work of his Finnish counterparts—Björn Weckström of Lapponia, among others—and he fashioned accomplished studio pieces, including heavy bracelets, rings, pendants, and cufflinks, which topographically evoked glaciers, tundra, and the occasional moon crater.[19]

Indeed, across the material and cultural landscape of the 1970s and 1980s, the taste for Scandinavian styling continued to dominate. There were always competing trends for home décor and for the style of everyday objects. And while the mass character of the appeal may have come at the expense of the cultures of making that celebrated the craftsperson, the core values that people saw exemplified in Nordic-inspired things remained important because they seemed appropriate to the conditions of life in Canada.

III

"The notoriously difficult question of national and regional design styles," contends historian Kjetil Fallan, "has long haunted design history and has taken on renewed importance in the wake of the massive increase in international trade and global production and consumption networks over the last several decades."[20] Fallan's insightful comments—written in 2012 in a radically revisionist essay about Scandinavian design—can easily be applied to Canada.

Ever since colonial Canada's popular outing at the Great Exhibition of 1851 in London, where slabs of wood, taxidermal moose heads, and impressive clumps of ore dominated, questions have been asked as to how best to represent the land, the people, and the evolving political and social order. The Canadian design on display in Milan—as sincere as it was theatrical—presented an image of a modern country that embraced the realities of its topography and seasonality. Eschewing the more bombastic symbols of statehood, it demonstrated a visual language that communicated an image of the nation as a place aware of itself, its affinities, and its character.[21]

But negotiations of identity are rarely finished. Each generation of politicians, makers, and citizens engages with questions of the semiotic errands of defining sovereignty through images, symbols, motifs, and materials. As constructs, all nations are the products of cultural processes where the contested realities of social existence, collective memory, and unevenly shared aspiration combine together in the making of functioning ideas and lived experience. In Canada's case, nature and ancestry have historically been dominant variables in the country's equation of selfhood. Accordingly, in light of the multicultural transformation of Canada since 1971 with the reform of emigration policy and subsequent passage of landmark legislation in 1988, the stakes have been raised, both officially and not, on identifying images, symbols, and other aesthetic forms around which the attending ideas about nationalism could coalesce.[22] For it is the act of translation that domesticates the natural world, and it is the mimetic act that transforms the observed world into representative and functioning entities. Scandinavian design objects have long been regarded as revealing of their conceptual and aesthetic origins—the realities of landscape and available resources—and indicative of the importance of traditional skills and ways of making, the relevance of craft and handmade things, and a communitarian emphasis on well-being and the work of fashioning tools to serve people. How else to explain the immense and respectful popularity of Scandinavian design and, specifically, Scandinavian design in the history of modern Canada and its millennial reinvigoration?

The resurgence across the country of artisans and craftspeople producing goods of exemplary conceptual and material quality and, in what is rightly described as a derived, modified, and stylistically Nordic idiom merits close consideration. What can be framed as "contemporary" design practice in Canada—meaning the design culture after the events of 9/11 and its palpably galvanizing effects on people around issues of place and culture and identity—represents an important study in a type of liberating capitulation or an unanticipated opportunity to consider the values of nation and nationality. Makers, often working at intimate scales across media, have turned their skills and attention to fabricating what operate economically as small-batch goods that are often luxurious. Indeed, Canadian design of the millennium—contemporary because of the fact of temporality (or its place in chronological time), revealing prevailing sensibilities (the ways that expressive culture functions as sign and symbol), and destined to pass into history (the short-lived status of the object as "new" and its reconfiguration as simply something from the past)—demonstrates both a resurgence in artisanal practices and a confidence in the embrace of materials, forms, and motifs that are at once referential and self-aware. Additionally, the expansion in the cultures of studio, craft, and artisanal practices in the first decades of the twenty-first century is tied to a maturity of thinking about place and country in the contexts of levelling globalism and the ubiquity of mass consumption.

> But sensitive and innovative historicism represents just one dimension of the tenor of millennial design in Canada.

Constituting a return to the types of philosophical and stylistic convergences that marked the modernist movement, makers such as Derek McLeod of Toronto, Shawn Place of Prince George, and Jeff Martin of Vancouver, for example, have drawn thoughtful inspiration from the distinguished history of twentieth-century Danish cabinetmaking. McLeod's maple, steel, and leather sling chair of 2012 (cat. 105)—designed along with a companion low round maple table and maple tray—is both new and deferentially tied to the 1950s. The carefully detailed construction of the frame, the distinct cant of the back legs and the precision of the front-facing understructure, (reminiscent, as it is, of the PK22 lounge chair by Dane Poul Kjærholm) reveal McLeod's careful rigour as a designer-maker and his informed, sensitive inventiveness. In corresponding ways, Place's furniture also recalls the mid-century aesthetic of designers such as Hans Wegner and Finn Juhl. Self-taught and inventive, Place openly acknowledges that it was a visit to Inform Interiors, the Vancouver design store owned by distinguished Danish-Canadian designer Niels Bendsten, and his encounter with what he called "Danish modern furniture" that propelled him to his work. "I said to myself," explained Place, 'I'm going to do that,' and just started researching furniture and design."[23] Place's walnut and rattan rocker from 2004—curvilinear, gentle, and efficient—acknowledges its lineage while likewise articulating its stylistic autonomy. (cat. 97) The same can be said of the work of Jeff Martin. His *Coastal Credenza* (cat. 115) is a grounded and serious object. Designed in 2015, it is clearly reminiscent of the domestic and architectonic mainstays of stylish and modernized mid-century suburban living rooms and assuredly current. The refinement of the millwork, the quiet patina of the metal substructure, the complementing wooden feet (akin to one of Juhl's signature forms), and potent architectonic presence of the low-slung cabinetry, all nod towards the expansive legacy of this particular historic form and render it augustly anew.

Significantly, the active engagement with historical forms functions in sympathetic contrast to the deliberate evocations of the geographical and meteorological conditions of the northern half of the North American continent.[24] Jenna Stanton's studio-made ceramic drinking sets for the Medalta International Artists in Residence Program in Medicine Hat, Alberta, hearken back to the functionalist agenda of the modernist movement, with their pleasingly repetitive and colourful patterning being reminiscent of the graphic work of such Swedish designers as architect Sven Markelius and polymath Stig Lindberg. (cat. 117) In a related instance of historical referencing, the shape and aesthetic import of Andrew Jones's Fleurt chair of 2014 proclaims its debt to the graphic and "Pop" sensibility of classic Marimekko textiles from the 1960s—and especially Maija Isola's vibrant Unikko from 1964—and to the important ergonomic investigations of Charles and Ray Eames in the 1950s. (figure 6 and cat. 112) Lightweight, stackable, and graced with a pleasingly cheeky double entendre of a name, Jones's chair exemplifies the ways that ideas and precedents can be rewardingly referenced and reconfigured.

But sensitive and innovative historicism represents just one dimension of the tenor of millennial design in Canada. A considerable number of makers working across the country have looked to landscape and the natural world for inspiration. The work of Loyal Loot Collective—originally comprised of four female designers divided between Edmonton and Calgary who, as the members have explained, make things with "integrity and beauty"—constitutes a smart study in the willingness to reference winter and forests in the making of things. The collective's birch coat rack (cat. 94) reads simultaneously as a bunch of cross-country skis leaning against a wall and as the wood shavings occasioned by an axe being taken to a tree. It is as genially wry as it is functional. The collective's bright and affecting log bowls—

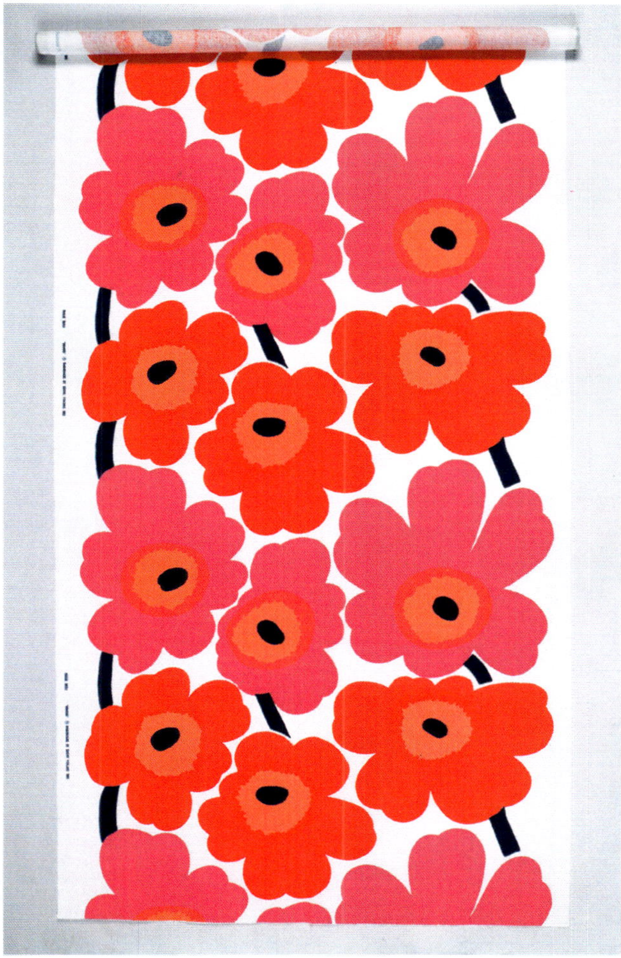

6 Maija Isola, "Unikko," textile, 1965 (introduced in 1964), manufactured by Marimekko, Helsinki, Finland. Cooper Hewitt, Smithsonian Design Museum, gift of Marimekko, Inc., 1979-89-7 Photography by Matt Flynn © Smithsonian Institution / Art Resource, NY

designed by Doha Chebib Lindskoog—succeed because of the way the bark of sliced log is perfectly preserved with the interior being hollowed out and painted. Here the palette of deep of winter is cheered by vibrant colour. (cat. 93)

And other Canadian designers similarly embrace the motifs of the natural world. Glass-blower Brad Copping's *Barkbird* decanter and *Stumpware* cups from 2015 are about the textures of trees and the transparency of water and ice. (cat. 118) The Toronto-based Brothers Dressler's 2009 *Branches Chandelier* riffs off of nineteenth-century antler lighting while capturing the experience of looking up to the sky through a thicket of trees. (cat. 101) Rob Southcott, likewise a Toronto maker, references the tangle of the backwoods and the trackless forests of Canada in his four-seat chair/bench *United We Stand* from 2007. (cat. 100) With the antler-like branches extending beyond and above the seatback, Southcott's chair conveys, in poetic and stylistic ways, the transforming journey of a natural resource to inviting, arguably affable, domestic implement.

But while the translation of raw materials into goods for everyday life defines social existence, it is the creative spark—the marshaling of intellectual and cultural resources in the fabrication of domestic goods—that is of critical importance. One of the more significant developments in contemporary design in Canada takes the form of a set of collaborative projects sponsored by Toronto retailer Mjölk that have provided several designers the opportunity to have their works produced in Canada. Established in 2009, Mjölk's unexpected transnational production model has yielded results noteworthy on the level of both economics and aesthetics. The partnership with the Norwegian design duo of Torbjørn Anderssen and Espen Voll (known as A&V), for example, resulted in the creation of several striking products for the home. The *Water Bulb* boasts two asymmetrically positioned large orbs on a hollow tapered stem, which once filled and inserted into the soil in a planter, releases the water slowly and steadily. (cat. 116) Made in Toronto by master glass-blower Gregor Herman and reminiscent in form of the whimsical work of Oiva Toikka for Nuutajarvi, the historically important Finnish glassmaking firm, the product is an example of what John Baker and Juli Daoust, the owners of Mjölk, call "localization," or the marriage of design expertise from one place (where manufacturing is "in decline") with the studio expertise of another.[25] In similar fashion, A&V's elegant "precision" brass and wood watering can demonstrates the promise of Mjölk's cultural entrepreneurship. (cat. 114) With its hand-spun body, long and extending spout, and carefully milled handle, the can displays its production pedigree: it was fabricated in Toronto by the fourth-generation owners of the venerable metalworking firm of Harnisch, established in Copenhagen in

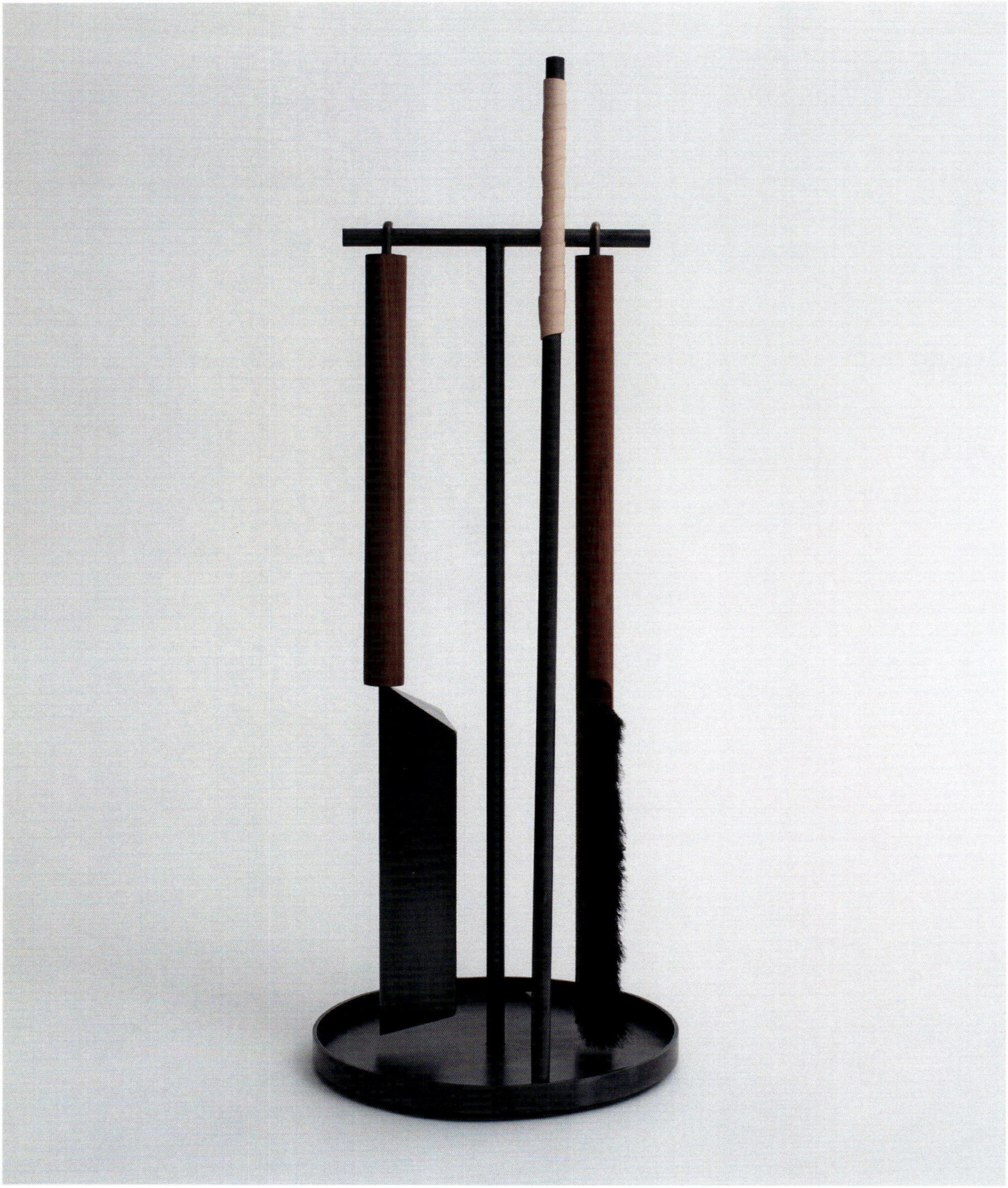

7 Thom Fougere, Fire Tools, Toronto, Ontario, 2015
Image courtesy of Thom Fougere

1842 and famous for the nautical lighting it produced for the Danish Royal Navy and for the Danish coast guard. Mjölk's other collaborative projects include an oil lamp with the Toronto-based firm Castor (the fabrication of which was also undertaken by Harnisch) and a set of Fire Tools by Winnipeg designer Thom Fougere.[26] (figure 7) Materially refined, enticing in form, and fundamentally humane in character, the prosthetic imperative of each device—meaning how each tool is an extension of the human body—is rendered in what constitutes an effective updating of the domestic aesthetic of mid-twentieth-century Scandinavian design.[27]

Yet, despite the complex prognoses around Canada's post-industrial future, there is something reassuring about emerging models of creativity and partnership that build on shared understanding and (perhaps quite literally) common ground with nations of proximate latitude and attending awareness, or what functions as a similar consciousness. If anything, the return by Canadian designers to a direct, guileless acknowledgement of nature and the realities of life in a sparsely settled and earnest land, seem appropriate and sincere. As Canada continues to diverge from the economic and cultural hegemony of the United States, so continues the need and the capacity to speak in its own metaphoric and material voice. That the influential *Financial Times* of London could run a story in late April 2015 with the title "Canadian Design: Nordic by Nature" suggests that the days of reducing the motifs of land, forests, and weather to caricatures might well be over.[28] Canadian design of the millennium—influenced by the cultures and aesthetic practices, some half a world away, and the legacies of their agents and offerings—constitutes a shared acknowledgement of the legitimacy and benefits of the tending and outfitting of one's own proverbial cabin first.

Endnotes

1 Bonne Zabolotney, "Anonymity and Authenticity: Everyday Canadian Design," *Current: Design Research Journal,* Issue 6 (2015): 4. See http://current.ecuad.ca/anonymity-and-authenticity-everyday-canadian-design.
2 "Triennale Canadian Exhibit," *Canadian Interiors* 1, no. 5 (August 1964): 13.
3 Ibid., 16–18.
4 Ibid., 16.
5 Historicism, or the embrace of the stylistic past, operated alongside aesthetic explorations that were frequently seen as the logical developments of trends within modernism. The result was a decades-long period in design history where the sureties of modernity gave way to a playfulness and wry culture of pluralist possibility.
6 In the context of design in Canada, there was a type of democratization of production. The interpretation and fabrication of objects styled on elite originals expanded, as did the creation of objects for which an original did not necessarily factor in the creative process, but where, significantly, the inference of the newly made thing was sufficient.
7 It is important to note that even in the face of the enormous popularity of Scandinavian modernism, historical styles—revivals and so on—never fell altogether out of favour. Traditional styles, in the same symbolic ways as contemporary ones, held the ability to conjure a place in time and to demonstrate one's character and social condition.
8 *Canadian Interiors* 2, no. 11 (November 1967): 56.
9 *Canadian Interiors* 2, no. 10 (October 1965): 63. The advertisement shows a low and long storage chest. There are nine drawers each with two inset handles. The legs are tapering spindles. Advertisements for Canadian-made Scandinavian-styled furniture were plentiful. See *Canadian Interiors* 5, no. 10 (October 1968): 93.
10 *Canadian Interiors* 4, no. 11 (November 1967): 47.
11 Huber, for example, used the tag line "upholstered furniture with a Scandinavian accent." See *Canadian Interiors* 5, no. 10 (October 1968): 93. In an earlier advertisement featuring a rounded sofa and chair set with distinctive teak legs arranged so that the front, back, and sides of each different piece were visible, Huber offered, "anyway you look at it, Canada's most exciting line of furniture." See *Canadian Interiors* 4, no. 1 (January 1967): 18.
12 *Canadian Interiors* 3, no. 9 (September 1966): 18–19.
13 See the website of Paul Epp, http://www.paulepp.com/row-prod.php.
14 *Canadian Interiors* 4, no. 11 (November 1967): 56.
15 Lillstina looms were also widely promoted and Anja's Weaving Supplies of Chelsea, Quebec, advertised almost continually in the pages of the journal between 1976 and 1983. In September 1976, Ms. Palvio, the owner of the import firm, wrote an open letter to her customers and the weaving community: "Your most beautiful weaving deserves the most beautiful yarns. My natural fibres selection from Finland gives you fine quality yarns suitable for home furnishings, personal apparel or tapestry." The letter explained that the company had secured the distribution rights for "100% pure wool worsted rya yarn" in 125 colours. The letter also made mention of the availability of "multi-harness counter marche looms of TOIJALAN KAIDETEHDAS of Finland (TOIKA). *Ontario Handweavers and Spinners* 20, no. 1 (September 1976): 15.
16 In June 1977, for example, the editors of *Ontario Handweavers and Spinners* suggested their readership secure copies of Martine Selander's classic 1961 texts *Weaving Patterns from Sweden* and *Swedish Handweaving*. See *Ontario Handweavers and Spinners* 20, no. 4 (June 1977): 77. In December 1980, an advertisement appeared for Glimarka looms. "Most Swedish Weavers Select a Glimarka Loom," read the notice, "for some very good reasons." *Ontario Handweavers and Spinners* 24, no. 2 (December 1980): 36. On Mäki's visit, see *Ontario Handweavers and Spinners* 20, no. 3 (March 1977): 53. Mäki spoke at the "Woven Structures" conference at the Holiday Inn on Kent Street. Copies of her speech were subsequently published by the organization. "This personal point of view by an outstanding artist is a work of art in itself," read the alert in the bulletin. "It is thought-provoking and very good reading." *Ontario Handweavers and Spinners* 20, no. 3 (March 1977): 53. Indeed, the work of Saskatchewan-based Finnish-Canadian weaver Kaija Sanelma Harris—trained at the Turku Textile Institute—was widely publicized and held up as an example of the successful translation of Nordic design sensibility to Canada. Harris's lyrical use of the double-weave in what was described as "lushly colored [and] sensuous work, whether commercial or commissioned." See "The Premier's Prize Winner," *The Craft Factor: The Magazine of the Saskatchewan Craft Council* 15, no. 2 (Summer 1990): 4–5 and 8. For examples of Harris's work, see "# 5 Spring Cloud" in "Dimensions 1988," *The Craft Factor* 13, no. 2 (Summer 1988): 6; and "Dimensions '89: The Premier's Prize Winners," *The Craft Factor* 14, no. 2 (Summer 1989): 7–8. Harris was often commissioned to make large-scale installation pieces. Her clients included architect Raymond Moriyama and the Toronto Dominion Centre in Toronto, Ontario, for which she made an enormous tapestry for the foyer of the main building. See "Introducing Some of the Award Winning Craftspeople: Dimensions '87," *The Craft Factor* 12, no. 2 (Summer 1988): 27.
17 Even in plastic, the Jakobsen version of the Arabia pot did manage to communicate a refined design sensibility in the spirit of the original.
18 An additional and important variable in the broad interest in what can be called affordable Nordic and Scandinavian style in Canada was due to the arrival of Ikea in 1976—the first store opened in Vancouver—and the company's aggressive expansion. The store's distinct approach to marketing—the catalogue, the restaurant, and its DIY sensibility—succeeded in reinforcing the aesthetic preferences to the budget-minded and introduced successive generations to the appeal and power of good design from Sweden.
19 Larin worked in pewter and plated base metals. One of the striking details of his practice was that he employed artisans with hearing impediments. In the heyday of his work, his factory on Rue Papineau had some twenty-five employees. See Roberta Peach, "Robert Larin," *Abstractions*, 2003, http://www.modernsilver.com/Abstractions.htm.
20 Kjetil Fallan, "Introduction," *Scandinavian Design: Alternative Histories* (London and New York: Berg, 2012), 4.

21 Indeed, that the design for a new Canadian flag was taking place at the same time as the cottage was on display and that Jacques St-Cyr played a key role in both is telling. See http://www.macleans.ca/news/canada/the-quebec-nationalist-who-designed-canadas-flag/.

22 Canada adopted multiculturalism as policy in 1971. The policy was formally made law in 1988. See Immigration, Refugees and Citizenship Canada, "Canadian Multiculturalism: An Inclusive Citizenship," last modified October 19, 2012, http://www.cic.gc.ca/english/multiculturalism/citizenship.asp.

23 See "The Method Behind: Shawn Place of Shawn Place Designs," Plastolux, May 23, 2011, http:www.//plastolux.com/the-method-behind-shawn-place-designs-modern-furniture.html#.VsZURb5jp95; and see Stacey McLaughlin, "Furniture Designer of the Year 2012: Shawn Place," *Western Living Magazine*, September 1, 2012, http://www.westernlivingmagazine.com/doty/furniture-designer-of-the-year-shawn-place-a-bike-shop-manager-walks-into-a-furniture-store-and-emerges-as-one-of-the-wests-best-new-design-talents/.

24 Stanton's interest in simple geometric shapes does reference Markelius's famous textile design of 1952 and is striking because of its similarities to designer Anna Svanfeldt's revisiting of Markelius patterning for her line of Ikea textiles designed in 2006.

25 *Anderssen & Voll + Mjölk*, (Toronto: Mjölk, 2015), 11.

26 See "Oil Lamp," Castor, http://www.castordesign.ca/oil-lamp/.

27 Fougere's Fire Tools for Mjölk were debuted at the 2015 Stockholm Furniture Fair. They were presented along with eight other products, including table and seating. As Fougere explains "The Fire Tools are the result of a long term study into man's historical relationship with fire, hearths, and the tools used for tending to a fire." "Our history with fire is an important one," he explains, and is:

> deeply embedded within our being. Fire itself is a tool that provides a means of warmth and nourishment; we are instinctively drawn to its presence. The design for the Fire Tools was inspired through studying tools of the past and how these tools have evolved over time. By examining this evolution and distilling the tools down to only the most essential components needed for modern day hearths—maintenance, cleanliness, storage, and tending to the fire—their forms emerged. Each tool was reimagined to address each of these necessities in a unique way. The set is comprised of a selection of natural materials that enrich with use and age—walnut, leather, and brass. Developed for the Toronto based gallery Mjölk.

See "Fire Tools Mjölk," Thom Fougere Studio, 2016, http://thomfougere.com/index#/mjolk-fire-tools/.

28 Trish Lorenz, "Canadian Design: Nordic by Nature," *Financial Times*, April 24, 2015, http://www.ft.com/cms/s/0/3c3d428a-e42b-11e4-9039-00144feab7de.html#slide0.

The author would like to thank the following: Elise Hodson, Allan Collier and the staff of the Shore + Moffat Library at the Daniels Faculty of Architecture, Landscape and Design, and the Thomas Fisher Rare Book Library at the University of Toronto.

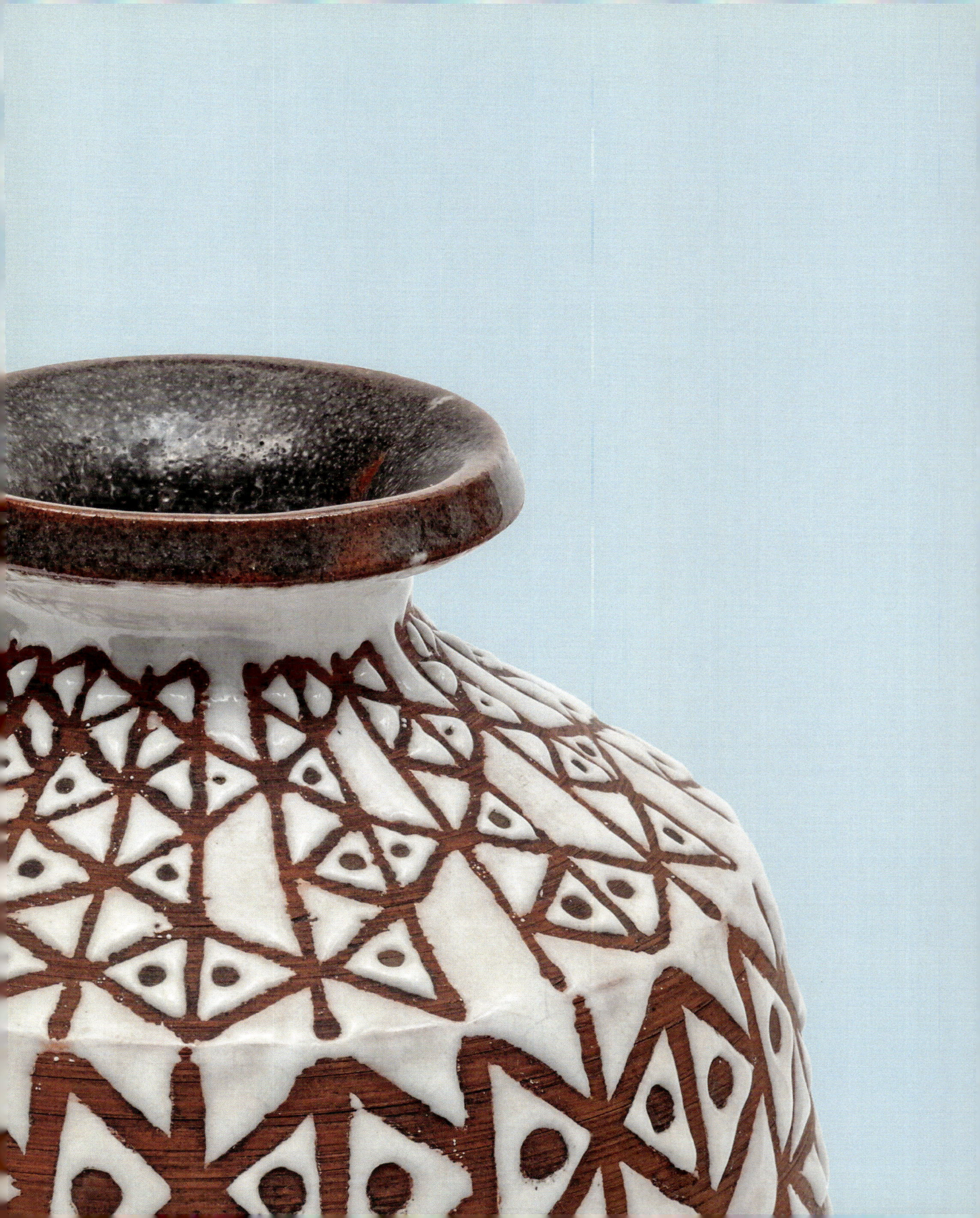

The Influence of Scandinavian Architecture and Design on Architecture in Central Canada

George Baird

The "Scandinavian design ethos," which influenced architecture in central Canada in significant ways, is largely associated with the careers of five major twentieth-century Scandinavian architects. In chronological order, they were Eliel Saarinen (1873–1950) of Finland and the US, Gunnar Asplund (1885–1940) of Sweden, Sigurd Lewerentz (1885–1975) also of Sweden, Alvar Aalto (1898–1976) of Finland, and Sverre Fehn (1924–2009) of Norway.[1]

Saarinen was one of the leaders of the National Romanticist movement in Finland—a cultural blend of Arts and Crafts and Art Nouveau—which flourished in Finland from the turn of the century until the ascendancy of what is called Heroic Period modernism, the movement characterized in the 1920s by the all-white, cubic buildings of Le Corbusier and Mies van der Rohe. Saarinen's progress can be tracked from the Arts and Crafts house he designed for himself at Hvitträsk, Finland, of 1902 to his ornate Helsinki Central Railway Station of 1919.

Asplund and Lewerentz, on the other hand, started their careers in the genre known as Nordic Classicism, a spare and very restrained Scandinavian version of the early nineteenth-century neoclassicism associated with Prussian Karl Schinkel. Asplund's famous Stockholm Public Library, which opened in 1928, would be a well-known example of Nordic Classicism. Gradually, Asplund and Lewerentz shifted away from its restrained formal vocabulary and material palette toward a more emotive modern architecture.

Alvar Aalto, far and away the most admired of this entire group, started his career under the influence of Asplund's work, but moved away from it in the early 1930s, first to his own version of Heroic Period Modernism and then eventually to the intensely material work of his mature period from 1938 to 1976. Fehn, the youngest of the group, in some respects extended the robust tradition running from Eliel Saarinen through Lewerentz to Aalto in his own career.[2]

It is the entwined consequences of these architectural traditions that had the greatest influence on Canadian architecture, especially in the period from the mid-1950s to the early 1970s, and particularly in Toronto and other parts of Ontario. The main defining features of this ethos were as follows: a strong engagement with the natural landscape; a striking counterpoint of rectilinear plan geometries, on the one hand, and of curvilinear or jagged rectilinear ones, on the other; an intense interest in such "natural" building materials as brick, timber, and copper; and last, but not least, a highly refined sense of material detail. All of these characteristic features are evident in a 1939 masterwork of Alvar Aalto: the Villa Mairea, a villa in Noormarkku in western Finland, the radical significance of which was disseminated widely in the European, British, and American architectural press.

First Evidence of the Influence in Ontario

Even with the decades-long movement of ideas and images of Nordic architecture to North America from roughly 1930 onwards, the midfifties are key in the history of Scandinavian influence in central Canada. Already by 1955, an Estonian immigrant to Toronto, the architect Michael Bach (1916–1972) had designed a remarkable church for the congregation of St. Peter's Estonian Evangelical Lutheran Church in north Toronto. With its rich dark red brick exterior and its dramatically sheltering copper-clad roof, it strongly evokes many of the Scandinavian design motifs cited above.

By 1957 the Danish silver retailer Georg Jensen opened a new shop on Bloor Street in Toronto. Designed by Finn Juhl (1912–1989), otherwise best known for his furniture designs, the building was a beacon of refined urbane and luxury objects with its clean glass cases and striking lighting. (p. 14, figure 6)

The same year, rebellious students at the University of Toronto's School of Architecture succeeded in persuading their influential teacher, Eric Arthur, to join their campaign against a traditional design for Toronto's new city hall, and to organize an international competition for the selection of a more contemporary one. The students' unlikely campaign proved successful. Arthur became the professional advisor for the competition that concluded with the selection of the design by Finnish architect Viljo Revell (1910–1964). (figure 1)

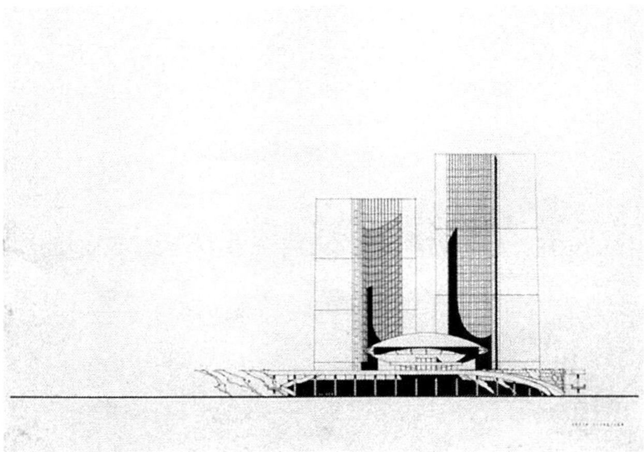

1 Viljo Revell, south elevation panel for the second-stage submission to the Toronto City Hall Competition, 1958. Courtesy of Toronto Public Library, Manuscript Collection, L 4B

Even with the decades-long movement of ideas and images of Nordic architecture to North America from roughly 1930 onwards, the midfifties are key in the history of Scandinavian influence in central Canada.

Interestingly, the young associates of Viljo Revell, who conceived the first version of their design for the Toronto City Hall, were obviously pitching their entry to Eero Saarinen, the son of the famous Eliel, and probably the most influential of all the jury members for the Toronto City Hall Competition. Ironically, however, the younger Saarinen was not really a participant in the same design ethos as his father, having been educated in an entirely American architectural system not much influenced by Scandinavia at all.[3] By 1958, he had just completed the dramatically curvilinear TWA Terminal at Idlewild (now JFK International) Airport in New York. This said, it is still true that there is a quite distinctively Scandinavian motif included in Revell's second-stage competition drawings: the depiction of hanging vines on the raised exterior walkways that formed part of their design is utterly Aalto-esque. So even though Revell had moved away from Aalto over the span of his career, in his entry to the Toronto City Hall Competition, some evidence of his influence can still be seen.

Significantly, the movement of people and ideas was not always from Europe to North America. The story of Carmen Corneil (b. 1933), a talented Canadian graduate from the University of Toronto architecture program, is particularly telling. For in 1958 Corneil made his way, shortly after his graduation, to work in the office of Alvar Aalto, and the consequences of his experience are evident in the form of several significant buildings and projects he designed in Toronto in the early and mid-1960s.

By 1957 the long-term development of the bold new Toronto suburb of Don Mills was becoming publicly visible, at the same time revealing the tensions in architectural culture between what might be called Scandinavian humanism, on the one hand, and corporate modernism, on the other. Most of the institutional and commercial buildings that would eventually make up Don Mills—many of them designed by the major Toronto modernist firm of John B. Parkin Associates—largely did not follow a Scandinavian design direction, but rather, one influenced by German modernist Ludwig Mies van der Rohe. In contrast, many of the houses designed for Don Mills, especially those by either James A. Murray or Henry Fliess, reflect a notable, if rather generalized, Swedish

> Significantly, the movement of people and ideas was not always from Europe to North America.

influence. The single and split-level houses with pitched roofs exhibit crisp profiles and minimalist details that characterize Swedish contemporary design.

The Main Period of the Scandinavian Influence: the 1960s

By 1959 Corneil had returned to Toronto from Finland, and had commenced his professional career as an architect. He divided his practice working on projects under his own name as well as on projects under the auspices of William McBain, one of his former teachers from University of Toronto. Over the next few years, Corneil designed a number of projects that clearly demonstrate the powerful influence Aalto had on him and his design thinking. Some of the projects were constructed, such as the headquarters building for the Association of Girl Guides. Completed in 1962, with its angular volumetric form, its very rough red brick cladding, and its wood-louvred windows, it stands to this day as the most Aalto-esque building erected in Toronto. (figure 2)

In 1960 Corneil was one of the invited participants in a limited competition for the design for a new Massey College to be erected on the campus of the University of Toronto—a competition that included submissions by Arthur Erickson and the eventual winner, Ron Thom. (figure 3) In 1963 Corneil participated in the competition for the design of a cultural centre to commemorate the Fathers of Confederation in Charlottetown. (figure 4) Even though Corneil won neither competition, these remarkable entries, similarly to the Girl Guides' headquarters, show Aalto's strong influence on his thinking. This is particularly evident in the geometries of the proposed buildings in plan and in section, and in the deployment of such natural materials as brick masonry.

The Scandinavian ethos in architecture was also evident in the new residence building of the same period for New College at the University of Toronto, designed by Macy DuBois (1929-2007) of the firm Fairfield and DuBois. Built between 1964 and 1969, the building combines a jagged rectilinear exterior form with a sinuously curvilinear interior form in its inner courtyard, and is also clad in a characteristically Aalto-esque red brick. (figure 5)

The work of several other Toronto architects during this period also exhibits evidence of the influence of Aalto's work. The Group Health Centre, commissioned by the steelworkers' union in Sault Ste. Marie, Ontario, and designed by Jerome Markson (b. 1929) in 1963, exhibits an adaptation of Aalto's ideas about massing and materials to the conditions of Ontario. The building incorporates a second storey in the jagged rectilinear style typical of Aalto. Constructed of light-coloured brick at grade and sheathed in white ceramic cladding on the second floor, it represents a clear example of the adaptation of Nordic form in the decades after 1950. (figure 6)

The Central Place in this History of Janis Kravis and his Karelia Studio

Another architect with Baltic origins, who helped to bring the influence of Scandinavia to central Canada, is Latvian Janis Kravis (b. 1935). Upon graduating from the University of Toronto's architecture program in 1959, he almost immediately opened a small retail area in the reception of a hairdressing salon on Bayview Avenue, in the Toronto suburb of Leaside. At the time, Kravis was working in the office of John B. Parkin Associates—the Toronto firm that served in the capacity of associate architects with Viljo Revell on the Toronto City Hall project. It was at the Parkin office, Kravis reports, that he first met Revell. The Finn encouraged him to visit Finland as well as to import more Scandinavian products than he was already doing. The result of this mentoring conversation was

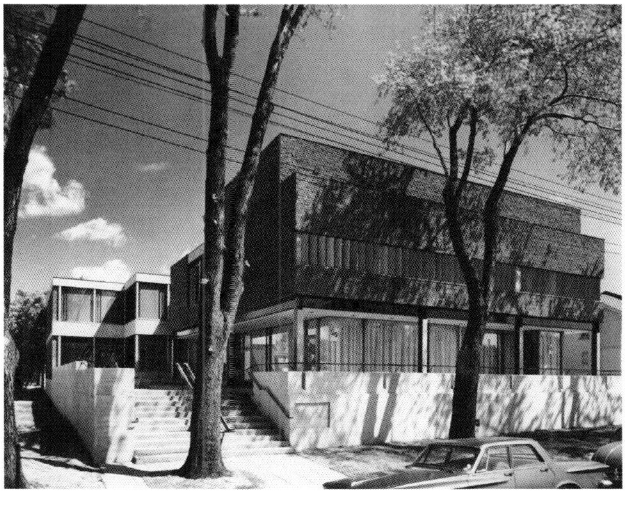

2 Carmen Corneil, Headquarters building for the Girl Guides of Canada, completed in 1962. Carmen and Elin Corneil fonds, Canadian Architectural Archives, University of Calgary

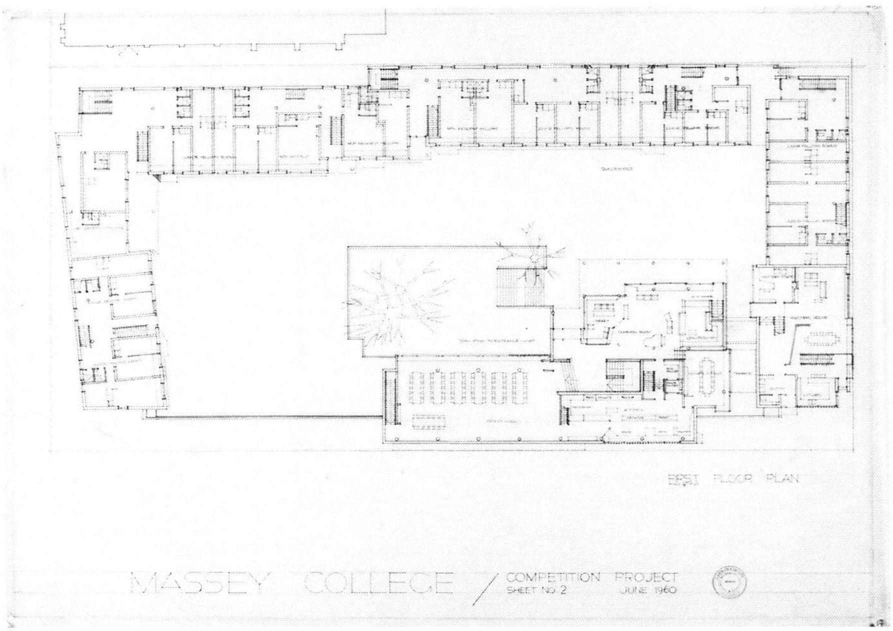

3 Carmen Corneil, plan drawing, entry to the Massey Hall Competition, University of Toronto, 1960. Carmen and Elin Corneil fonds, Canadian Architectural Archives, University of Calgary

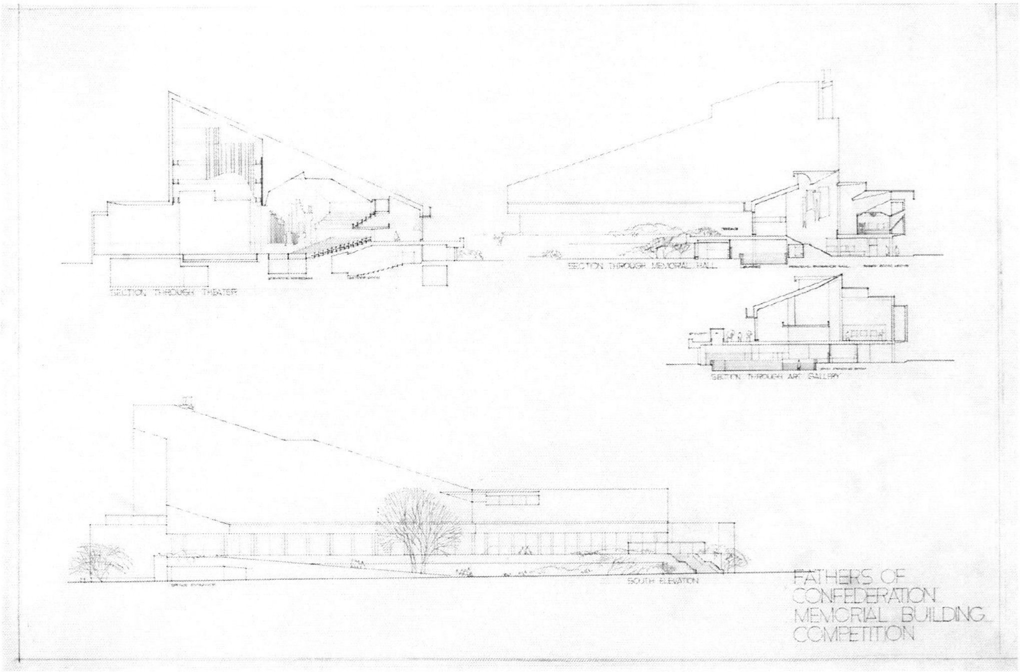

4 Carmen Corneil, section drawing, entry to the Fathers of Confederation Memorial Building Competition, Charlottetown, 1963. Carmen and Elin Corneil fonds, Canadian Architectural Archives, University of Calgary

significant for Toronto: Karelia Studio soon moved to its own independent space in the thriving Gerrard Street Village, between Bay and Elizabeth Streets in downtown Toronto. There Kravis stocked stainless steel by Gense, glassware by Karhula-littala, Marimekko fabrics, and a wide range of household Scandinavian-made products.

The Gerrard Street shop eventually also proved too small, and Kravis moved again to Lothian Mews, a small, new, and very precocious infill shopping mews behind a building on Bloor Street, across from the Georg Jensen shop. Lothian Mews, a small grouping of shops disposed on two levels around a courtyard and fountain, was famous not just for Karelia Studio, but also for the Coffee Mill. Opened in May 1963 by Martha von Heczey, the eatery quickly became not only fashionable but also culturally important. It operated as the powerful social focus of the significant expatriate Toronto Hungarian community. Lothian Mews, demolished in 1984, has to be seen as the seed of the remarkable small-scale retail explosion that eventually came to define the village of Yorkville in midtown Toronto.

The 1960s proved important in terms of the Scandinavian-inflected cultural life of Toronto. Kravis became a major boutique retailer in Toronto, at his peak managing two large shops, one in the Manulife Centre at Bloor and Bay Streets in midtown Toronto, and a second one in the newly reviving St. Lawrence Market neighbourhood on Front Street East. Notably, in the mid-1960s Kravis also received the major commission to design and to outfit a new restaurant being created in the Windsor Arms Hotel, a venerable small Toronto hotel just off Bloor Street. The hotel had been purchased by Kravis's lawyer's son, the young George Minden, who was intent on turning the modest 1920s Gothic-revival hostelry into Toronto's first fashionable boutique hotel. Opening in 1966, the Three Small Rooms was instantly one of the most glamorous and successful Toronto restaurants. Kravis designed the rich interiors of brick, wood, and copper and much of the restaurant's furniture. He selected the china, glassware, and cutlery as well.[4] Elegant and intimate, the three differently styled rooms with their discrete food offerings presented a distinctly northern and cosmopolitan sensibility.

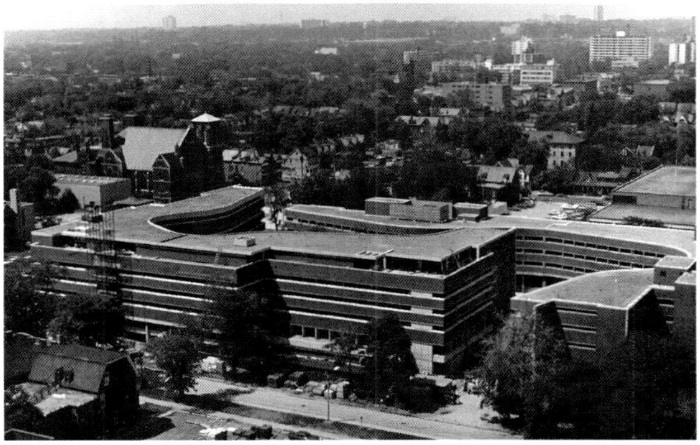

5 Fairfield and DuBois, New College Residence, University of Toronto, constructed in two phases between 1964 and 1969. Image courtesy of Helga Plumb

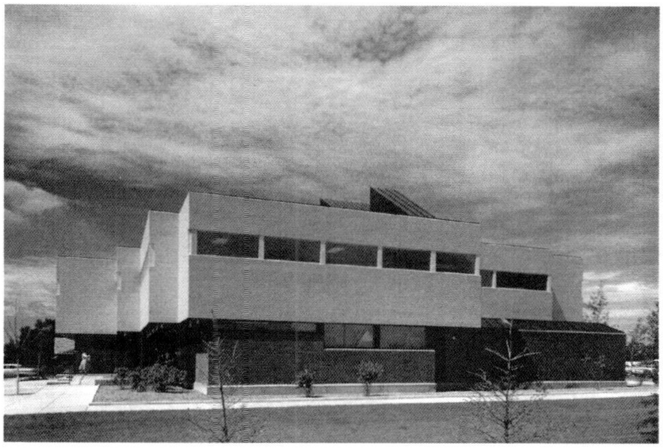

6 Jerome Markson, Group Health Centre, Sault Ste. Marie, Ontario, completed in 1962. Image courtesy of Jerome Markson

The 1960s proved important in terms of the Scandinavian-inflected cultural life of Toronto.

But such Nordic progressivism had already been publicly affirmed in 1965, with the official opening of Revell's new Toronto City Hall. From then on, the new city hall—and more so, the encompassing new Nathan Phillips Square—quickly transformed the social and political life of the city. Arguably, Revell's new city hall, with its radical form and materially sensitive interiors, and the much-praised retailing and hospitality efforts by Kravis quickly came to be seen as major new Toronto cultural and architectural landmarks influenced by Scandinavia.

The After-Effects of the Scandinavian Influence in Central Canada

Tellingly, perhaps, the peak of the influence of the Scandinavian design ethos on central Canada—decidedly a specific regional phenomenon—was already in decline. It was superseded in successive waves by such international design

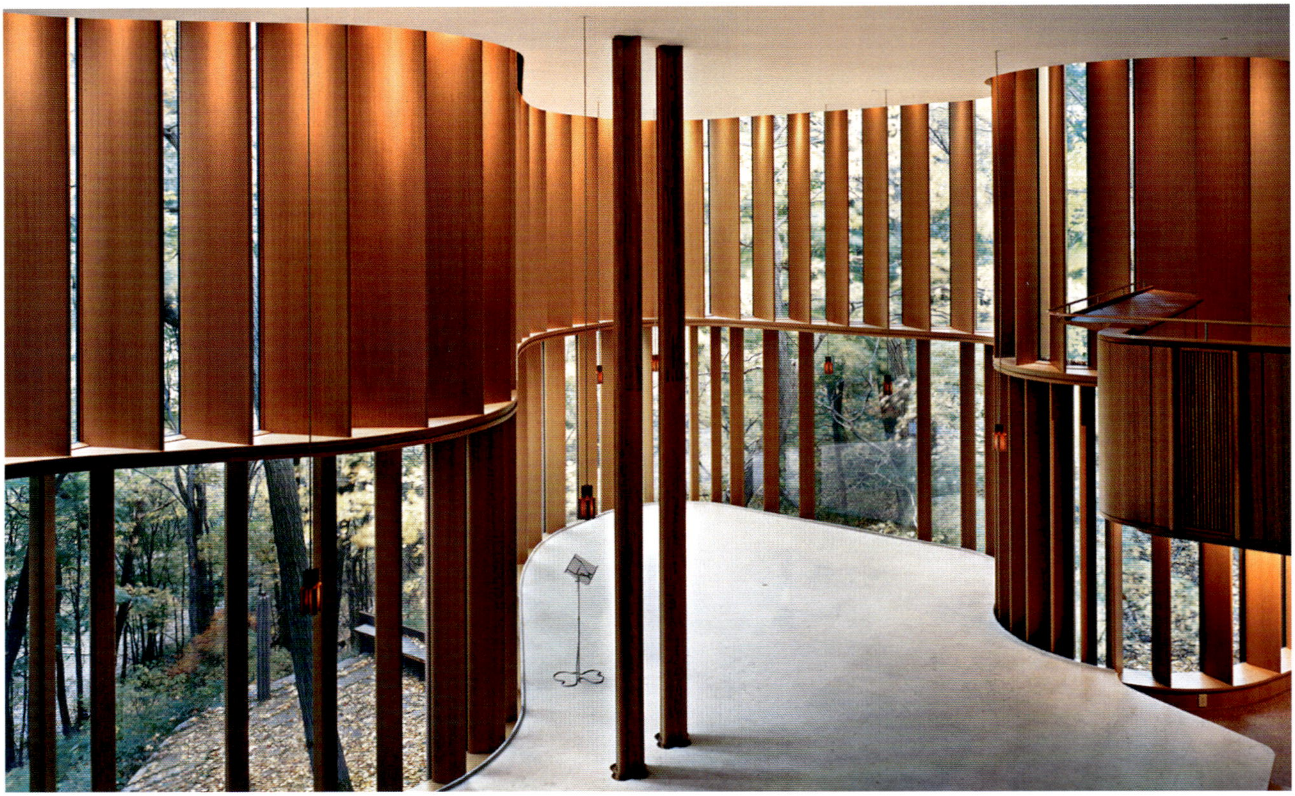

7 Brigitte Shim and Howard Sutcliffe, interior view of Integral House, Toronto, 2003–2009. Photography by Ed Burtynsky

tendencies as "high tech," the "megastructure," and eventually even postmodernism.[5] It is true that recent times have seen projects designed by architects with Scandinavian names erected in Canada. Notable examples would be the new Student Learning Centre for Ryerson University by Snøhetta (2015), Vancouver House condominium by Bjarke Ingels (2016–2018), and the new Halifax Central Library by Schmidt Hammer Lassen (2014). However, the design approach of all of these firms is only very tangentially influenced by the Scandinavian ethos described at the beginning of this text. At their core, all such firms as these have to be described not as Scandinavian, but as post-Koolhaasian—given the overwhelming influence of that charismatic Dutch designer on them.

Still, as late as 2009, the Toronto architects Brigitte Shim and Howard Sutcliffe—both of them participants in Alvar Aalto Symposia in Finland—unveiled their famous Integral House in Toronto's fashionable Rosedale neighbourhood. (figure 7) In this project, designed for the mathematician and philanthropist James Stewart (1941–2014), Shim and Sutcliffe reprised the geometrical lessons they had learned from Aalto, even fifty or so years after his most active influence. Distinguished by the sweeping curvilinear geometry of its main living space, which was designed to accommodate the musical performances to which Stewart was so devoted, and with a two-storey glass and wood rear façade (an inversion, in certain ways, of the form of Fairfield and DuBois's courtyard at New College), and its masterful massing and its storied cascade down a ravine hillside, Integral House reads as a timely material and stylistic revisiting of the principles that defined Scandinavian architecture in the 1930s and 1940s.

For a decade and a half from the mid-1950s onwards, a striking influence from Scandinavia can be seen in the new architecture of Toronto and its environs. At the present time, some half a century later, the appropriate direction for Canadian architecture in the future is not altogether clear. The set of compelling Canadian projects described in this essay cast an eloquent and highly suggestive light on that future.

Endnotes

1 The Danish architect Arne Jacobsen (1902–1971) might be thought an appropriate addition to this list, as he is certainly a figure of historical importance. However, his design sensibility was a more corporate one than that of any of the others listed here and thus less central to the design ethos under discussion.

2 For details of Fehn's career, see Christian Norberg-Schulz and Gennaro Postiglione, *Sverre Fehn: Works, Projects, Writings 1949–1996* (New York: Monacelli Press, 1997).

3 The elder Saarinen, having won second place in the 1922 competition for a new building for the *Chicago Tribune* newspaper, moved from Finland to the United States to become the professor of architecture and the designer of most of the buildings for George Booth's famous Cranbrook Academy in Bloomfield Hills, Michigan. It was at Cranbrook where Eero Saarinen spent his youth.

4 With the 1991 sale by Minden of the Windsor Arms for a condominium development, a long and memorable social tradition of dining at the Three Small Rooms came to a sad end.

5 During the same decade and a half from the midfifties to the early seventies, there were a number of architects in other parts of Canada who expressed their admiration for Scandinavian design in general, and for Aalto in particular. The evidence of actual design motifs in the buildings they designed are not nearly as intensely affected as is the group in the general vicinity of Toronto discussed above.

The author gratefully acknowledges the assistance of Professor Michael Milojevic of the University of Auckland in the preparation of this text, in particular for his generous provision of the reproductions of the images of Carmen Corneil's entries to the Massey College and Fathers of Confederation design competitions.

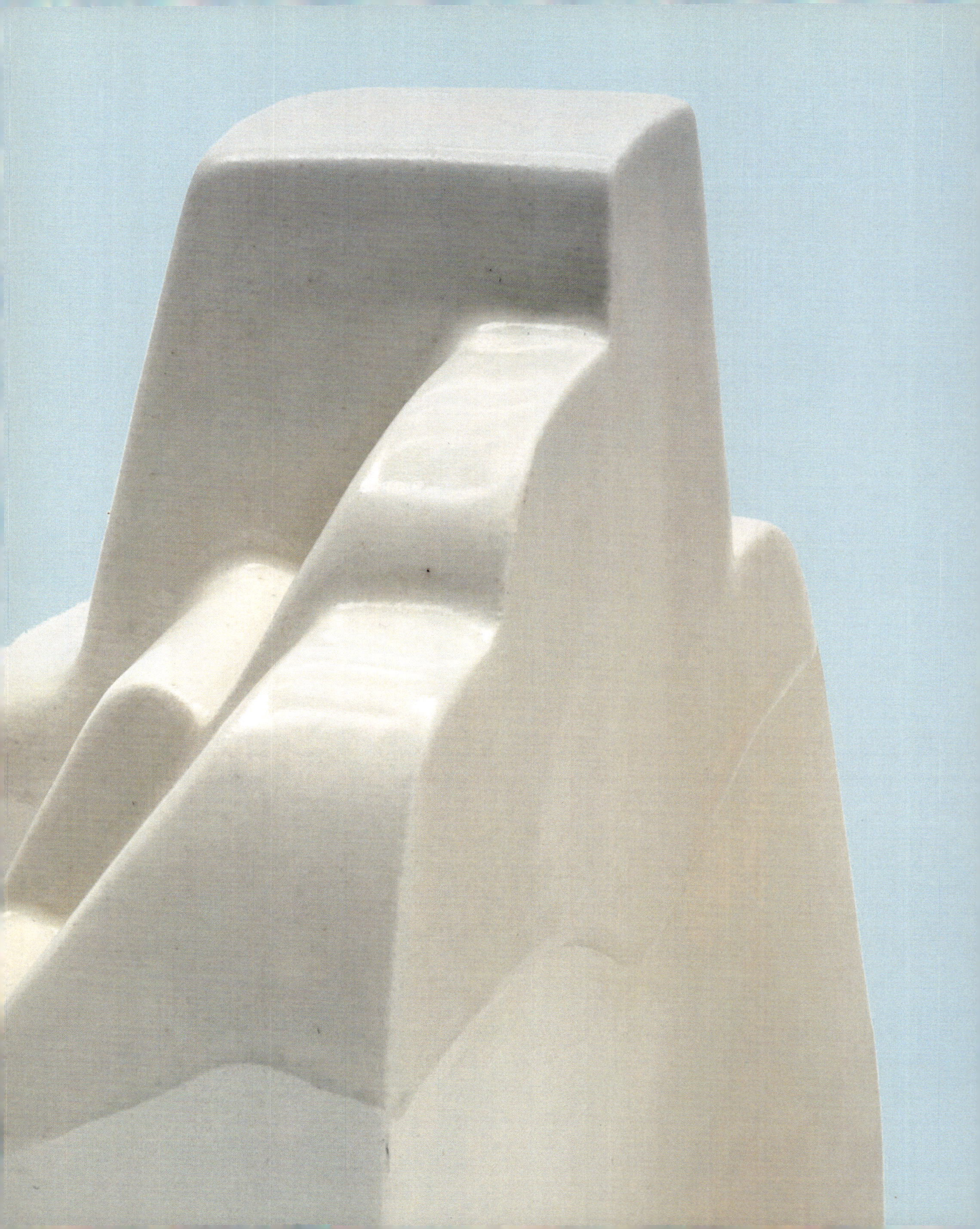

The Idea of North Revisited: Nordic Myths and Modernisms

Mark Kingwell

It is a well-worn cliché that the iconic imagery of Canada is all wintry. Snowshoes and igloos, toques and down parkas, the boreal forests, icebergs, and frozen oceans at or near the Arctic Circle—the land known, even unto the title of a not very good television series—as "North of Sixty." (The Arctic Circle itself lies at just over 66.5° north.) The nation's most widely praised national artists are seven painters who mostly did not visit this land and who people in the rest of the world still, despite the interest of comedian/collector Steve Martin in the work of Lawren Harris, do not recognize. (figure 1) From ubiquitous ice sports, such as hockey and curling, to the full let's-go-camping wardrobe of the Roots clothing chain, almost everything about the national mythology references the outdoors, preferably during periods of snow and intense cold.

Harris has become our de facto national painter, in part because, to quote the novelist and critic Russell Smith, he is "the Adele of Canadian visual art"—which is to say popular, inoffensive, and successful.[1] Smith finds Harris's "stylized, bulbous, glowing glacierscapes to look a lot like children's book illustrations.... They are pretty and smooth, and perhaps inspiring to people who prefer the idea of a magical, spiritually pure, people-free, dream-like, crystallized North—a place like the planet Krypton—to real places."

Smith has the better of this argument. The fanciers of what he mocks as "the raw majesty of the Canadian landscape" depicted by the Group of Seven are trapped in a web of national mythology. And while we might dispute the aesthetic judgment that Harris's icebergs "would be great on posters advertising breath-freshening gum," the real places are indeed otherwise. The actual north is unknown to the overwhelming majority of Canadians. They live in a handful of large cities that cling to the southernmost edge of the vast geographical territory as if their lives depended on it.

Perhaps this is literally true, since Canada's largest trading and foreign-policy partner has been and remains the United States. There are endless debates—indeed, endless debates about these debates—concerning whether and how Canadians are different from Americans, but the hard fact is that in many important ways they are not. They drive the same cars, live in similar neighbourhoods, shop for and eat the same food, and largely watch the same films and television shows. Marginal variances in culture are important, to be sure, especially when a very small country exists alongside a very large one with a tendency to bulldoze the Other. Canadian music, film, radio, and even food—hello poutine, you yummy delight!—make for identity. So, too, do deeper-running differences, such as the ongoing presence of a French-speaking minority, the demographic diversity of those cities, and of course the socialized health insurance of which we make so much.

Still, much of the agonizing that goes on about Canada's place in the world is a function of what Sigmund Freud called "the narcissism of minor differences."[2] A far more illuminating, though also

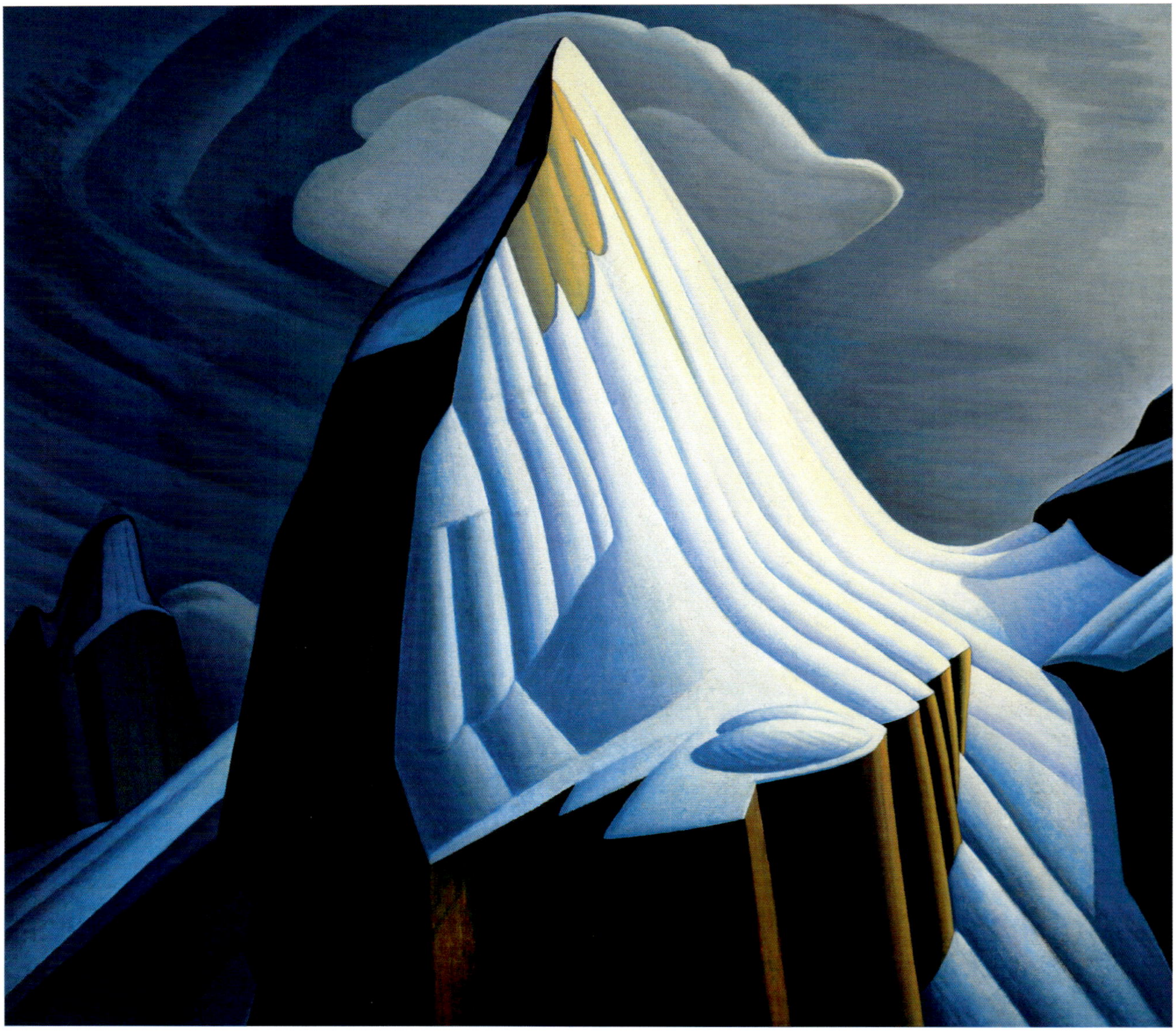

1 Lawren S. Harris (1885–1970), *Mt. Lefroy*, 1930, oil on canvas. McMichael Canadian Art Collection, purchased 1975, 1975.7

depressing, contrast can be found between the southern stretch of urban Canada and the benighted towns of the True North, which are not as strong and free as our national anthem would like us to believe. Here you find endemic poverty and unemployment, elevated murder and suicide rates, rampant abuse of drugs and alcohol, and a general malaise that can come only with the sense, generation after generation, that there is no future here. Because many of these towns are populated by Métis, Inuit, and First Nations citizens who bear the memory of past and present injustices

> It is a well-worn cliché that the iconic imagery of Canada is all wintry.

plus lack of political influence, you can add racism to the roll call of awful that marks the reality of Canada's North. No wonder the spiritualized Krypton-North is also people-free. The real people are just not decorative. Not to pile on, but even Harris's definitive "outdoor" aesthetic sometimes seems to owe more to American architect and architectural draftsman Hugh Ferriss's influential *Metropolis of Tomorrow* urban landscapes (published in 1929, and first exhibited in 1922) than to the actual Mount Lefroy (painted in 1930) or other peaks in the Rockies (painted from 1930–1934). (figure 2) Ferriss's radical "setback" skyscraper designs, drawn in response to the 1916 New York zoning code to control vertical density, somehow feel like the dark döppelganger to Harris's almost too-bright abstracted arrangements of peaks and shadows. Here, the cityscape literally shadows the landscape.

II

Thus a curious fact, which might be called ironic if it weren't so bleak: despite all the trumpeting of Canada's status as a northern nation, it really isn't one. The majority of Canadians will never set foot north of perhaps 52° north, let alone 60°.

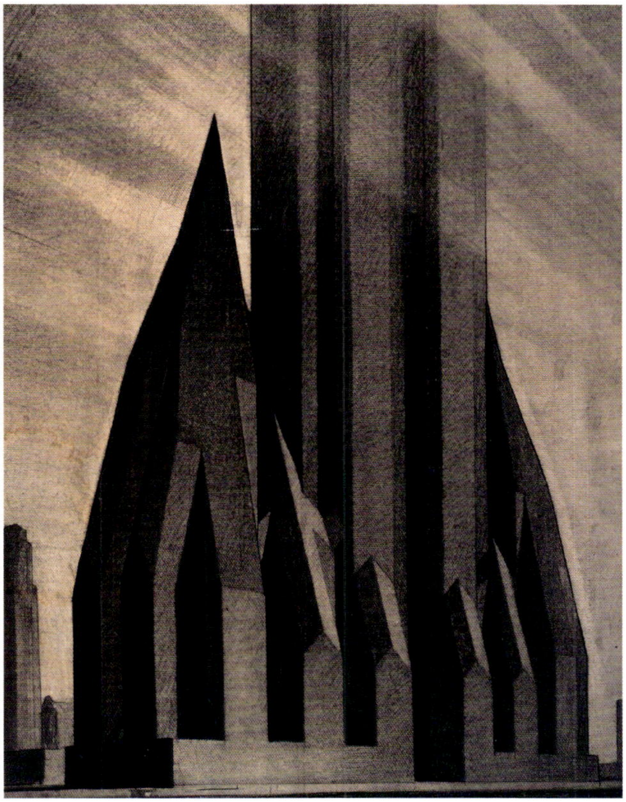

2 Hugh Ferriss (1889–1962), study for maximum permitted by the 1916 New York zoning law, stage 2, New York, NY, 1922. Cooper Hewitt, Smithsonian Design Museum / Art Resource, NY

Thus a curious fact, which might be called ironic if it weren't so bleak: despite all the trumpeting of Canada's status as a northern nation, it really isn't one.

Edmonton and Saskatoon are the only major cities up that far, and the Greater Toronto Area, with 6 million of the country's 35 million souls, just touches 44°. Toronto has trying winters, but nevertheless maintains an attitude of deep denial about both the weather and the sprawling tracts of hostile land, with its scatter of sad settlements, that stretch beyond. Meanwhile, those very same demographic shifts that make Canadian cities so diverse have created new population groups—predominantly from East Asia and South Asia—which will swell the population to more than 42.5 million by the middle of the century. These people have no obvious concern with the North as North, or with the Canadian mythology concerning that wide boreal strangeness.

And so a second irony: even as the real Canadian North is suffering material decline and progressive abandonment, as young people who possess the means flee a crumbling region, the Idea of North seems stronger than ever. The idiosyncratic pianist Glenn Gould—himself an iconic figure in the Canadian pantheon—created in 1967 an odd, compelling CBC radio documentary about this idea, which is still a dominant frame for the concept. (figure 3) Gould was fascinated by northernness and used his well-known penchant for adopting multiple voices and personas to create a work of what he called "contrapuntal radio." The first program would join two later ones, produced over the next ten years, as Gould's *Solitude Trilogy*. They compose, in effect, an autobiographical essay performed in the public medium that joined modern Canada together.

"The Idea of North" remains the best-known of the three, and Gould's introduction to the piece offers a clear sense of the philosophical stakes:

> I've long been intrigued by that incredible tapestry of tundra and taiga which constitutes the Arctic and sub-Arctic of our country. I've read about it, written about it, and even pulled up my parka once and gone there. Yet like all but a very few Canadians I've had no real experience of the North. I've remained, of necessity, an outsider. And the North has remained for me, a convenient place to dream about, spin tall tales about, and, in the end, avoid.[3]

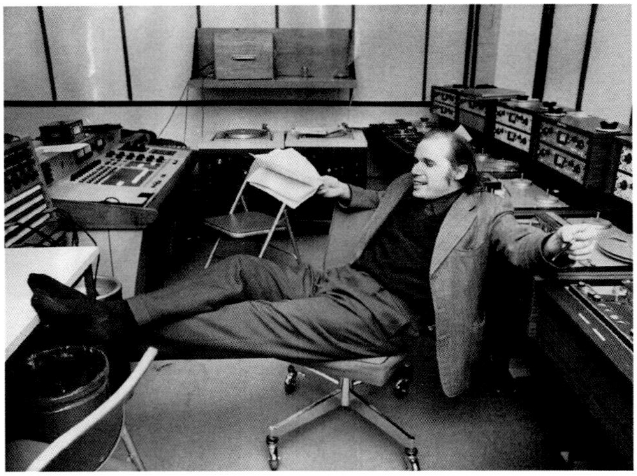

3 Glenn Gould in his studio, *Toronto Star*, November 26, 1973
Photography by Ron Bull / *Toronto Star* / Getty Images

That phrase "in the end" captures Gould's keen sense of Canada's uneasy relationship with itself: tall tales combined with rituals of evasion. And note the honest "once" before mentioning his trip up to 60°. In the documentary Gould would note the competitive "Northmanship" performed by travellers who brave the upper reaches of the national land mass: how many trips? How far north? How long the stay? This is a game without a winner. Canada's North is, finally, still *terra incognita*. There be not dragons there, instead bears and seals and—above all—a small number of fellow citizens about whom the rest of us know almost nothing.[4]

III

The countries of Scandinavia have a relationship with their geography that is no less complicated, even if they lie clearly in the globe's northern reaches according to the maps. Here we encounter, in more compact and deeply rooted form, some of the same things that shape the Canadian imagination: port cities, a forbidding landscape, a royal heritage, parliamentary democracy, and socialized health care; also, low overall population density combined with significant concentration in southern cities. (For example, 85 percent of Sweden's population of 10 million reside in urban areas clinging to the lower edges of the land mass, principally Stockholm, Gothenburg, and Malmö.[5]) Given Finland's ethnic differences and former conjunction with Sweden—Finland gained independence in 1809, though would not break free of Russian influence under its Declaration of Independence in 1917—there is even a sort of analogy to what Canadians call "the French fact." Except, of course, that Quebeckers maintain their own national status within our federation of provinces and territories. And yes, we all play hockey obsessively.

At the same time, there is an ethnic and linguistic purity to the Scandinavian nations that is entirely foreign to the Canadian experience, a still-young nation driven by wave after wave of immigration. The heritage of social justice in Scandinavia has meant that they could not ignore the 2015 Iranian migrant crisis, for example, but also that anti-immigration politics are a strong force, ranging from extreme neo-Nazi groups remaining mostly underground to slick electoral success stories such as Sweden's Social Democrats. The fear of "Islamization" in the region is clearly racial as much as religious or political, generating in ethnic Swedes and Norwegians a feeling that they are no longer comfortable in their own homes. Even the extraordinary effort to help during the migrant crisis by accepting record numbers of refugees has fallen on the hard rocks of political and economic reality: some 80,000 of the 163,000 refugees admitted in 2015 are likely to be deported before the middle of 2016.[6]

Meanwhile, the latitude itself makes for a very different circadian rhythm, something which is hard to describe: the day-long duskiness of a crepuscular winter, never really emerging from twilight; the startling, almost drugged feeling of the late-night summer sun. For reasons nobody can quite fathom, Scandinavian novelists have recently, and extravagantly, dominated the genre of neo-noir detective fiction. There is no Canadian parallel to this, but one is hard-pressed to substantiate the claim that it's to do with the dark winters. Noir was born, after all, on the sun-drenched streets of Southern California.

These comparative markers are fascinating enough, but they are more suggestive than solid. We can say who the winners and losers are when it comes to international hockey, but we can hardly say which country in pursuit of its version of Northern Justice is faring best, simply because basic circumstances are so different. No, if we want to explore the affinities between Canada and Scandinavia further, there are more subtle mechanisms than these; and so let us consider the range of beautiful objects that are gathered in this exhibition.

IV

True Nordic is a design show in a museum dedicated to objects that almost always belong to the indoor spaces of human life, but right away I am struck by the thought that there is a reason they called them "shelter magazines." Again and again, we realize that the result of northern living is intense urbanization. The city and its promises of comfort, security, and warmth define the experience of the north. And yet, these promises are themselves precarious. Every doorway forms an airlock between the livable interior and the threatening outdoors. Except during brief summers—surprisingly hot and humid in Toronto, to visitors' surprise—we cannot saunter blithely out to the lanai and take our ease in shorts and T-shirt. Even then it would be silly to have a lanai; you *might* have a porch or patio. In any season, we must always be thinking about thresholds, permeabilities, energy expenditures. Is that a draft? Do we have enough insulation in the attic? How long will it take to shovel my way to the garage so I can liberate the frozen automobile cached there like an escape vehicle in a disaster movie? The comforts of the interior are thus at the centre of life in northern cities in a manner that suggests higher stakes than elsewhere. Hence, I think, the combination of lushness and clean functionality we see here, and in other canonical Scandinavian designs. This is an independent Nordic or Scandinavian modernism that is now as instantly recognizable as Deco or Nouveau. It owes something to the International Style curated by Philip Johnson, that fancier of Nazi Youth, and yet possesses a distinctive sleekness that feels more organic, less machined, and forbidding. One writer dubs it "glacial glamour," which seems about right, if perhaps glib. It is a style easy to replicate, tempting in its simplicity, but also ripe for overuse and even unconscious self-parody.[7] The first, still unfamiliar, version was also the modernism that blew a

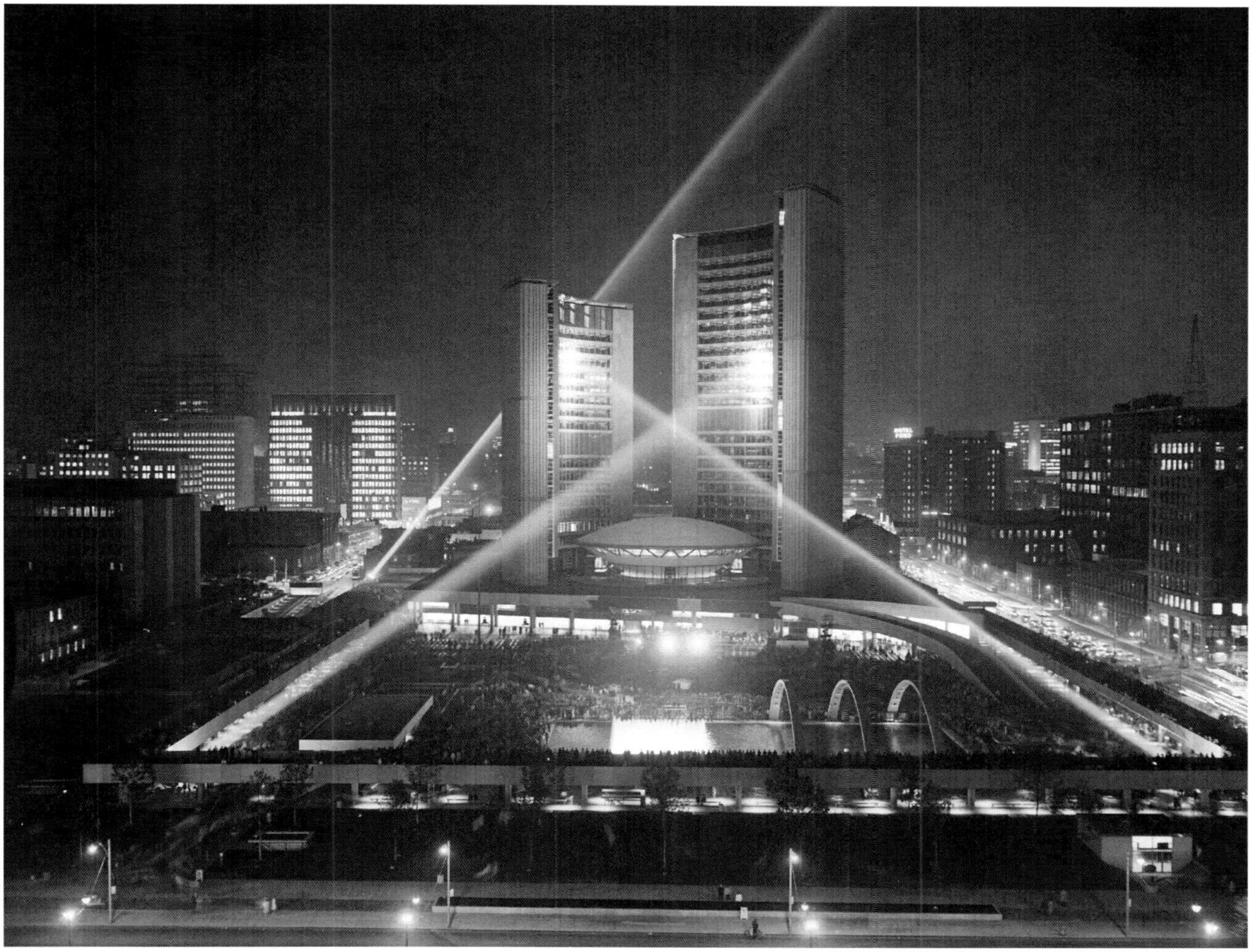

4 The Opening of Toronto's City Hall, designed by Viljo Revell, 1965
City of Toronto Archives, Series 374, File 799, Item 17

cold gust of refreshing air through the stuffy drawing rooms and overstuffed parlours of the Canadian home during the 1930s and after. The more recent Ikea invasion of North America, whatever its merits to consumers with limited budgets, is a pale, ready-to-assemble ghost of the same aesthetic. (Plus more Allen keys than any sane person could ever need.)

Was this a matter of regional kinship? In part, yes. The appeal of light teak sideboards and tables or bentwood chairs executed in body-hugging curves, for example, is almost instinctive for the inhabitants of a land of forests. Likewise the asymmetrical and sometimes pod-like ceramics, vases, and bowls that not only defy previous norms of propriety but almost seem to have been gathered from the forest floor and glazed. The objects are instantly haptic, warm, ready to be in place. They welcome our bodies' touch.

Canada may yet accept its strange status as a not-quite-northern northern nation in the emerging constellations of global power and creativity.

We might note, finally, some clear middle terms in this suggestive logic of affinity. One was Danish-born artist and designer Thor Hansen. Transplanted to Canada after the Second World War, Hansen took up a position as art director for the British-American Oil Company. Designing the company's office interiors from 1948 to 1968, Hansen created and curated textiles, murals, rugs, and other decorative forms. His playful use of typical national icons—geese, eagles, mountains, trees—in a then-contemporary idiom of craft production created a short-lived but distinctive Canadian Modern.[8] (cat. 25–26) All petroleum companies should be so lucky, especially in these days when the plunging barrel price and collapsed Canadian dollar make the very idea of an in-house art director, let alone one of surpassing talent, a laughable prospect.

An even more obvious example, at least to the thousands of citizens who walk or drive past it every day, is Finnish architect Viljo Revell's unsurpassed Toronto City Hall. (figure 4) Opened in 1965, it defines in a single functionalist gesture the optimism and modern sensibility of the newly open, ambitious city. Stretching the geographical point a bit, one could begin to discuss Estonian-Canadian architect Uno Prii and his beautiful modernist apartment towers, scattered around the city.

New Canadian styles have of course emerged since this heyday leading up to and celebrating the Canadian centenary in 1967. They feel less and less obliged to confront the national symbology, or find inspiration in the chilly outdoors. One of the most successful design teams of contemporary Toronto, for example, a redoubtable young group known collectively as Partisans, found inspiration for an award-winning downtown bar interior in the work of Spanish architect Antoni Gaudí. The result is a mini-cathedral of dark, smooth-flowing mahogany in organic shapes that feels entirely unrelated to the boreal. This is advanced post-national design for the new century.

Canada may yet accept its strange status as a not-quite-northern northern nation in the emerging constellations of global power and creativity. In the meantime, we have this history, this shared geography, and these exquisite objects from daily life to consider and enjoy.

Endnotes

1 All quotations from Russell Smith, "Lawren Harris is the Adele of Canadian Visual Art," *Globe and Mail,* December 2, 2015, http://www.theglobeandmail.com/arts/art-and-architecture/russell-smith-lawren-harris-was-the-adele-of-canadian-art/article27565059/.

2 Freud discusses what he labelled "der Narzissmus der kleinen Differenzen," based on some earlier work by anthropologist Ernest Crawley, in *Civilization and Its Discontents,* Standard Edition, trans. James Strachey (London: Hogarth Press, 1994). Originally published as *Das Unbehagen in der Kultur* (1930).

3 Glenn Gould, "'The Idea of North': An Introduction," in Tim Page, ed., *The Glenn Gould Reader* (New York: Vintage, 2004).

4 I discuss these issues, along with a range of other Gould-sourced philosophical and cultural conundrums, in *Glenn Gould* (Toronto: Penguin, 2009). French translation by Alain Roy as *Glenn Gould* (Montreal: Boréal, 2011).

5 See http://www.geohive.com/earth/pop_urban.aspx.

6 David Crouch, "Sweden Sends Sharp Signal with Plan to Expel up to 80,000 Asylum Seekers," *The Guardian,* January 28, 2016, http://www.theguardian.com/world/2016/jan/28/sweden-to-expel-up-to-80000-rejected-asylum-seekers.

7 This is especially true in the global profusion of hotel and restaurant designs that offer a depressingly similar array of smooth wood, angular furniture, sleek metal surfaces, and the standard taupe-to-beige palette of Globalized Nothingness. One writer noted recently that, owing to the success of Denmark's Noma restaurant—repeatedly voted best in the world—food purveyors everywhere are acting in the approved chilly manner. "We're deep into tweezer food territory," he said of a fashionable Australian restaurant, "a place where the fare is surgically spectacular, the chefs coax ingredients onto plates with the help of pincers and pipettes, even the tiniest leaf receives a program of pastoral care to smooth the passage from stem to mouth, and the menu prose is so austere and liturgically rhythmic it could pass for late Beckett." The menu style is one he calls *degustation laconic,* a preposition-free zone of comma-separated ingredients: scallops, kohlrabi, yukari; beetroot, black sesame, cream; etc. See Aaron Timms, "Degustation Laconic: The Language of Menus," *The Monthly,* February 2016, https://www.themonthly.com.au/issue/2016/february/1454245200/aaron-timms/degustation-laconic.

8 The work Hansen executed for British-American Oil Company was celebrated in a 2005 exhibition at the Textile Museum of Canada, curated by Rachel Gotlieb (also the present exhibition's co-curator). The exhibition and Hansen's work are beautifully documented in Rachel Gotlieb, *Thor Hansen: Crafting a Canadian Style* (Toronto: Textile Museum of Canada, 2005).

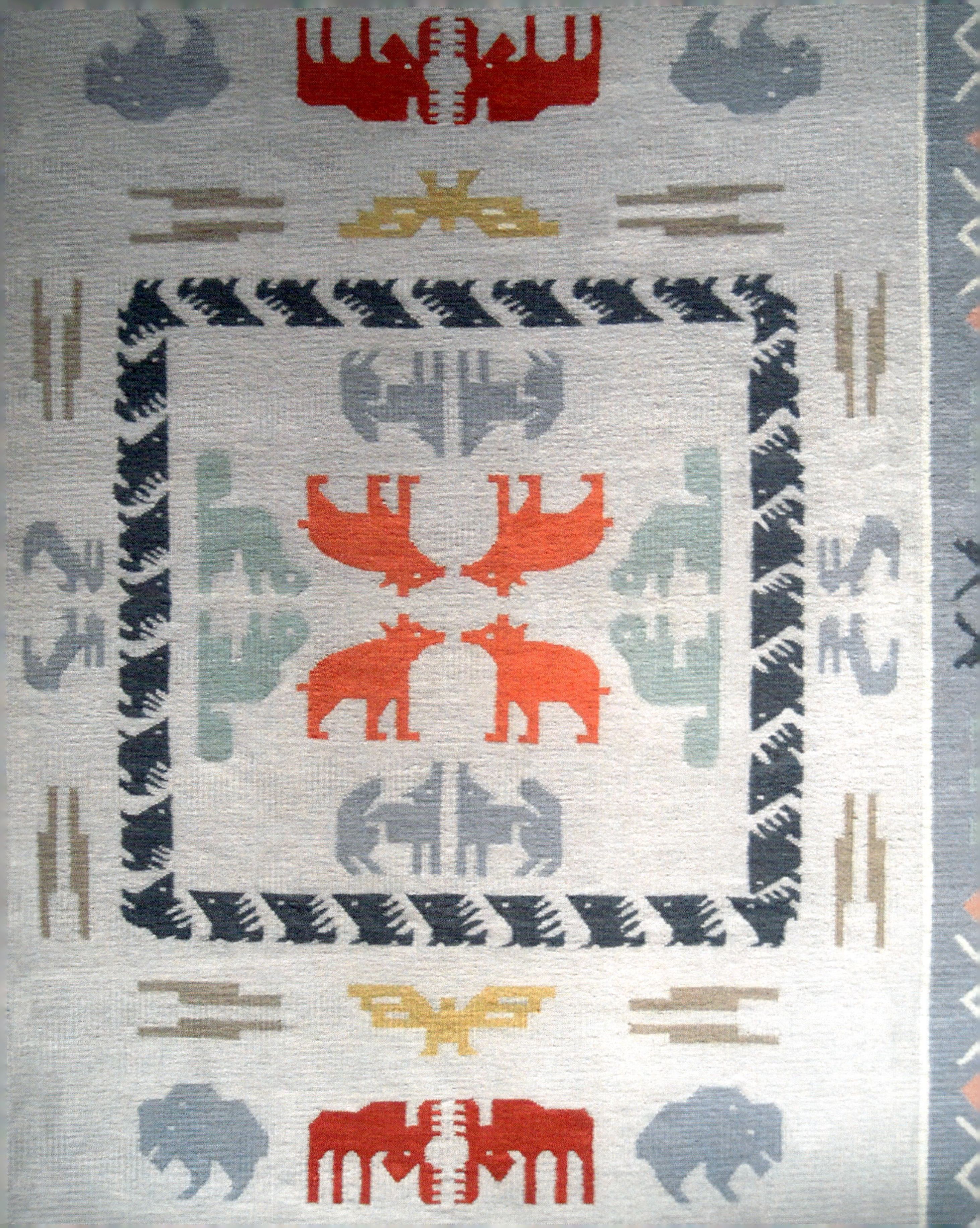

True Nordic

How Scandinavia Influenced Design in Canada

Exhibition Catalogue

This landmark exhibition examines the ways that modern Scandinavian design was introduced to Canada and how the aesthetic principles and material forms that defined it were adopted and adapted by Canadians artisans and designers. *True Nordic* documents more than seven decades of the marked influence of Scandinavian design on Canadian craft and design. The foundation of all Nordic design lies equally in the notion of what has been called "fitness of purpose"—the functionalism and rationality of objects for everyday life—and the acknowledgement of the conditions of place. Here, the thought and practice of design seeks to serve people and holds the potential to stimulate beneficial social and democratic change.

For both clear and complex reasons, Scandinavian design resonated with Canadians as evidenced first in the importing and domestic manufacturing of goods, in the extensive coverage in the press and the response by consumers to the array of functional and decorative products including furniture, ceramics, textiles, and metalware. Both critics and the general public broadly admired the style of Scandinavian design—modest, pleasingly utilitarian, and materially logical—and judged it to be appropriate for the conditions of Canadian living. It met the needs of Canadians seeking a new and contemporary look for their lives. At once progressive, and genial, Scandinavian design easily and effortlessly fit Canada's modernizing needs. Both elite and middle-class consumers saw Canadian designer's interpretation of Scandinavian aesthetics as a new material culture for living and wellbeing.

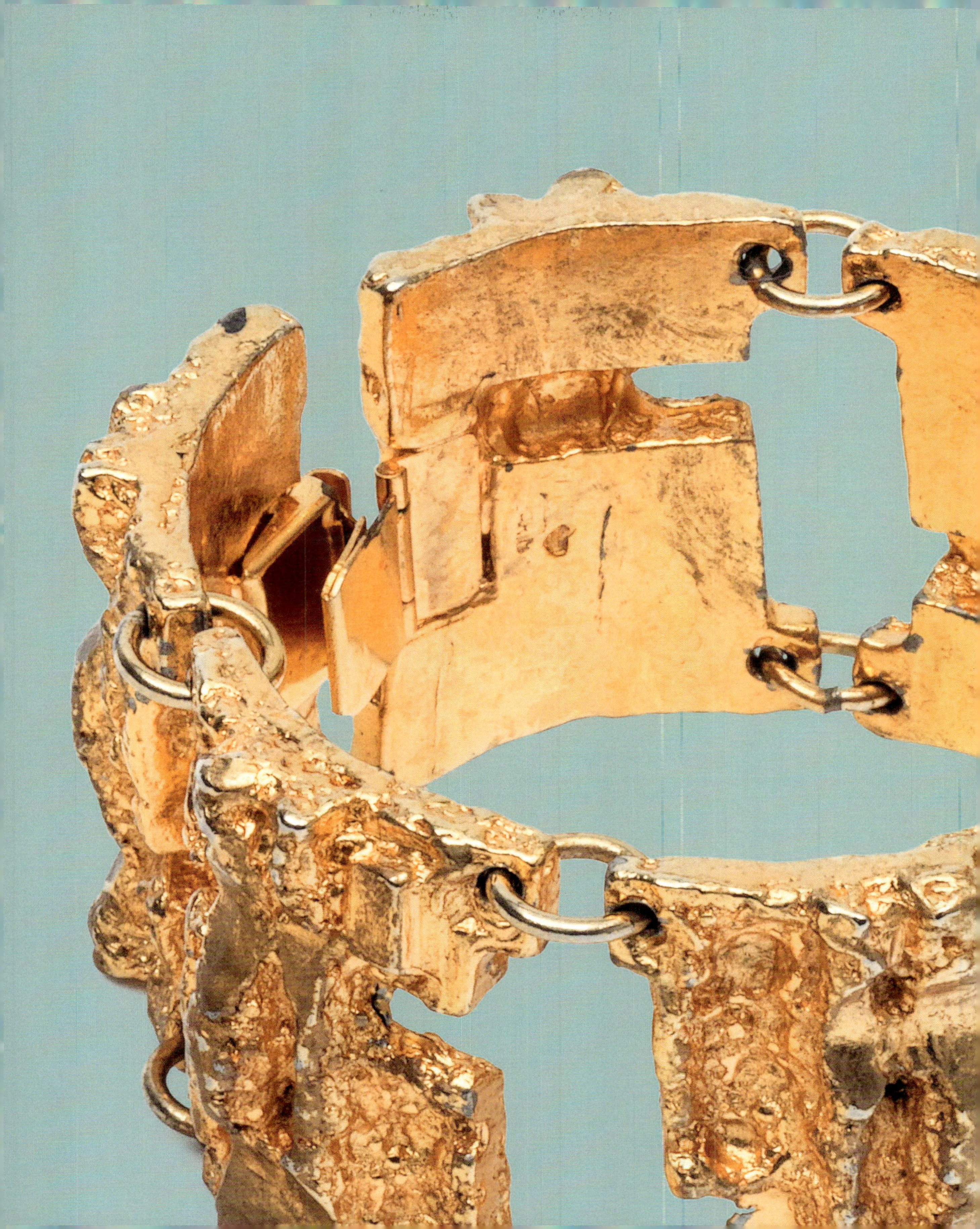

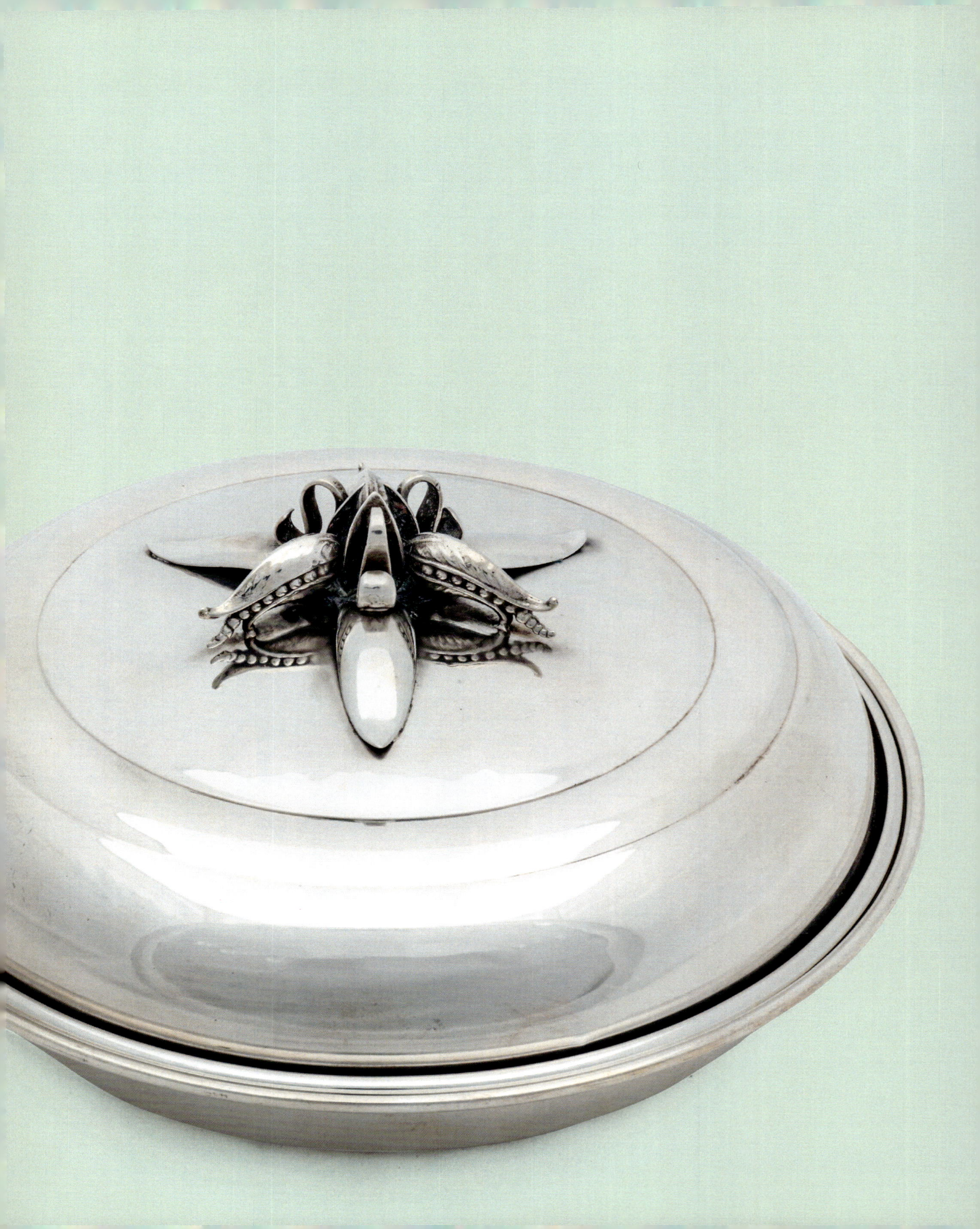

Arrival and Consequences
1925–1956

Best understood as a more humane and regional variation of the larger trans-Atlantic modernist movement—and one where historical studio practices and traditions easily co-existed with progressive aesthetic and material tenets—Scandinavian design arrived in Canada in the early decades of the twentieth century. The imports from Scandinavia made significant and longstanding contributions to the nation's material and visual culture. In a country where domestic interiors and patterns of taste had been long tied to traditional British and French models and where the striving design culture of the United States also held appeal, the consequences of the design of the nations of Denmark, Sweden, Finland, and Norway coming to Canada cannot be underestimated.

Scandinavian modernism initially reached Canada's elite consumers and style-makers via museum and gallery exhibitions, designer showrooms, small retail shops, and articles and photographic essays in popular decorator magazines. In turn, designers who came from Denmark and Sweden in the 1920s and 1930s—many of whom were trained in prominent workshops and ateliers—carried with them skills and sensibilities that resulted in the production of goods in Canada exhibiting the properties of Scandinavian design culture. In addition, other makers across the country—aware of the power and promise of such thinking and practice—were likewise responsible for adapting Scandinavian motifs and principles in the design of everyday household furnishings for the Canadian marketplace. The result was a new national design language that spoke in resonant ways to the public.

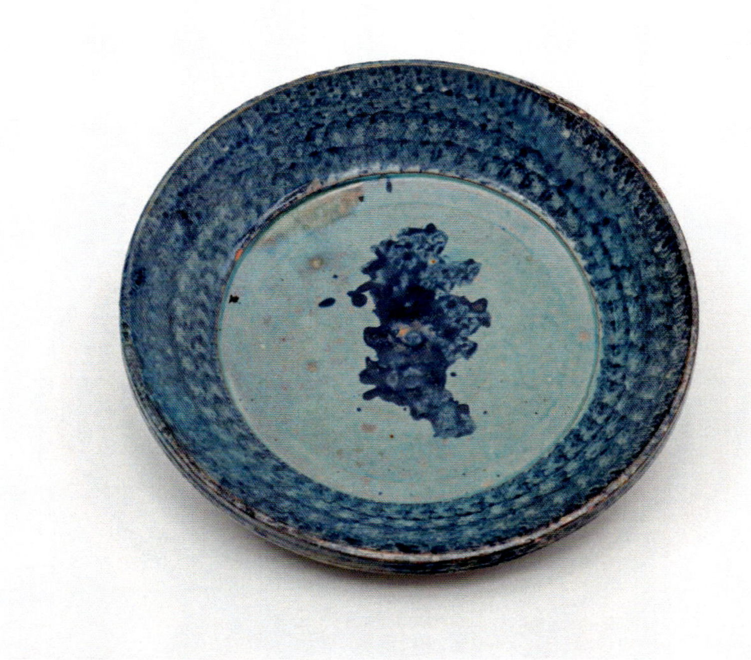

1 | **Axel Ebring (1869–1954)**
Charger, c. 1925. Glazed earthenware, 5.5 x 28 cm
Collection of John David Lawrence. Photography by Toni Hafkenscheid

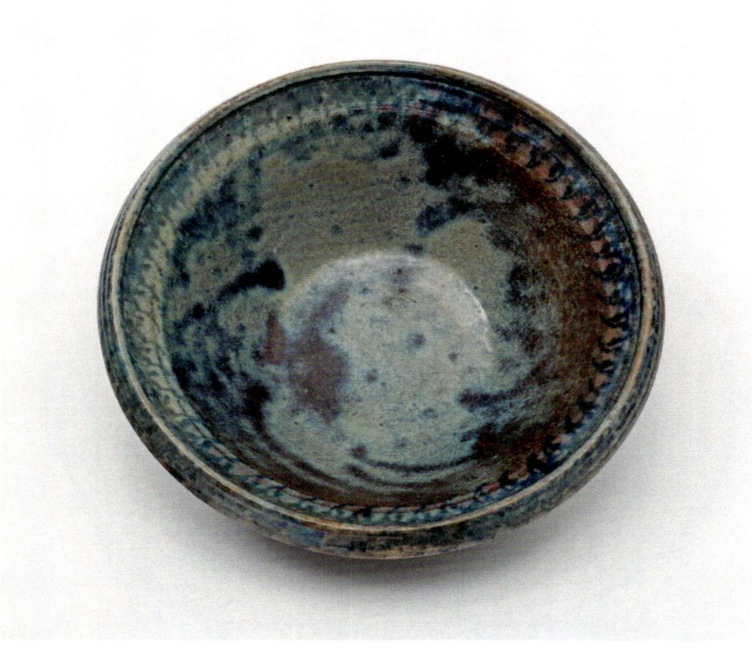

2 | **Axel Ebring (1869–1954)**
Bowl, c. 1928. Glazed earthenware, 10 x 27 cm
Collection of John David Lawrence. Photography by Toni Hafkenscheid

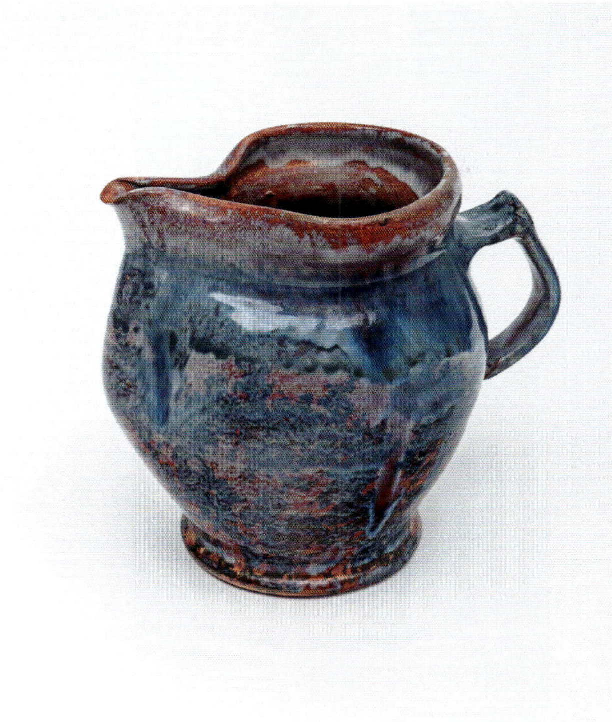

3 | **Axel Ebring (1869–1954)**
Pitcher, c. 1938. Glazed earthenware, 19.5 x 21 x 17 cm.
Private collection. Photography by Toni Hafkenscheid

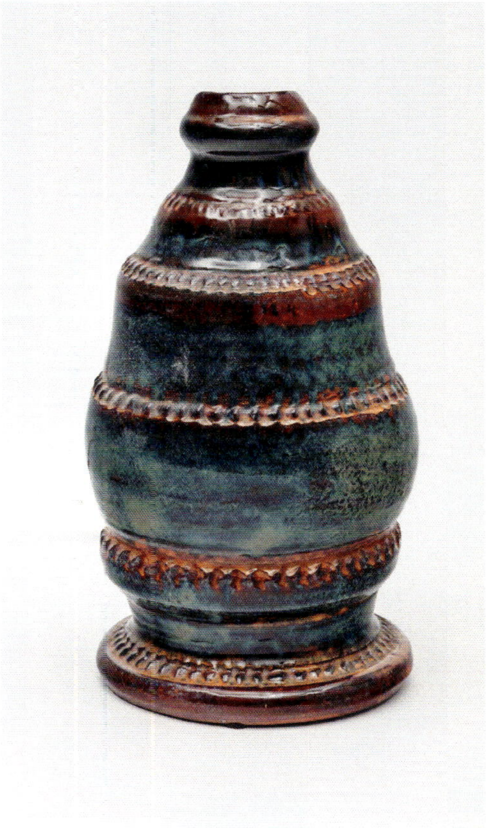

4 | **Axel Ebring (1869–1954)**
Lamp base, c. 1938. Glazed earthenware, 45.5 x 13 cm
Private collection. Photography by Toni Hafkenscheid

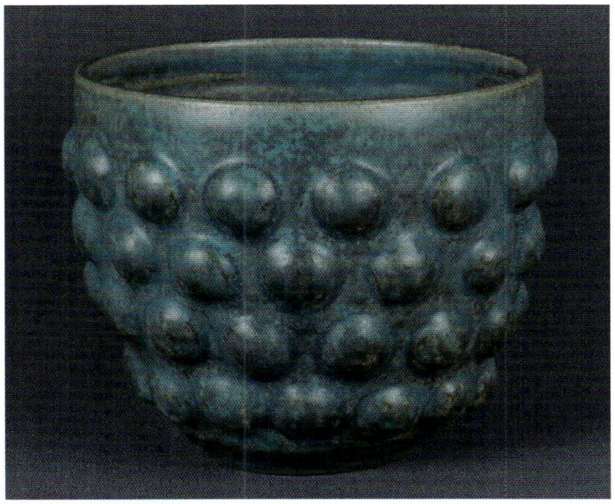

5 | **Kjeld Deichmann (1900–1963)**
Erica Deichmann (1913–2007)
Bowl, 1950–1960. Stoneware, 17 x 19.6 x 19.6 cm
Bequest of Lorna C. Pearce, 2012, 2012.29.2, New Brunswick Museum / Musée du Nouveau-Brunswick

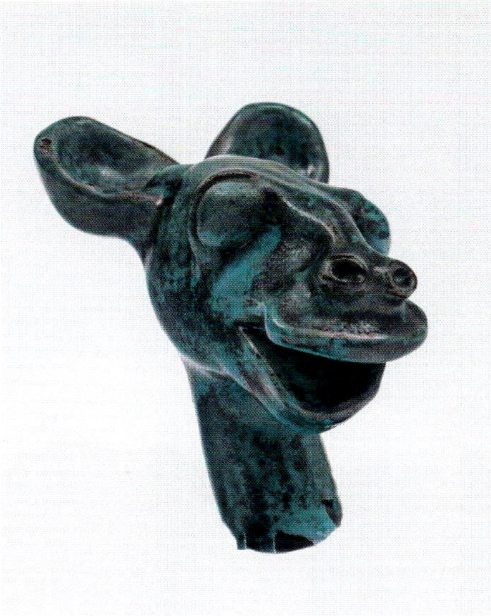

6 | **Kjeld Deichmann (1900–1963)**
Erica Deichmann (1913–2007)
***Goofus* (fragment), c. 1950**. Glazed stoneware, 12 x 8 x 10 cm. Collection of Peter Gorham
Photography by Toni Hafkenscheid

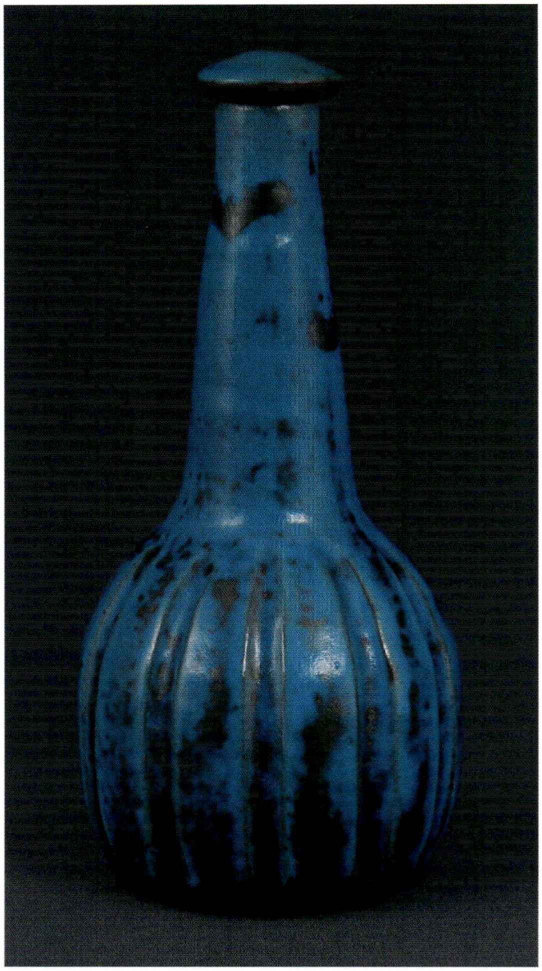

7 | **Kjeld Deichmann (1900–1963)**
Erica Deichmann (1913–2007)
Decanter, 1948. Stoneware, copper blue glaze, oxidation fired, 24 x 9.5 x 9.5 cm. Bequest of Lorna C. Pearce, 2012, 2012.29.4.1, New Brunswick Museum / Musée du Nouveau-Brunswick

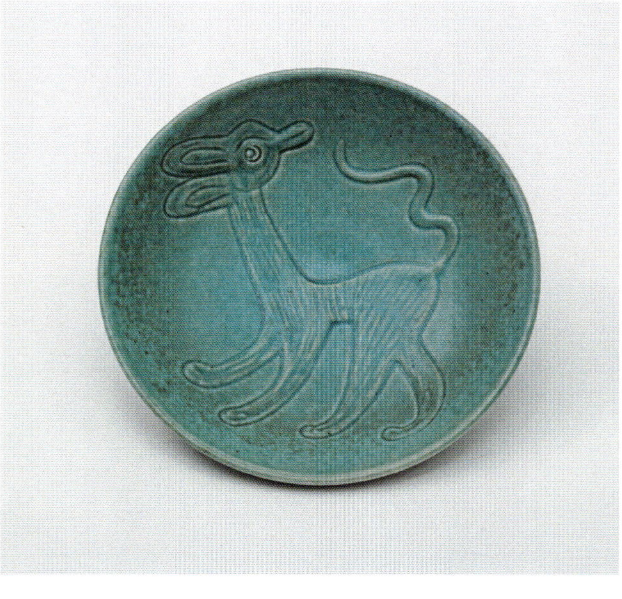

8 | **Kjeld Deichmann (1900–1963)**
Erica Deichmann (1913–2007)
Pin dish, 1950–1960. Glazed earthenware, 5 x 9.7 cm
Collection of the Gardiner Museum, donated by Bill Vrantsidis in memory of Tim Egan, G05.5.1
Photography by Toni Hafkenscheid

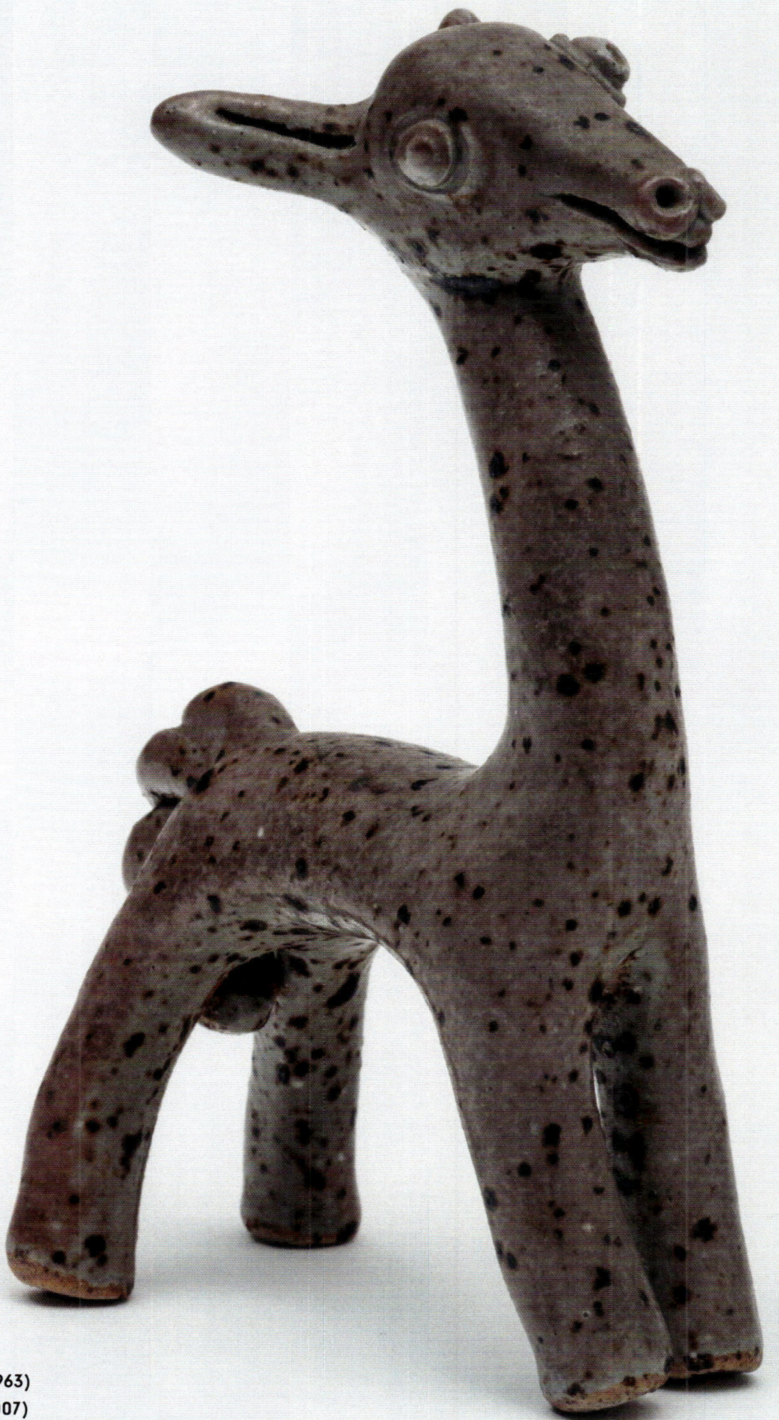

9 | **Kjeld Deichmann (1900–1963)**
Erica Deichmann (1913–2007)
***Goofus*, 1950–1963**, Stoneware with oatmeal glaze, 13 x 6.5 x 4.5 cm. Collection of the Gardiner Museum, gift of Gail and Gerry Crawford, G15.13.2
Photography by Toni Hafkenscheid

> Their combined population, as it happens, is just the same as ours. We resemble each other in habits, in ideas, in climate.
>
> **Governor General Vincent Massey, 1954**

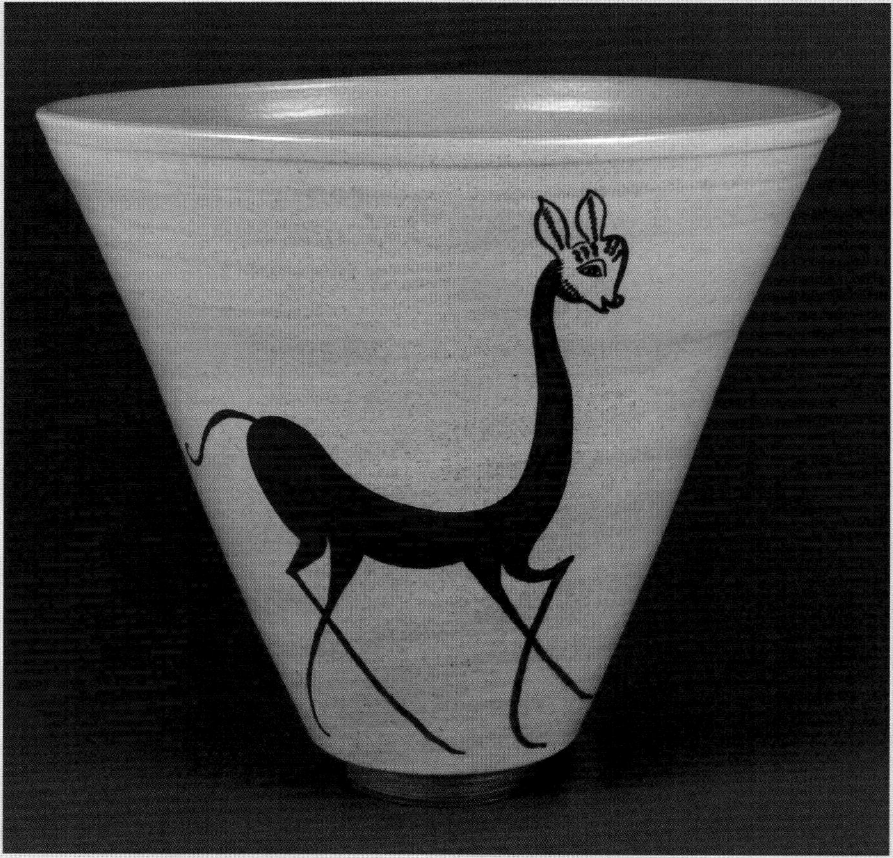

10 | **Kjeld Deichmann (1900–1963)**
Erica Deichmann (1913–2007)
Vase, 1962. Stoneware with cobalt underglaze, 33.8 x 34 x 34 cm. Purchased from the artists, 1967, A67.83, New Brunswick Museum / Musée du Nouveau-Brunswick

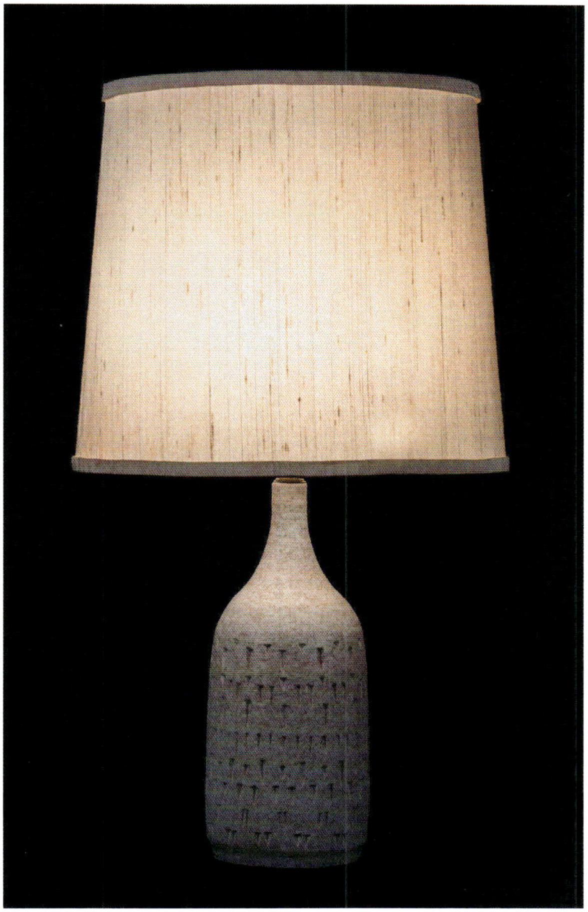

11 | **Kjeld Deichmann (1900–1963)**
Erica Deichmann (1913–2007)
Untitled (lamp), 1950s. Glazed stoneware, 57 x 26.2 x 25 cm. Art Gallery of Nova Scotia, gift of Dawn Bell Logan, Ottawa, Ontario, 2013, with assistance from the Jean and Lloyd Shaw Endowment Fund, 2013.34
Photography by Raw Photography

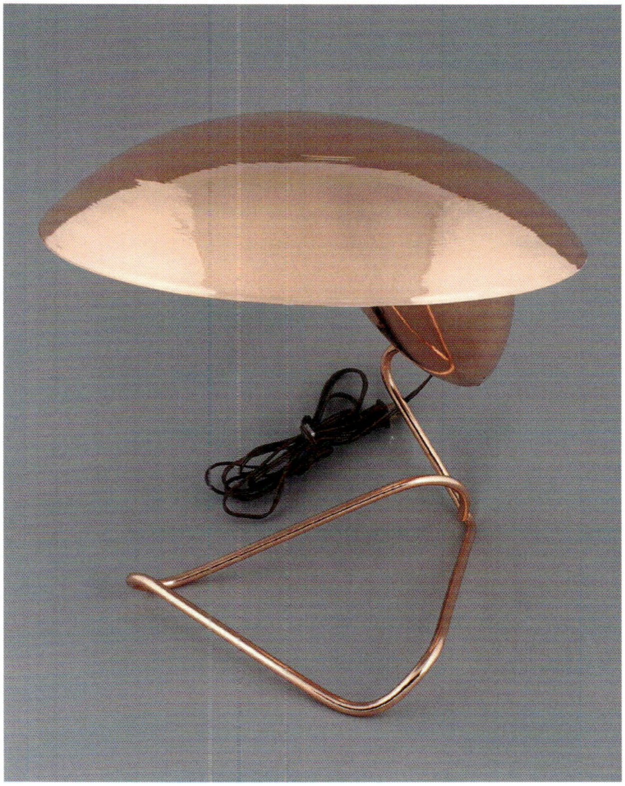

12 | **Murray Dunne (b. 1917), designer**
William Freeman and Son Ltd., BC, manufacturer
Electric lamp, 1949. Copper, electrical fittings, 37.3 x 37 x 41.2 cm. Canadian Museum of History, 2004.166.1, D2005-18114

A person who has talent in a certain craft or phase of craft will find greatest pleasure and productiveness in a position where that talent can be used to advantage. The nation needs all the natural talents available for its Industries, Arts and Sciences.... Handicrafts in the schools, churches, homes, Scout rooms, etc., will give to young people an opportunity to find the sort of work in which they will produce best and be happiest.

Rudolph "Rudy" Renzius, 1945

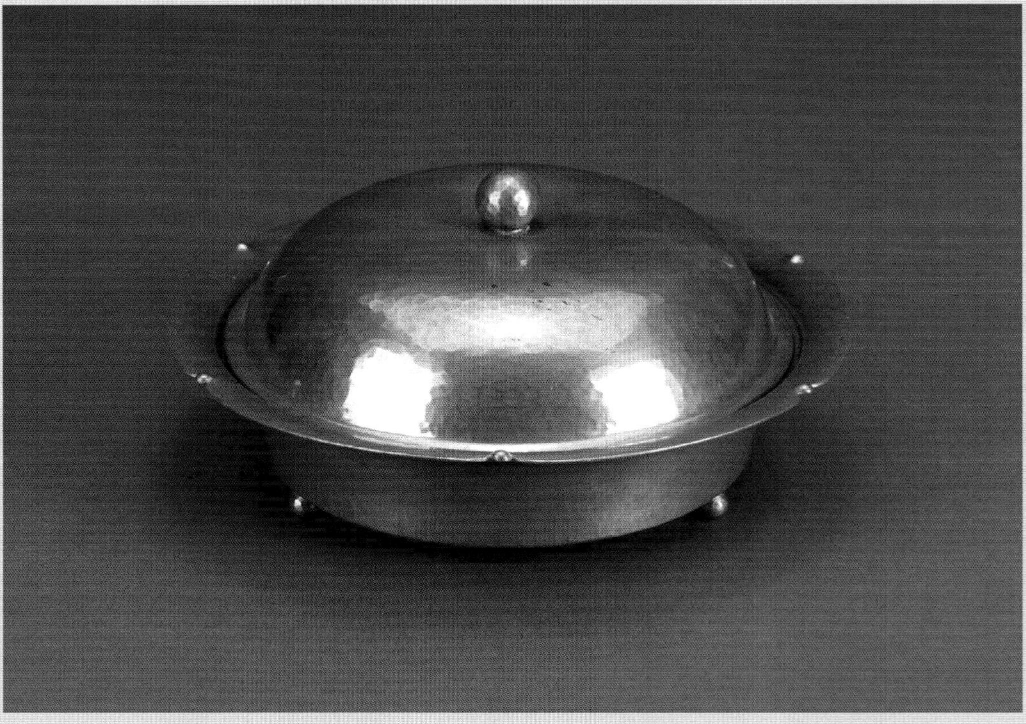

13 | **Rudolph "Rudy" Renzius (1899–1968)**
Covered dish, c. 1938. Pewter, 5 x 14 x 20 cm
Courtesy of Callie Stacey. Image courtesy of Waddingtons, Toronto

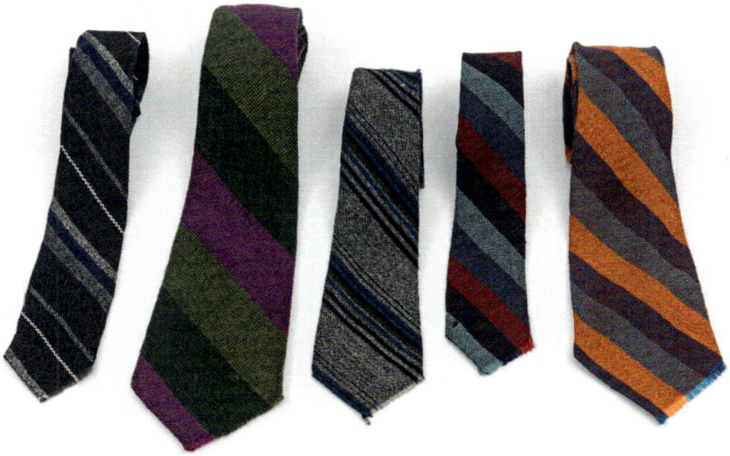

14 | **Karen Bulow (1899–1982)**
Neckties (five), c. 1955–1970. Wool, 5.7 x 131.5 cm
Private collection. Photography by Toni Hafkenscheid

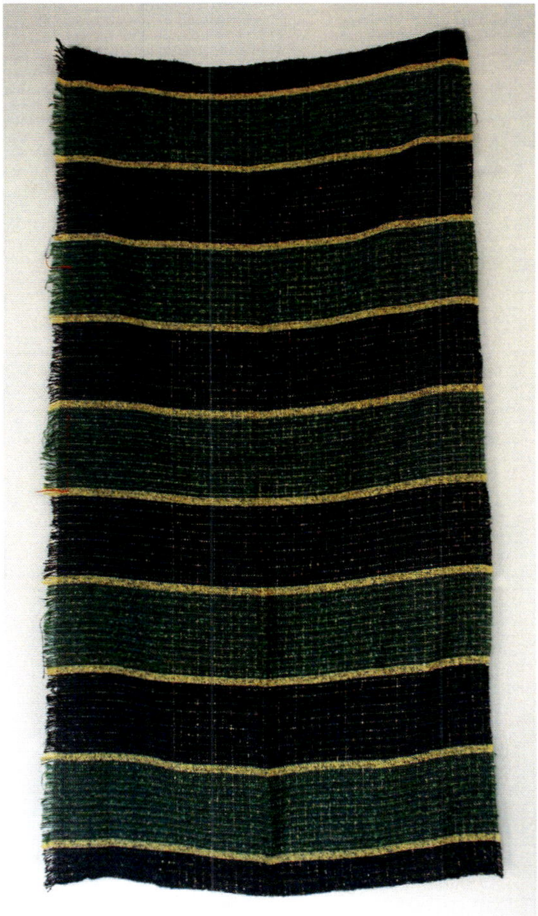

15 | **Karen Bulow (1899–1982)**
Fabric sample, c. 1954. Wool, gold, 64 x 128 cm
Design Exchange Permanent Collection, 999.6.2,
gift of Ted Steeves. Image courtesy of the
Design Exchange

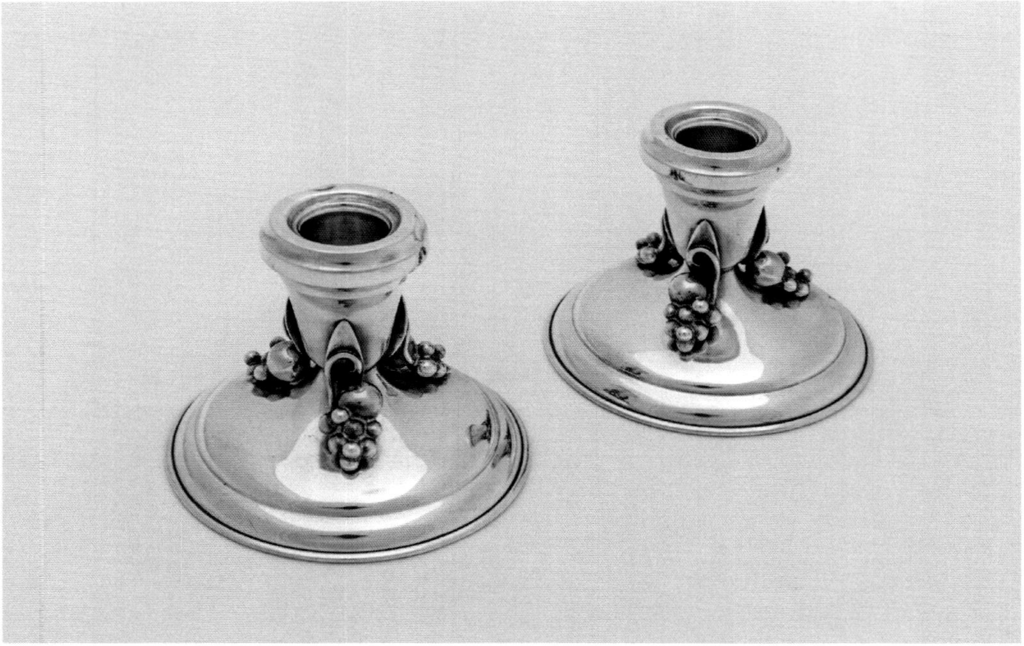

16 | **Carl Poul Petersen (1895–1977)**
Candlesticks, c. 1953. Silver, 8 x 10 cm each
Courtesy of Cynthia Findlay Antiques
Photography by Toni Hafkenscheid

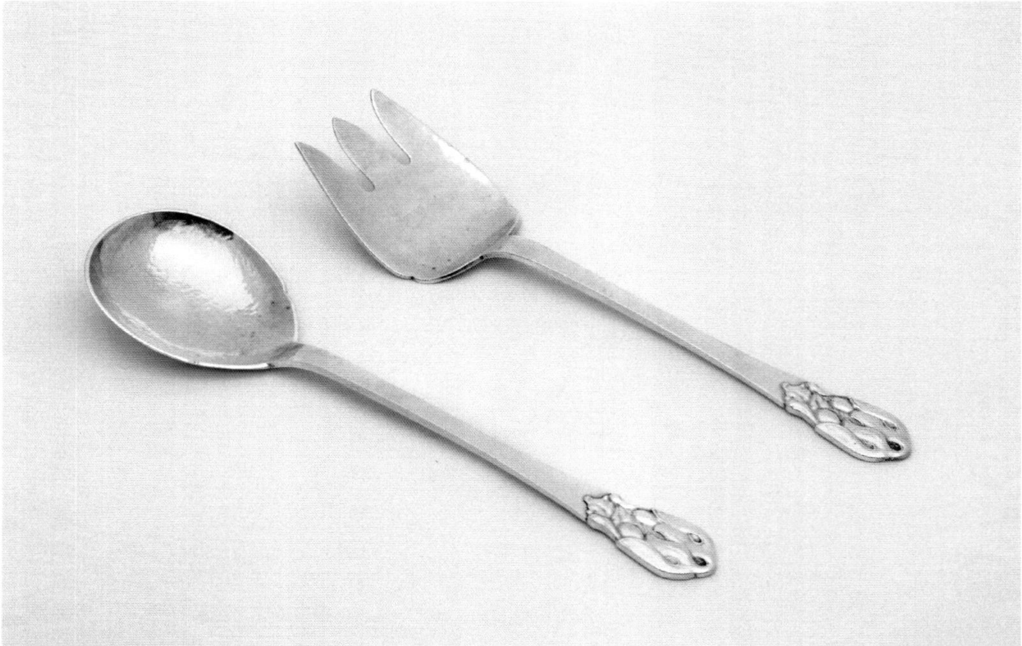

17 | **Carl Poul Petersen (1895–1977)**
Serving pieces, 1940–1970. Silver, 26 cm each
Collection of Dimitri and Catherine Anastakis
Photography by Toni Hafkenscheid

Good design in manufactured objects, as we understand it today, means a combination of simplicity, fine proportions and functional utility. It is not a question of ornamentation, but of the design of ordinary objects for everyday living. Grace of line and clarity of form are allied to fitness for purpose. This approach to fine design in mass production had some of its first advocates in Sweden and Finland, where many of the more important modern innovations in furniture design originated.

Donald Buchanan, 1947

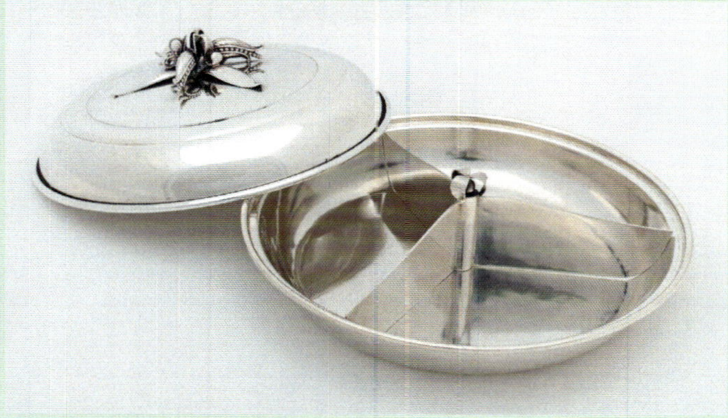

18 | **Carl Poul Petersen (1895–1977)**
Lidded dish, 1945–1946. Silver, 11.4 x 26 cm
Collection of Sheldon Parks. Photography by Toni Hafkenscheid

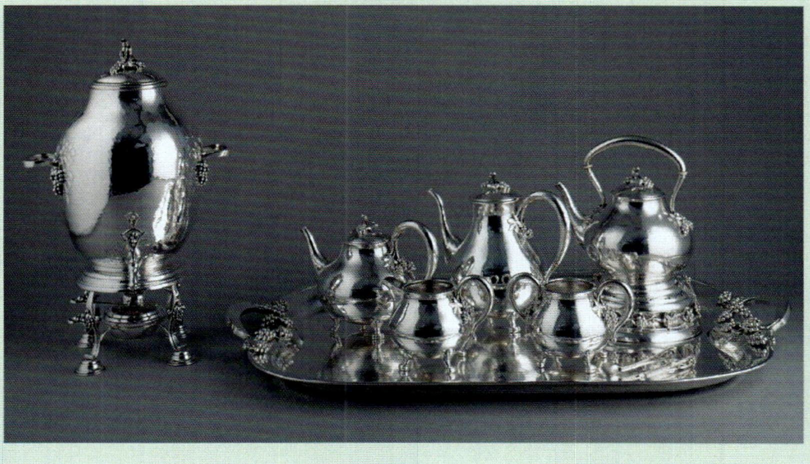

19 | **Carl Poul Petersen (1895–1977)**
Silver service, 1930–1945. Silver, 49 x 27.5 cm
McCord Museum, Montreal, M995.46.1-4; M995.46.6-7; M995.46.9; M995.46.41

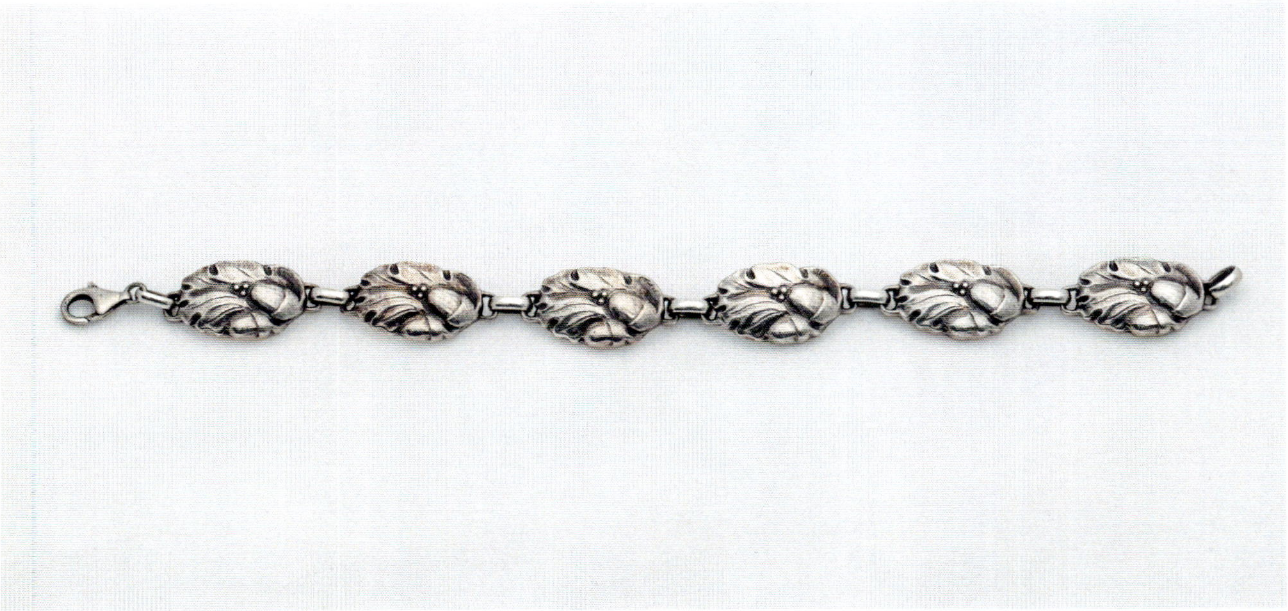

20 | Carl Poul Petersen (1895–1977)
Bracelet, 1940–1970. Silver, 19.5 cm
Collection of Dimitri and Catherine Anastakis
Photography by Toni Hafkenscheid

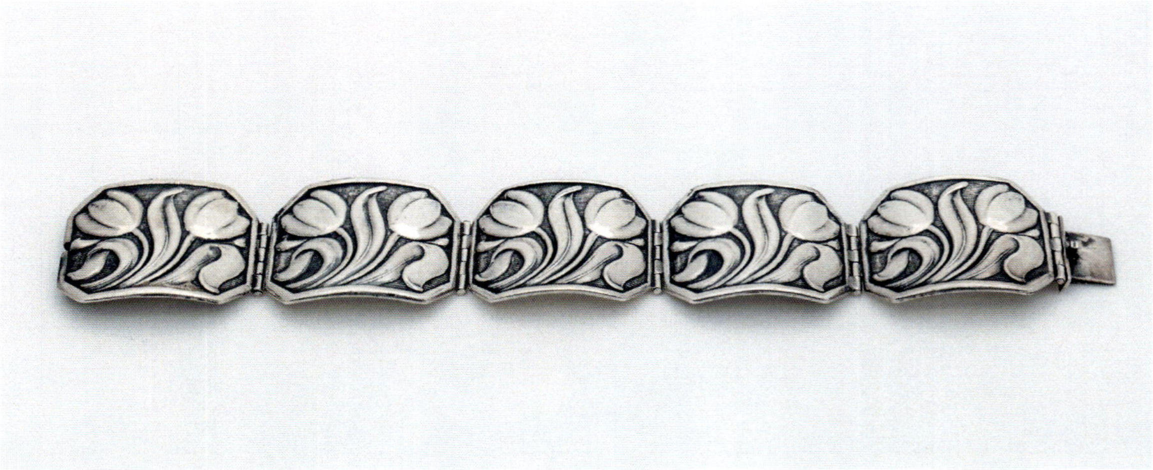

21 | Carl Poul Petersen (1895–1977)
Bracelet, 1940–1970. Silver, 19 cm
Collection of Dimitri and Catherine Anastakis
Photography by Toni Hafkenscheid

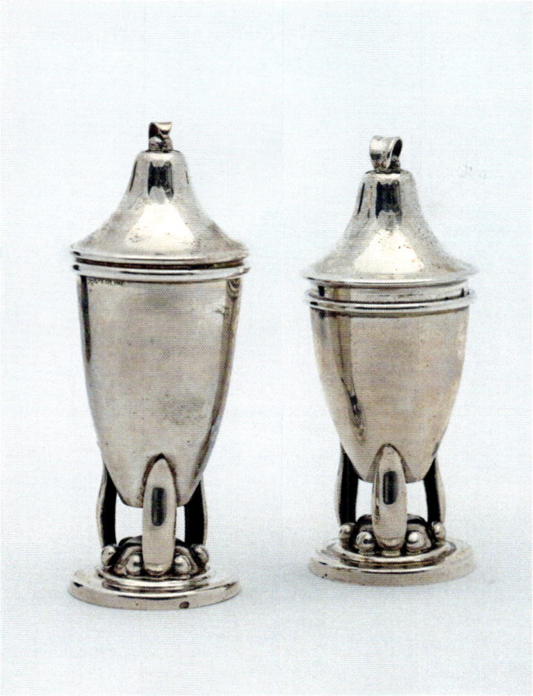

22 | **Carl Poul Petersen (1895–1977)**
Pepper pot and salt cellar, 1940–1970. Silver, 9 x 3.5 cm. Collection of Dimitri and Catherine Anastakis. Photography by Toni Hafkenscheid

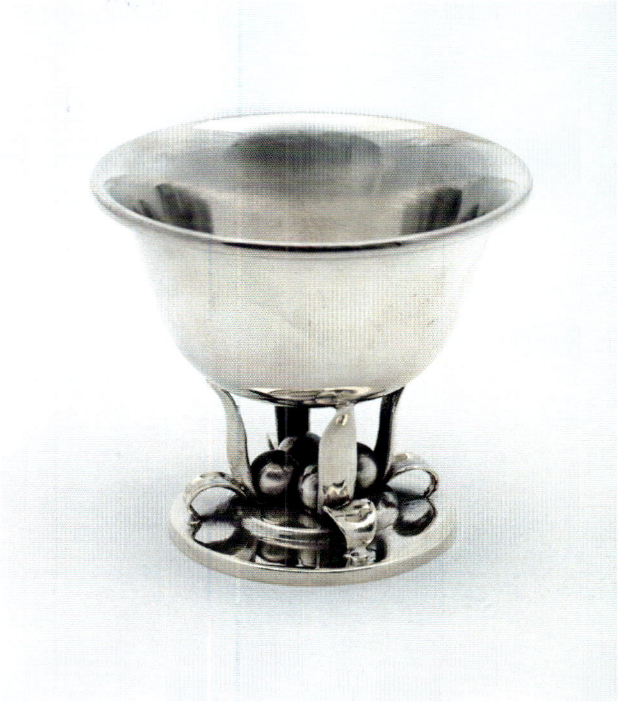

23 | **Carl Poul Petersen (1895–1977)**
Salt cellar, 1940–1970. Silver, 6.5 x 6.5 cm
Collection of Dimitri and Catherine Anastakis
Photography by Toni Hafkenscheid

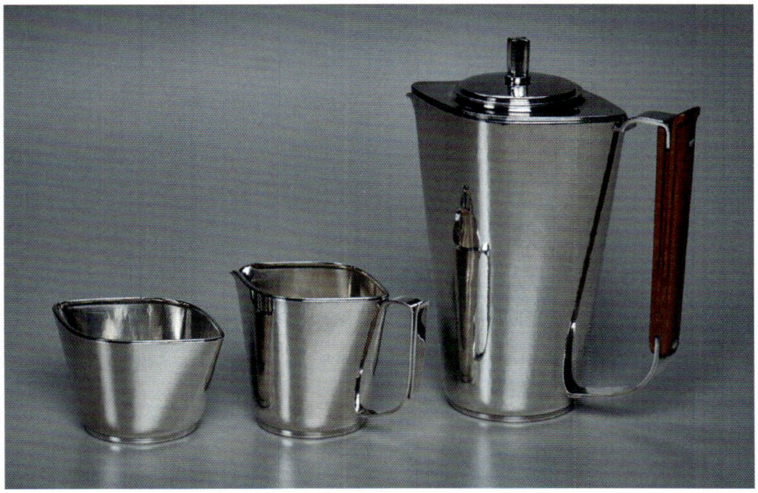

24 | **Harold Gordon Stacey (1911–1979)**
Coffee service, 1950. Silver and rosewood, coffee pot: 21.7 x 17.9 x 8.9 cm; sugar bowl: 6.4 x 11.3 x 3 cm; creamer: 8.5 x 13.2 x 7.2 cm
Purchased 2001, National Gallery of Canada, Ottawa
Photo © National Gallery of Canada

> Culture is something that evolves out of the simple, enduring elements of everyday life; elements most truthfully expressed in the folk arts and crafts of a nation.
>
> **Thor Hansen, 1955**

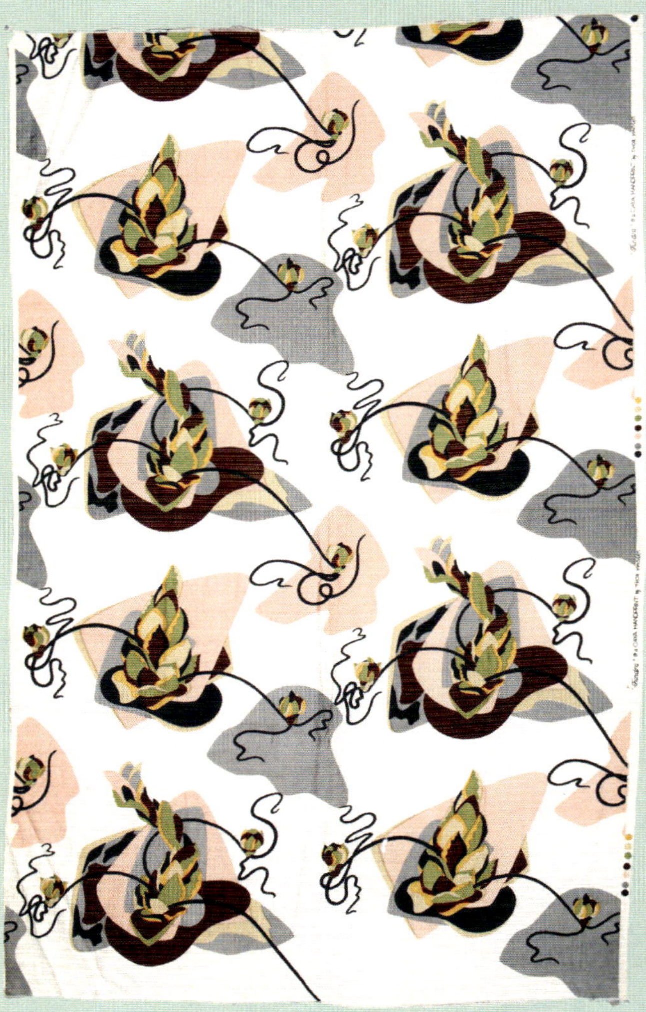

25 | **Thor Hansen (1903–1976), designer**
A. B. Caya Ltd., Kitchener, ON, manufacturer
***Tundra*, 1956**. Hand-screened fabric, 120 x 194 cm
Gift of Libby Toews, Textitle Museum of Canada Collection, T2012.26.1
Photography by Maciek Linowski

26 | **Thor Hansen (1903–1976), designer**
A. B. Caya Ltd., Kitchener ON, manufacturer
***Sunridge*, 1954**. Hand-screened fabric, 120 x 224 cm. Gift of Libby Toews, Textitle Museum of Canada Collection, T2012.26.4
Photography by Maciek Linowski

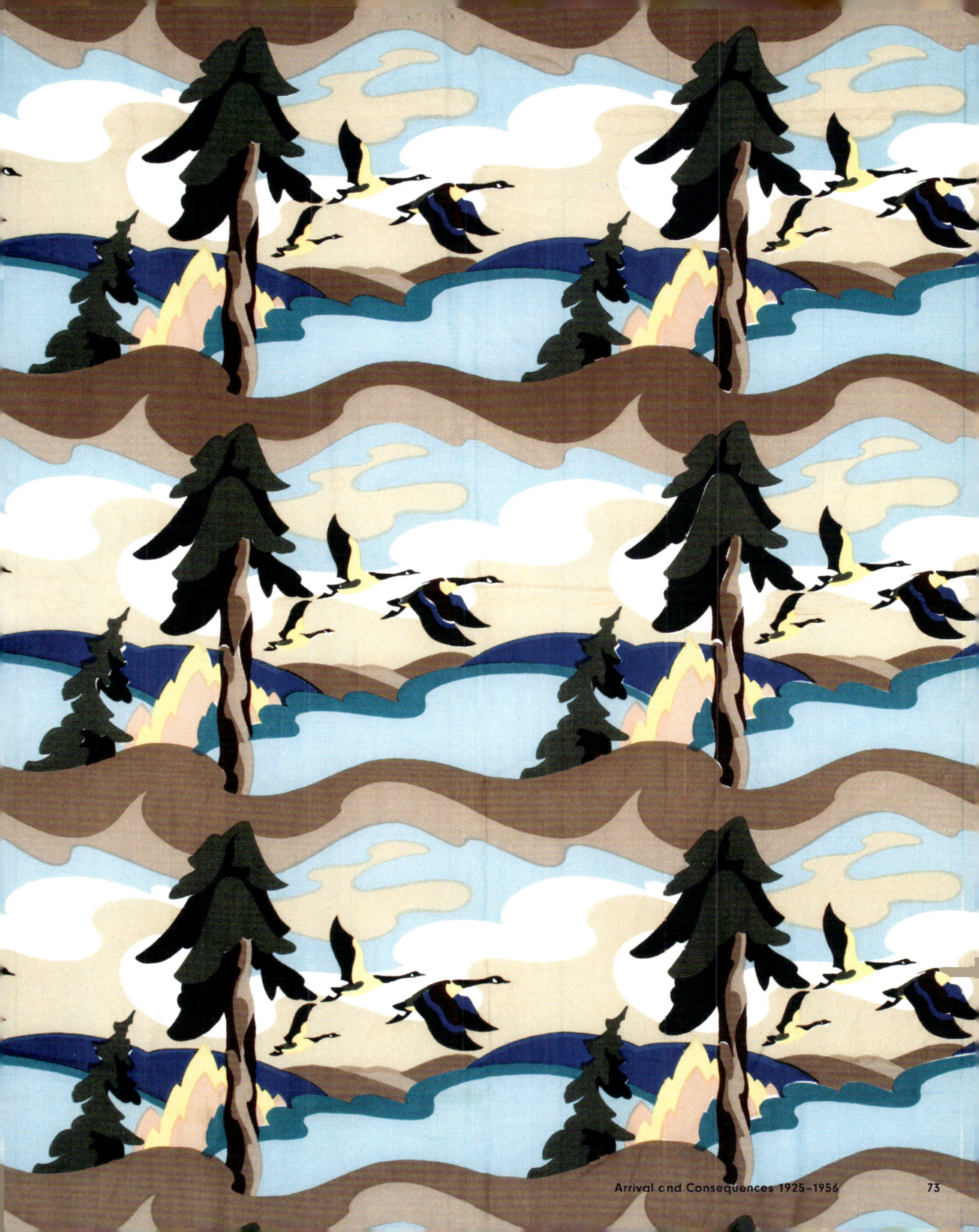

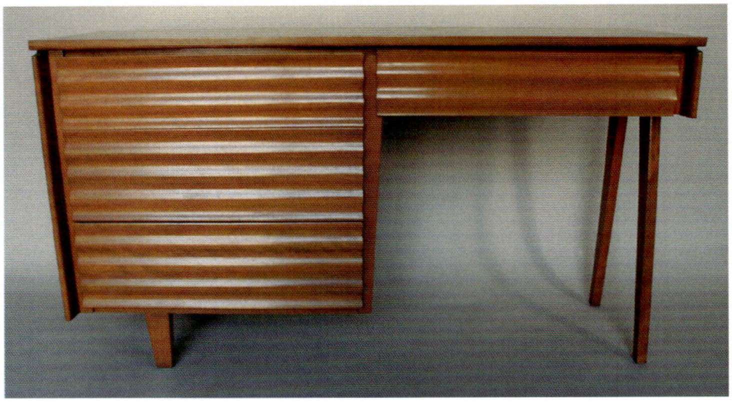

27 | Jan Kuypers (1925–1997), designer Imperial Furniture Manufacturing Co., Stratford, ON, manufacturer. Helsinki vanity/ Stavanger desk, 1952. Wood (yellow birch), 30 x 52 x 16 cm
Design Exchange Permanent Collection, 999.7.3
Image courtesy of the Design Exchange

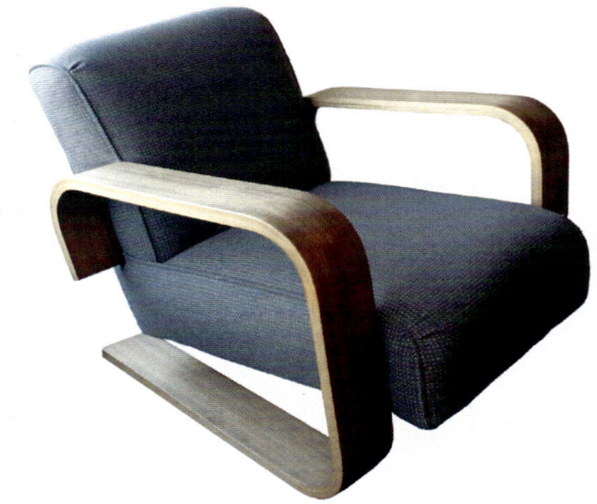

28 | Mouldcraft Plywoods Vancouver, BC, manufacturer Sky Bungalow side chair, 1946–1950
Plywood, upholstery, 81 x 43 x 46 cm
Collection of Jeannette and Jeff Wall
Image courtesy of Jeff Wall

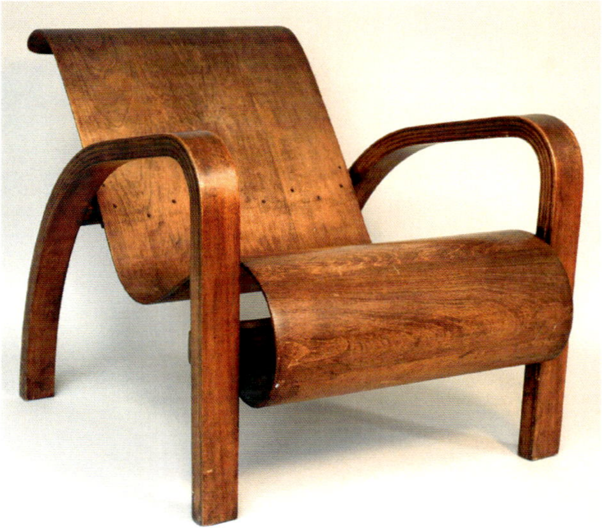

**29 | Waclaw Czerwinski (1900–1989)
Hilary Stykolt (1894–1974), designers
Canadian Wooden Aircraft Company, Stratford, ON, manufacturer. Armchair, 1946.** Plywood, 73 x 76.2 x 84 cm. Design Exchange Permanent Collection, 2002.1. Image courtesy of the Design Exchange

Scandinavian furniture is timeless and will blend with old periods very easily. It is designed to adapt to the human body. It has a functional design, an economy of line; and its most important purpose is comfort. Its line of beauty lies in the natural treatment of wood and simplicity of shape. Because it has no exaggerated forms or shapes put for the purpose of novelty, you are less apt to tire of it.

Sigrun Bülow-Hübe, 1957

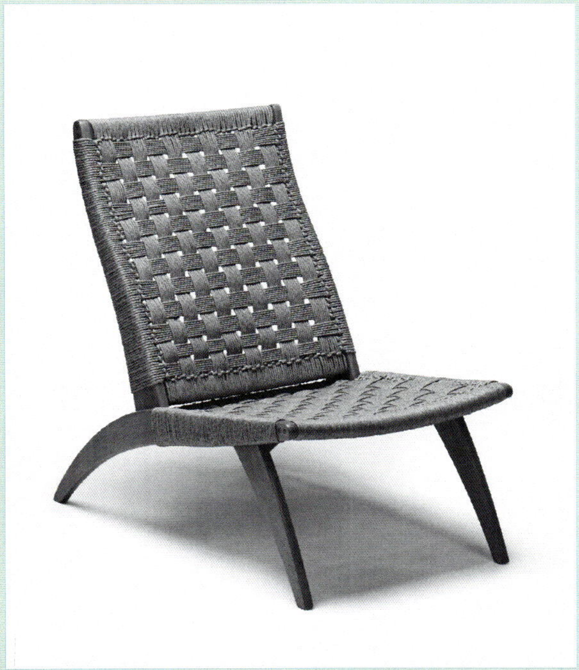

30 | **Earle Morrison (b. 1923)**
Robin Bush (1921–1982) designers
Earle A. Morrison Ltd., Victoria, BC, manufacturer
Occasional chair, 1951. Wood (birch), Rushtex, 86.5 x 57.2 x 90 cm. Collection of Allan Collier
Photography by Trevor Mills, Vancouver Art Gallery

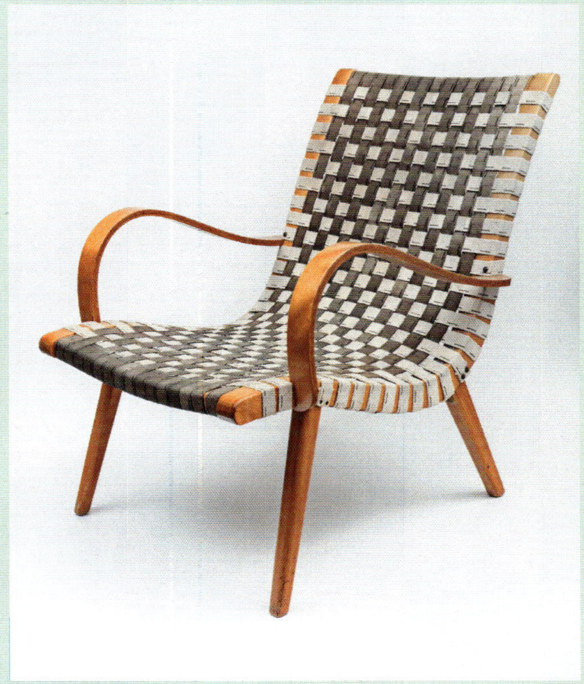

31 | **Attributed to Sigrun Bülow-Hübe (1913–1994), designer**
AKA Furniture Co. Ltd., Montreal, QC, manufacturer
***AKA Chair*, c. 1953.** Wood, 78.1 x 59.1 x 59.1 cm
Private collection. Photography by Toni Hafkenscheid

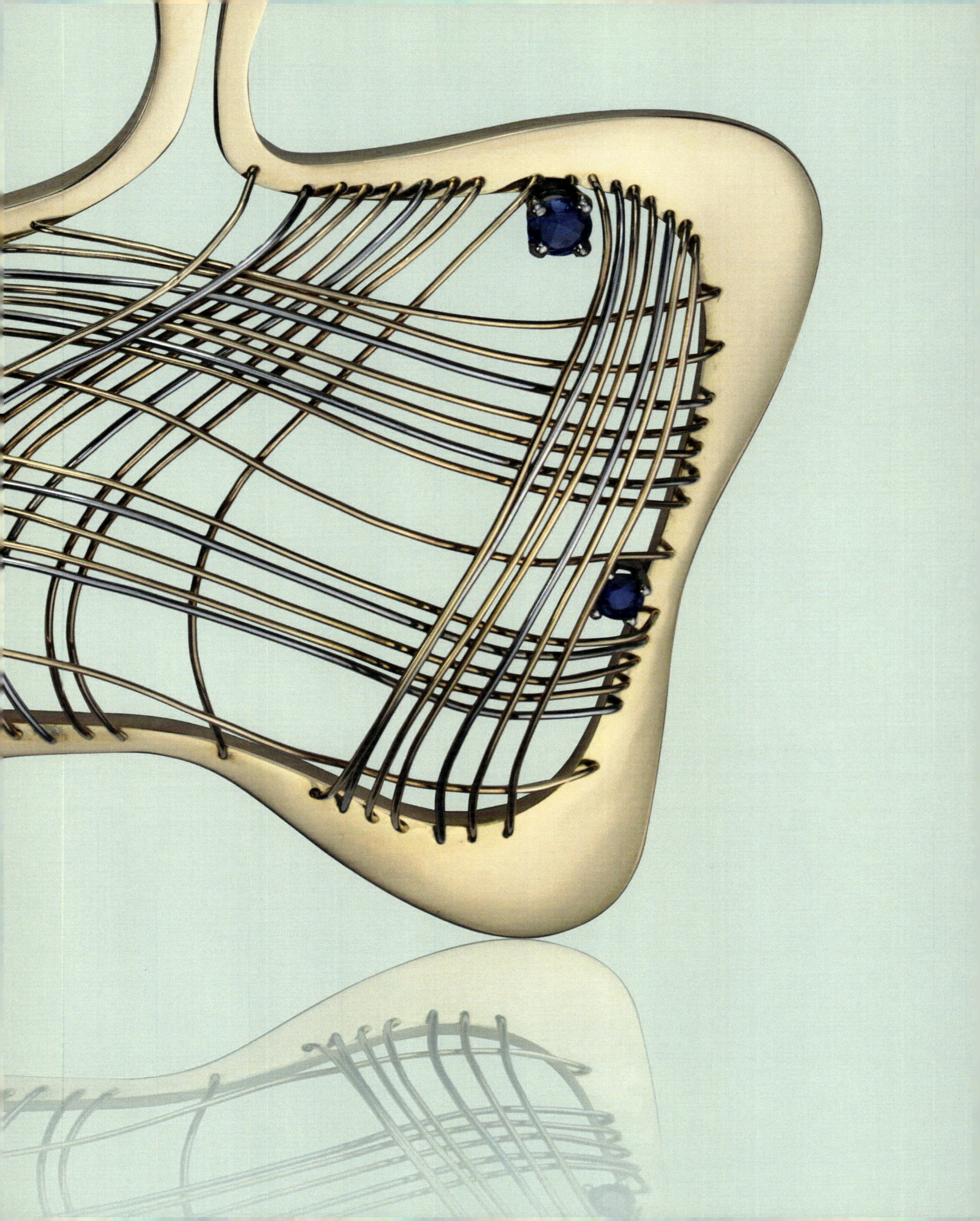

Exchange and Adaptation
1956–1990

Simultaneous with the second wave of Scandinavian émigrés who arrived in Canada after the Second World War and set up design practices, Canadian designers—some formally trained and others self-taught—further expanded the adaptation and commercial production of Scandinavian-inspired craft and design. Similarly, Canadian tastemakers writing for décor magazines and ladies' journals played significant roles in promoting the style. These editorials pronounced that it was progressive and comfortable without compromising elegance and taste, that it was affordable for budget-minded families and that it suited what was acknowledged to be changing patterns of middle-class life. The popularity of what was referred to as "Swedish Modern" and "Danish Modern" turned on these overlapping styles becoming synonymous with ideas about good design—a concern that echoed throughout North America—and the aspirational notions of domestic comfort and "gracious living."

Canadian interpretations of Scandinavian modern design functioned as visual and symbolic antidotes for those who sought something other than the traditional forms of furniture (whether pine Canadiana or overstuffed historical revival styles) that had long defined Canadian interiors. Capitalizing on the market opportunities presented, Canadian manufacturers added Scandinavian design to their conservative repertoire of colonial and historicist offerings and branded these lines with overtly Nordic names, *Helsinki*, *Stanvanger*, *Scanda*, and *Danesco*. Many designers produced sophisticated, materially accomplished, and original objects that evoked the character of modern Scandinavian design, while other makers and companies took a more pragmatic approach. By resorting to the production of cheaper versions and blatant "knock-offs" of Nordic originals—characterized by inexpensive materials and assembly techniques—such manufacturers nevertheless acted as promoters of the style's meanings in the country.

In these cases, while the shape of a chair, the tapering of a candlestick, the low profile of a sofa, the colourful printed graphics of a textile, and the solid boxiness of a credenza could be questioned because of the issue of originality and the implications of appropriation, the principles of utility, material integrity, and modesty that defined their lineage were maintained in significant and effecting ways. The 1970s saw the breaking of the tenets of modernism with ornamentation, irony, and whimsy increasingly present in design. Scandinavia and Canada were not immune from these shifts in thinking and practice. Leading Canadian furniture designers, while maintaining their adherence to Nordic design culture, likewise catered to the realities of casual and contemporary lifestyles and expanded the scope and repertoire of Scandinavian-inspired aesthetics in Canada.

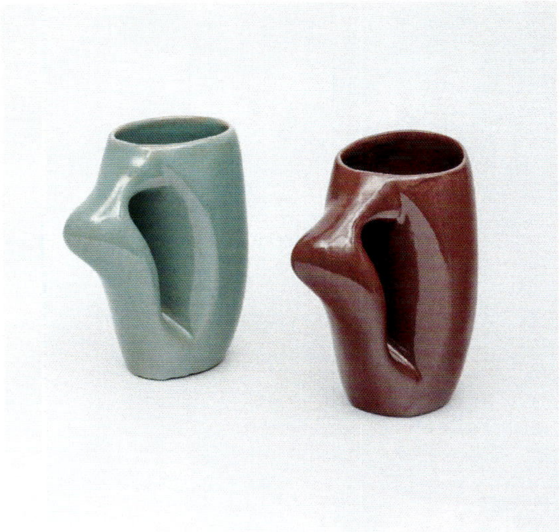

32 | **Gaétan Beaudin (1924–2002), designer Décor, Rimouski, QC, manufacturer. Mugs, 1950s**
Slip-cast earthenware, 15.5 x 12 x 9 cm each
Collection of the Gardiner Museum, gift of Léopold L. Foulem, G13.11.4.1-2. Photography by Toni Hafkenscheid

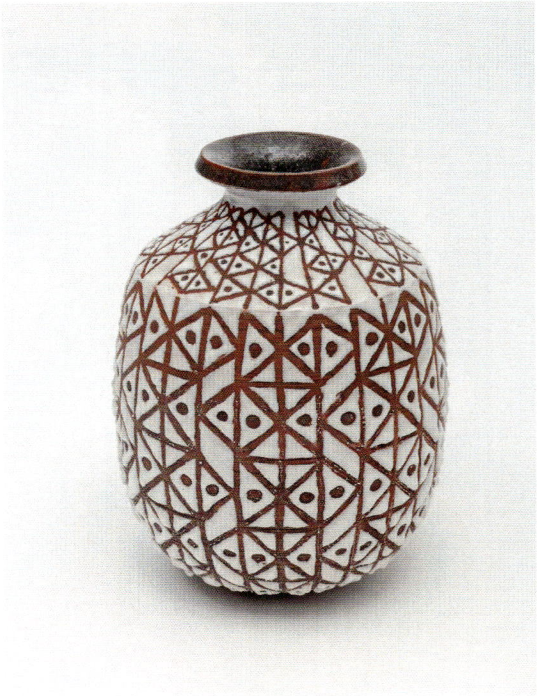

33 | **Jean Cartier (1924–1996)**
Vase, 1952. Thrown red earthenware, white glaze, wax resist decoration, 21.2 x 14.3 cm. Collection of the Gardiner Museum, gift of Léopold L. Foulem, G13.11.7. Photography by Toni Hafkenscheid

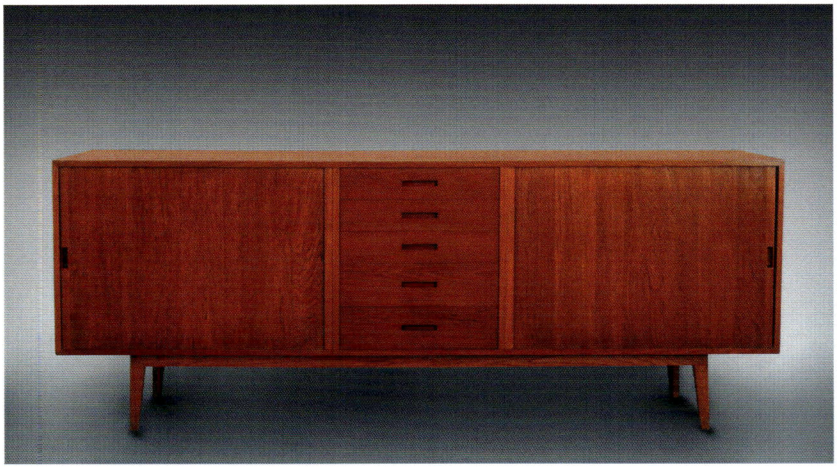

34 | **Vagn Petersen (1911–2002)**
Sideboard, 1956. Wood (teak, oak), 82 x 214.8 x 55.7 cm. The Montreal Museum of Fine Arts, purchase, William Gilman Cheney Bequest, 2000.118
Photography by Christine Guest

The conditions that mold Scandinavian furniture design are similar to our own. The people live in a northern climate with long winters; they live in apartments or small houses (somewhat like our subdivision houses, only smaller); they raise healthy children in a relaxed family atmosphere; and they have an inherent liking for the out of doors, summer and winter.

Mandel Sprachman, 1956

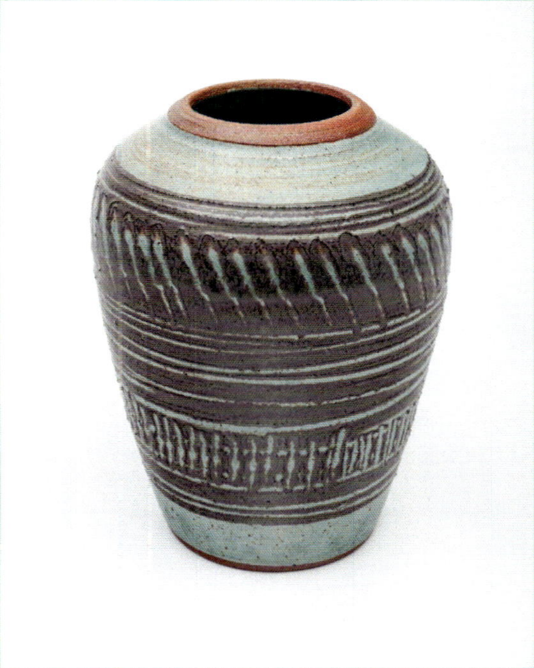

36 | **Walter Dexter (1931–2015)**
Vase, c. 1957. Ceramic, 21 x 16 cm. Private collection. Photography by Toni Hafkenscheid

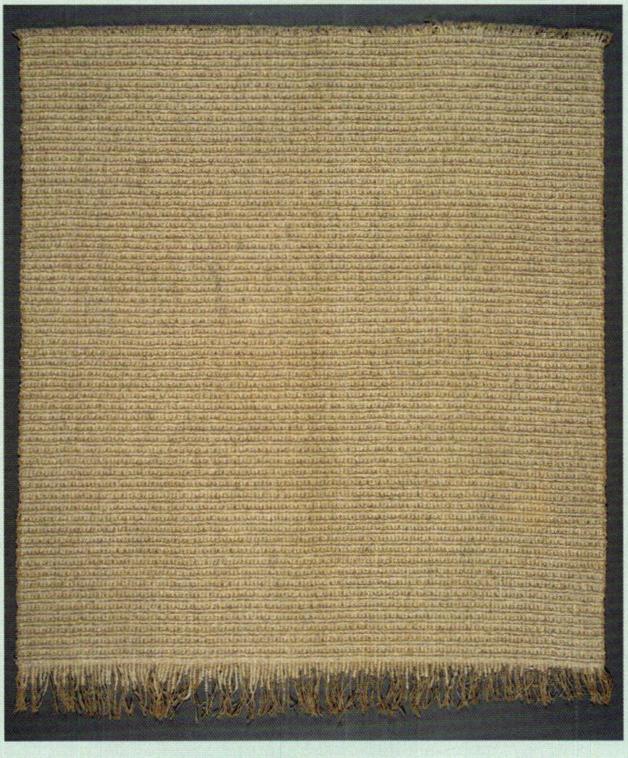

35 | **Harold Burnham (1912–1973)**
Upholstery width, 1957. Hemp, rayon, linen, 102 x 85 cm
Collection of the Royal Ontario Museum,
gift of Mr. and Mrs. Harold B. Burnham, 962.126.3
With permission of the Royal Ontario Museum © ROM

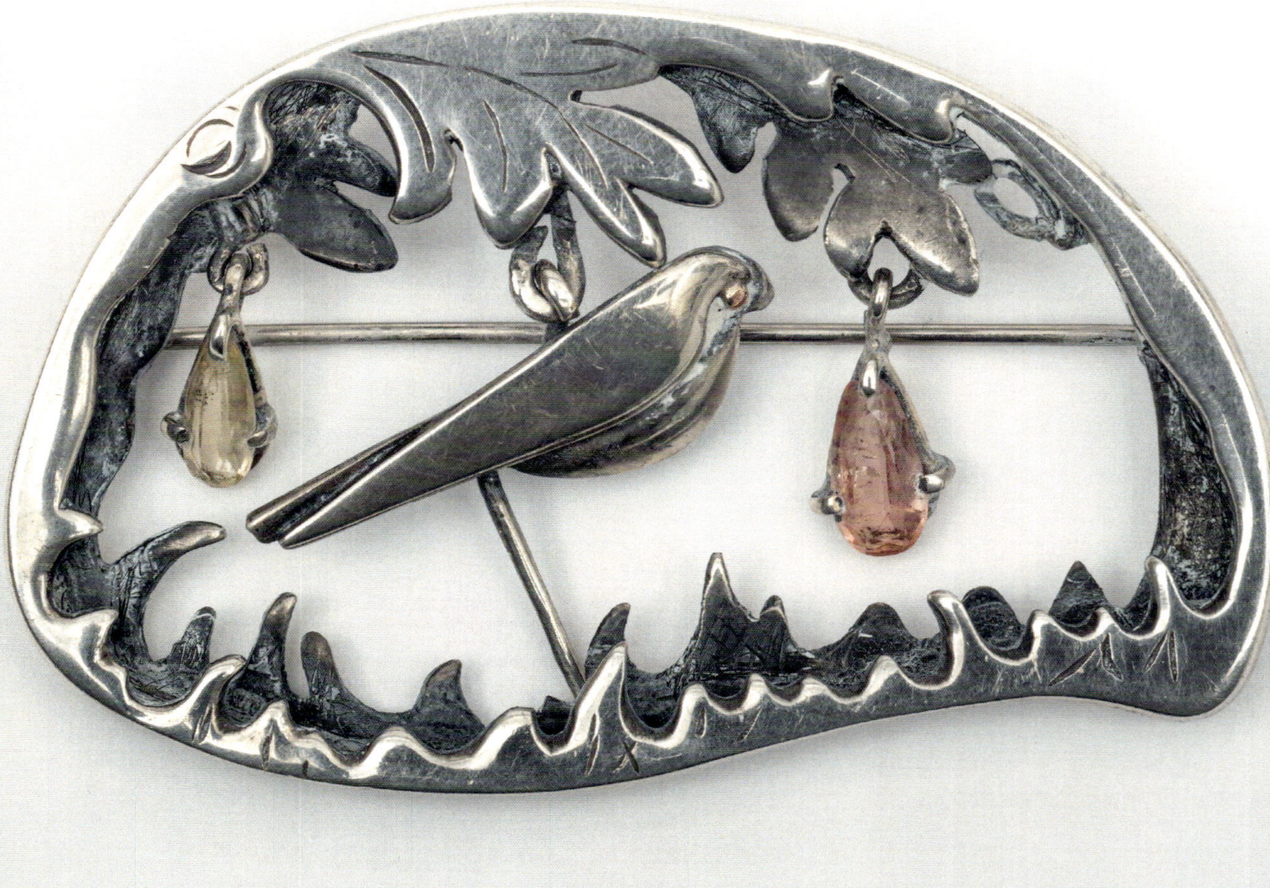

37 | **Nancy Meek Pocock (1910–1998)**
***Garden in the Rain*, 1960s**. Sterling silver, semi-precious stones, 5.1 x 2.5 cm. Private collection
Photography by Toni Hafkenscheid

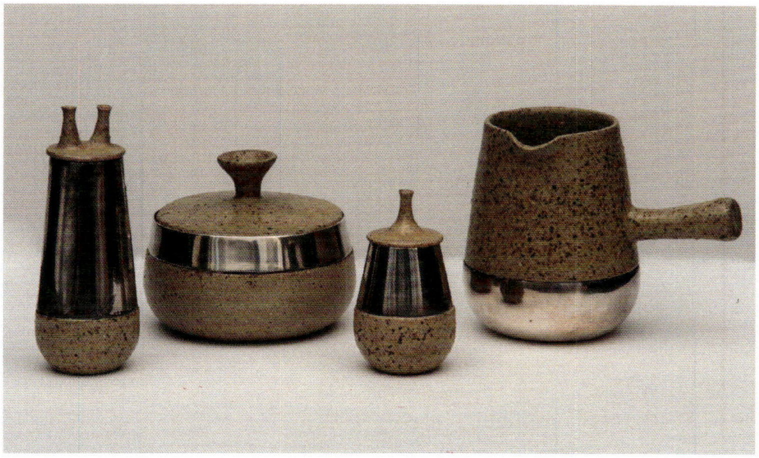

38 | Roman Bartkiw (1935–2010)
Cream jug, sugar pot, salt shaker, and pepper pot, c. 1960. Stoneware, silver, varied dimensions
Roman Bartkiw Estate, courtesy of the Art Gallery of Nova Scotia. Photography by Raw Photography

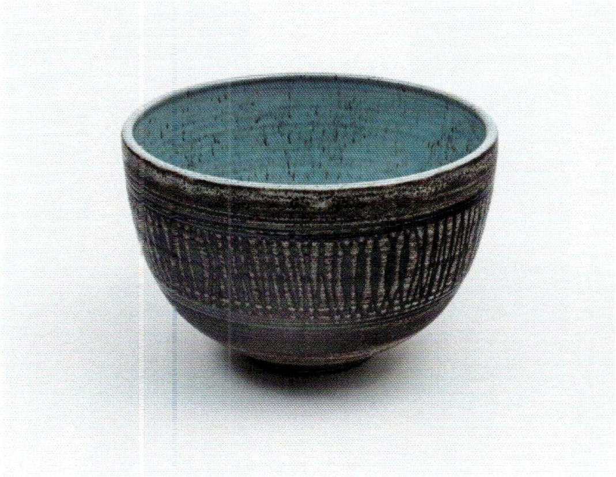

39 | Jack Herman (b. 1927)
Bowl, c. 1960. Ceramic, glaze, 17.5 x 24 cm. Private collection. Photography by Toni Hafkenscheid

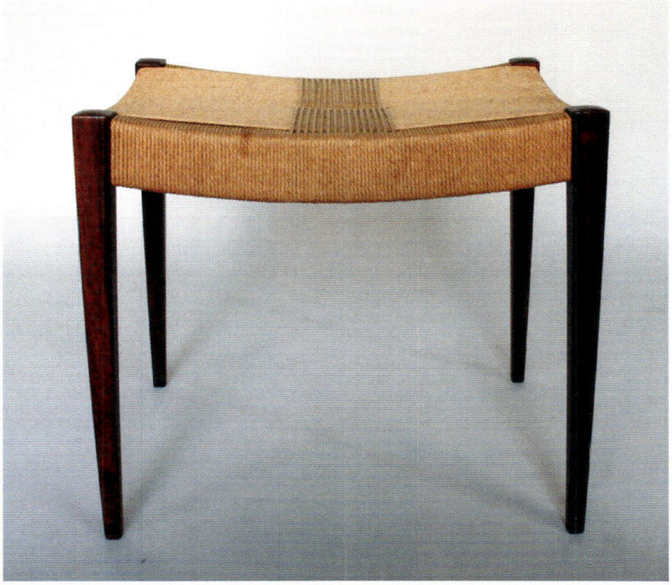

40 | John Stene (1914–2008), designer, Brunswick Manufacturing Co. Ltd., Toronto, ON, manufacturer. Stool, 1958. Wood (stained oak), paper twine, 46.9 x 49 x 33 cm. Design Exchange Permanent Collection, 2001.01, gift of John Stene
Image courtesy of the Design Exchange

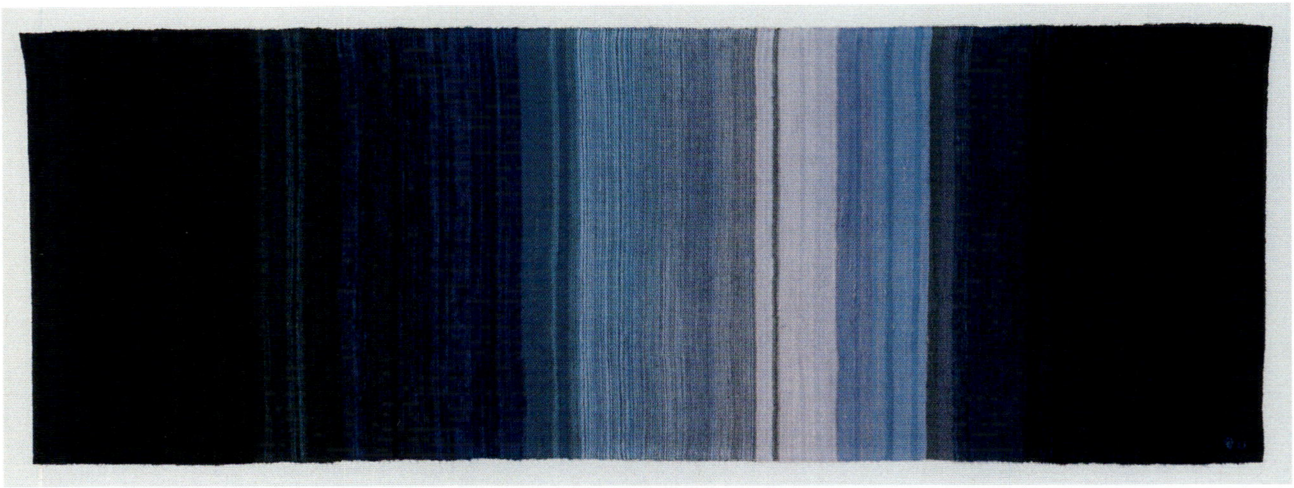

41 | **Mariette Rousseau-Vermette (1926–2006)**
***Hiver canadien*, 1961**. Wool, 540.7 x 213.3 cm
Musée national des beaux-arts du Québec, purchase, 1963.70. © Estate of Mariette Rousseau-Vermette and Claude Vermette. Image courtesy of MNBAQ, Jean-Guy Kérouac

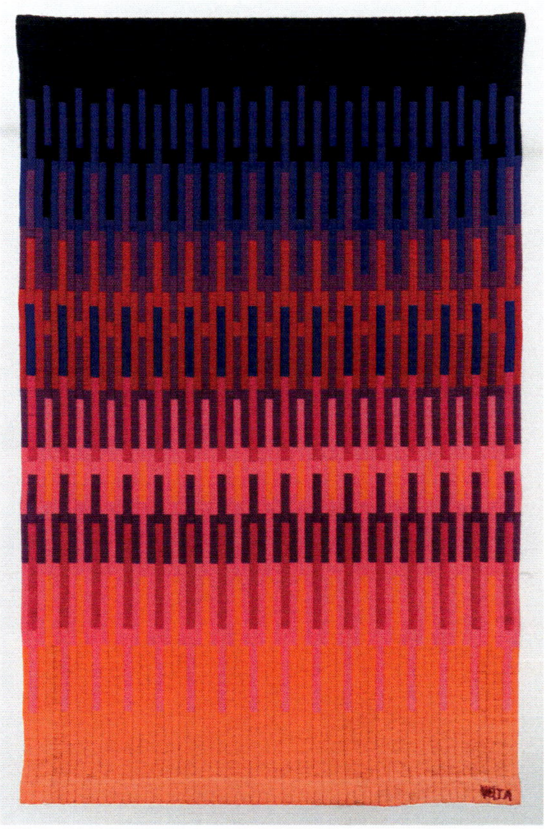

42 | **Velta Vilsons (b. 1919)**
Wall hanging, 1965–1970. Wool, 146.1 x 90.2 cm
Collection of Gail and Gerry Crawford
Photography by Toni Hafkenscheid

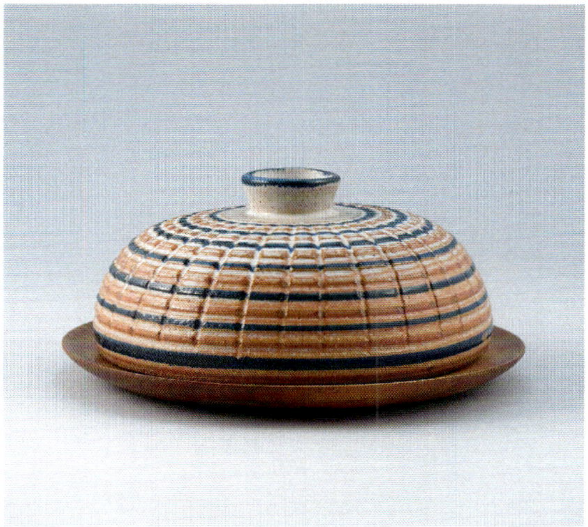

43 | **Folmer Hansen (1930–2014)**
David Ross (1925–1974)
Hansen-Ross Pottery, Fort Qu'Appelle, SK.
Cheese bell with plate, 1963
Clay, glaze, and wood, 10.5 x 22.5 cm
Saskatchewan Arts Board Permanent Collection
Photography by Gabriela Garcia-Luna. Photograph was taken at the Moose Jaw Museum and Art Gallery as part of the Hansen-Ross Retrospective Exhibition

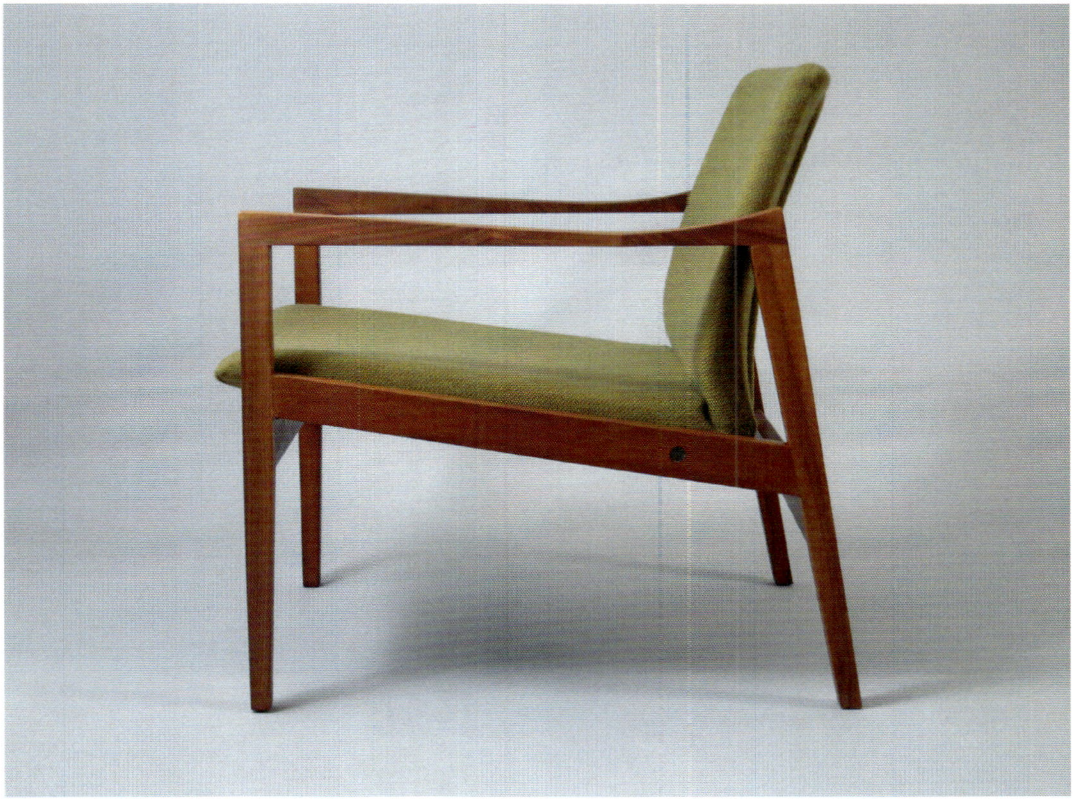

44 | **Walter Nugent (b. 1913), designer Walter Nugent Designs Ltd., Oakville, ON, manufacturer. Armchair, 1964.** Wood (walnut), fabric, 71 x 63 x 68 cm. Collection of Mary-Lynn Ogilvie
Photography by Allan Collier

I got to know Viljo Revell and his team of architects when they working on Toronto City Hall in 1960. They literally opened up their kitchen cabinets and showed me dishes by Kaj Franck for Arabia, glassware from Iittala, as well as fabric and cushions from Marimekko.

Janis Kravis, 2012

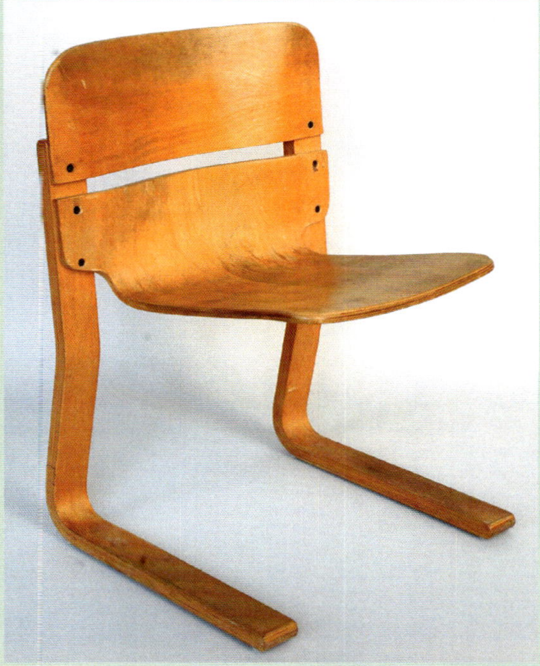

45 | **Thomas Lamb (1938–1997), designer**
Curvply Wood Products, Orono, ON, manufacturer
***Roo Chair*, 1970.** Moulded plywood, 77 x 52 x 50.5 cm
Design Exchange Permanent Collection, 2001.3.1
Image courtesy of the Design Exchange

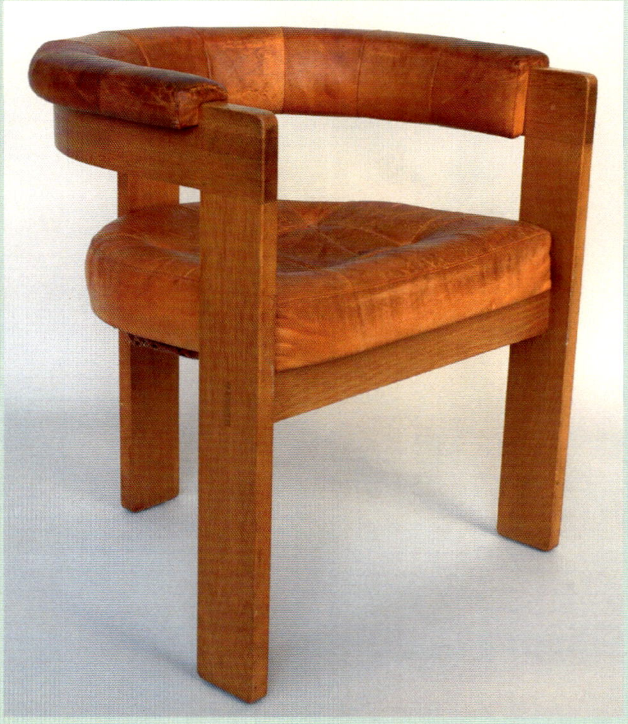

46 | **Janis Kravis (b. 1935)**
Armchair, 1964, Wood (teak), 71 x 61 x 53 cm
Design Exchange Permanent Collection, 002.5, gift of Janis Kravis. Image courtesy of the Design Exchange

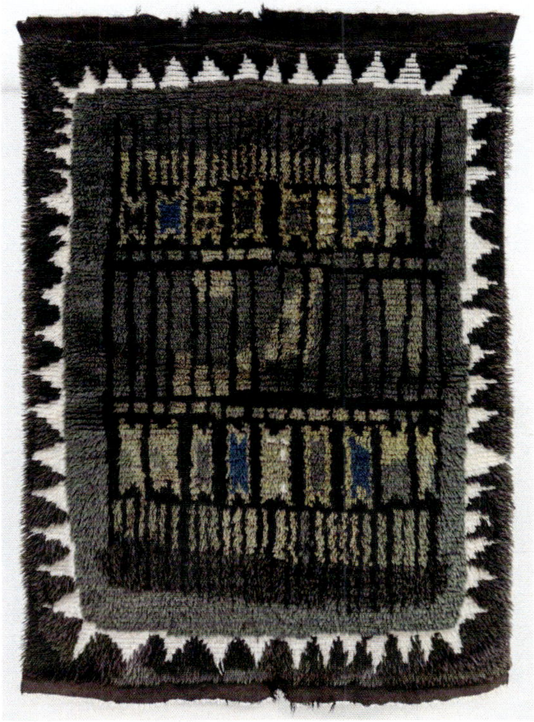

47 | **Marion Smith (1918–2009)**
Woven textile, c. 1965. Wool and linen,
173 x 119 cm. Private collection
Photography by Toni Hafkenscheid

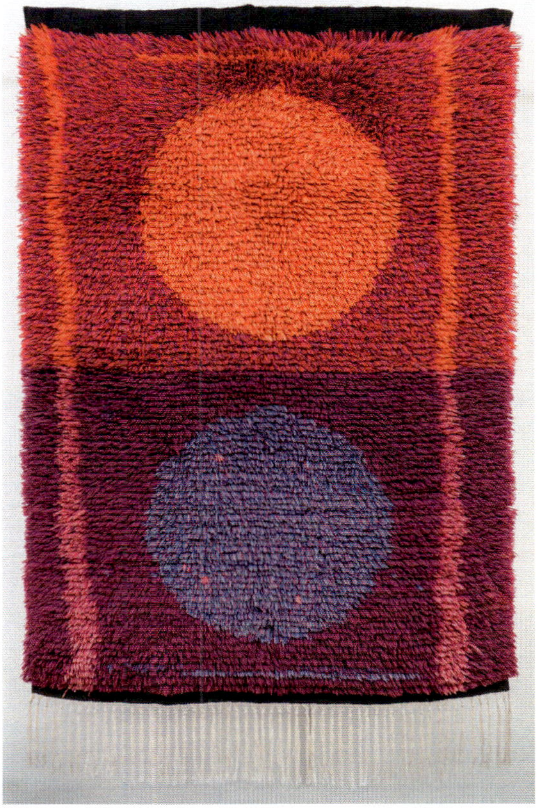

48 | **Marion Smith (1918–2009)**
Woven textile, c. 1964. Wool and linen,
150 x 102 cm. Private collection
Photography by Toni Hafkenscheid

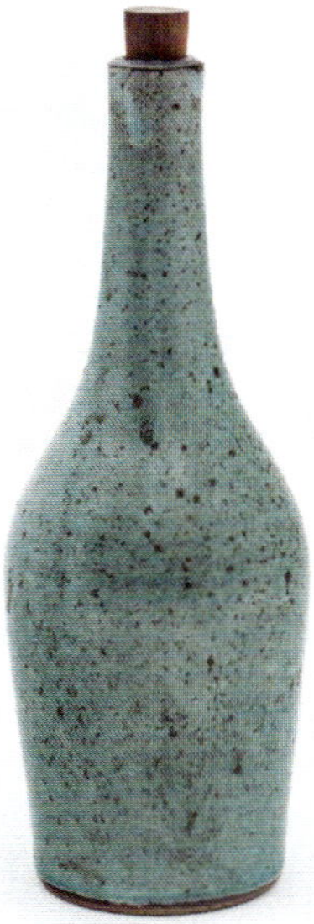

49 | **Jack Herman (b. 1927)**
Bottle with stopper, c. 1965, Ceramic, teak,
22 x 7.5 cm. Private collection
Photography by Toni Hafkenscheid

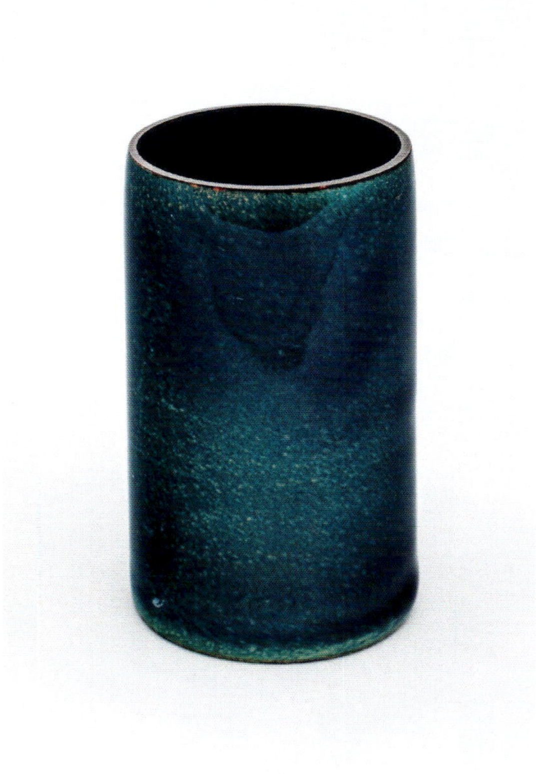

50 | **Alan Perkins (1915–2005)**
Enamel vase, c. 1965. Ceramic, enamel, 10 x 5 cm
Private collection. Photography by Toni Hafkenscheid

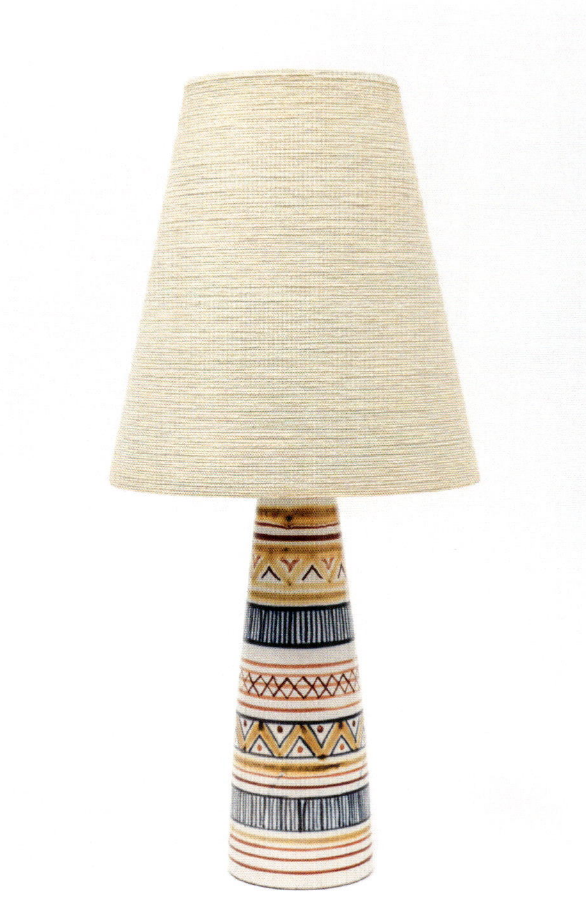

51 | **Lotte Bostlund (1919–1999), designer**
Bostlund Industries, Oak Ridges, ON, manufacturer
Lamp, c. 1964. Ceramic with paint, spun nylon, 69 x 27 cm
Private Collection. Photography by Toni Hafkenscheid

[M]any Canadian homes have already achieved the light airy look without sacrificing naturalness or warmth—thanks to Scandinavian originals or domestic reproductions.

Patricia Lamont, 1956

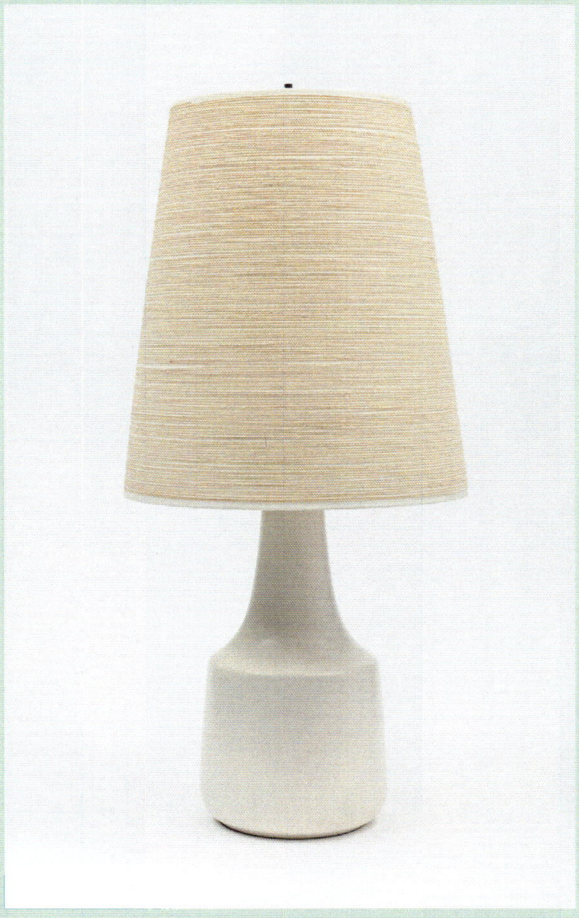

52 | **Lotte Bostlund (1919–1999), designer**
Bostlund Industries, Oak Ridges, ON, manufacturer
Table lamp, c. 1965. Slip-cast stoneware, glaze, spun nylon, brass, electrical cord, 75 x 35 cm
Courtesy of Dr. Robert Buckingham. Photography by Toni Hafkenscheid

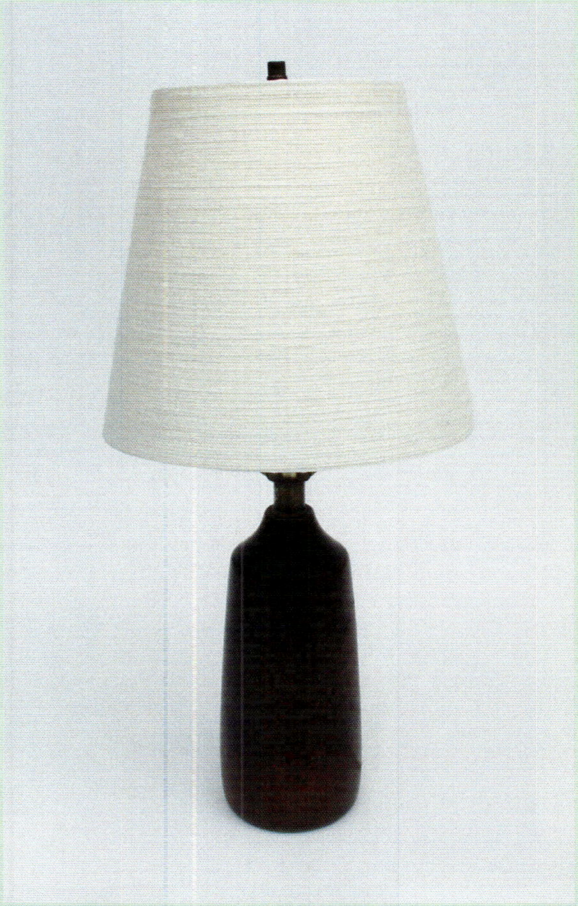

53 | **Lotte Bostlund (1919–1999), designer**
Bostlund Industries, Oak Ridges, ON, manufacturer
Table lamp, c. 1965. Stoneware, glaze, spun nylon, brass, electrical cord, 50 x 24.5 cm. Private collection. Photography by Christina MacDonald

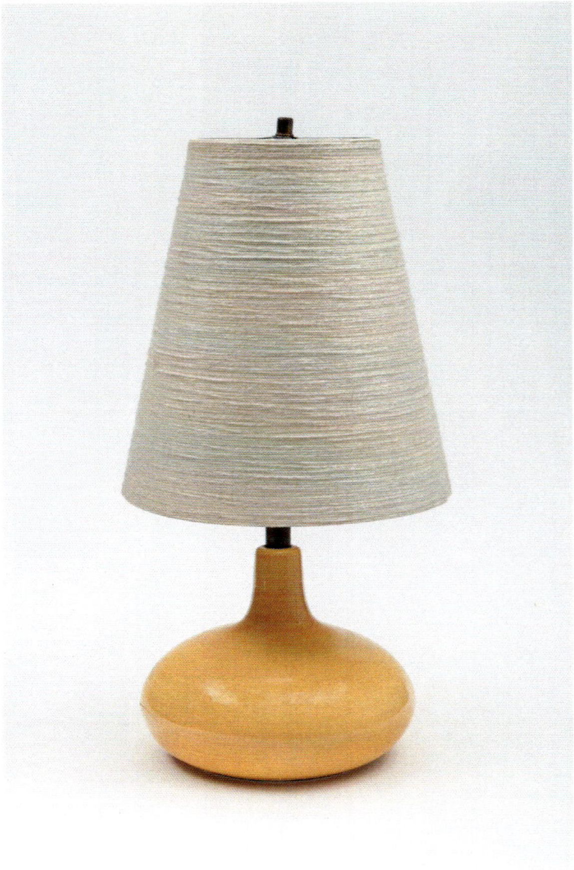

54 | Lotte Bostlund (1919–1999), designer
Bostlund Industries, Oak Ridges, ON, manufacturer
Table lamp, c. 1965. Slip-cast stoneware, glaze, spun nylon, brass, electrical cord, 63 x 24 cm
Courtesy of Sarah Keenlyside. Photography by Toni Hafkenscheid

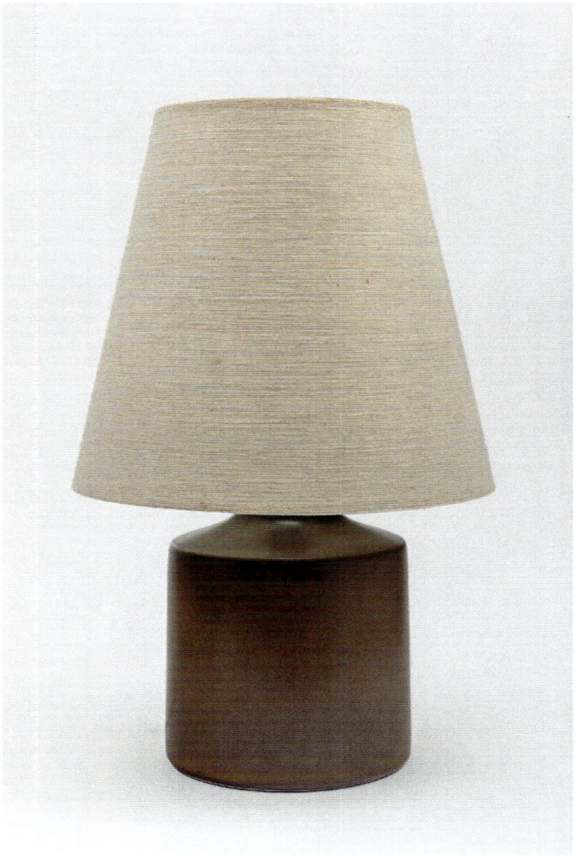

55 | Lotte Bostlund (1919–1999), designer
Bostlund Industries, Oak Ridges, ON, manufacturer
Lamp, c. 1965. Stoneware, glaze, spun nylon, brass, electrical cord, 75 x 46 cm. Courtesy of Sarah Keenlyside. Photography by Toni Hafkenscheid

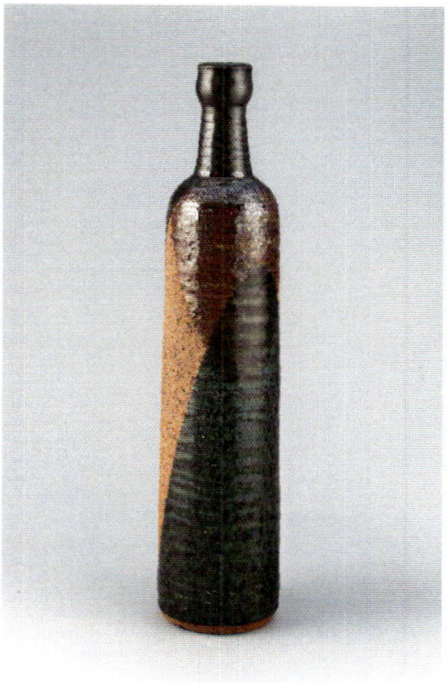

56 | **Folmer Hansen (1930–2014)**
David Ross (1925–1974)
Hansen-Ross Pottery, Fort Qu'Appelle, SK
Bottle vase, 1967. Ceramic, 53 x 11.6 cm. Saskatchewan Arts Board Permanent Collection, C68.12. Photography by Gabriela Garcia-Luna. Photograph was taken at the Moose Jaw Museum and Art Gallery as part of the Hansen-Ross Retrospective Exhibition

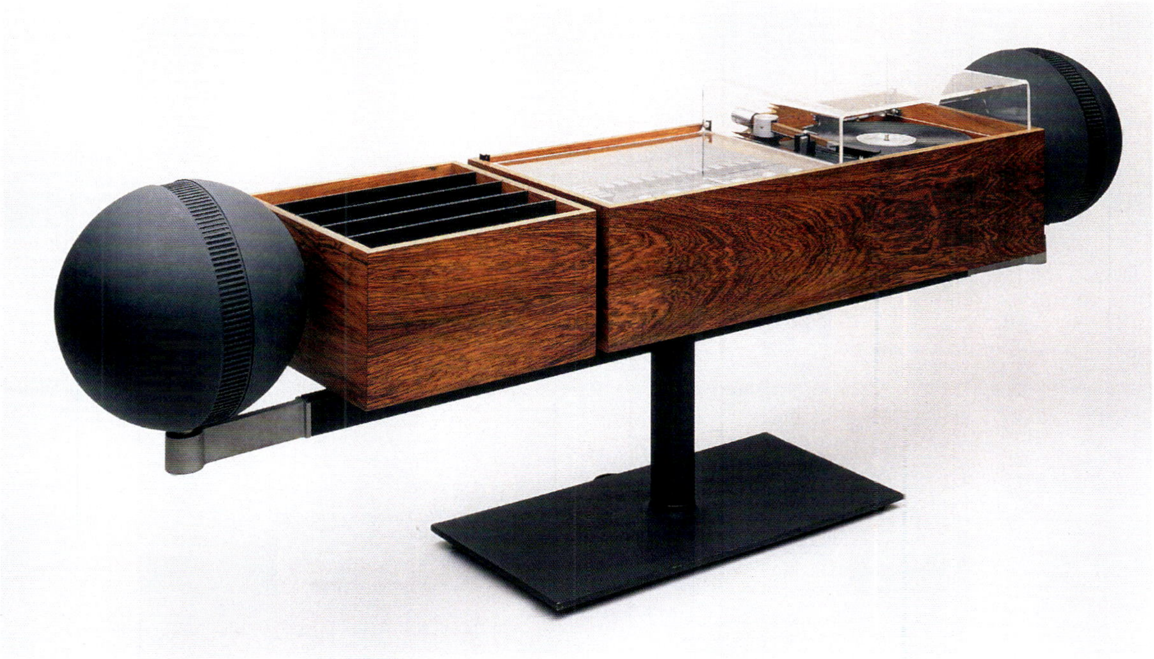

57 | **Al Faux (1931–1978)**
Hugh Spencer (1928–1982), designers
Clairtone Sound Corporation, Toronto, ON, manufacturer
***G2 Stereo*, 1966.** Wood (rosewood) chassis, painted cast aluminum speakers, plexiglas dust cover, brushed aluminum base, 68 x 199 x 37.5 cm. Design Exchange Permanent Collection, 991.1, gift of Frank Davies
Image courtesy of the Design Exchange

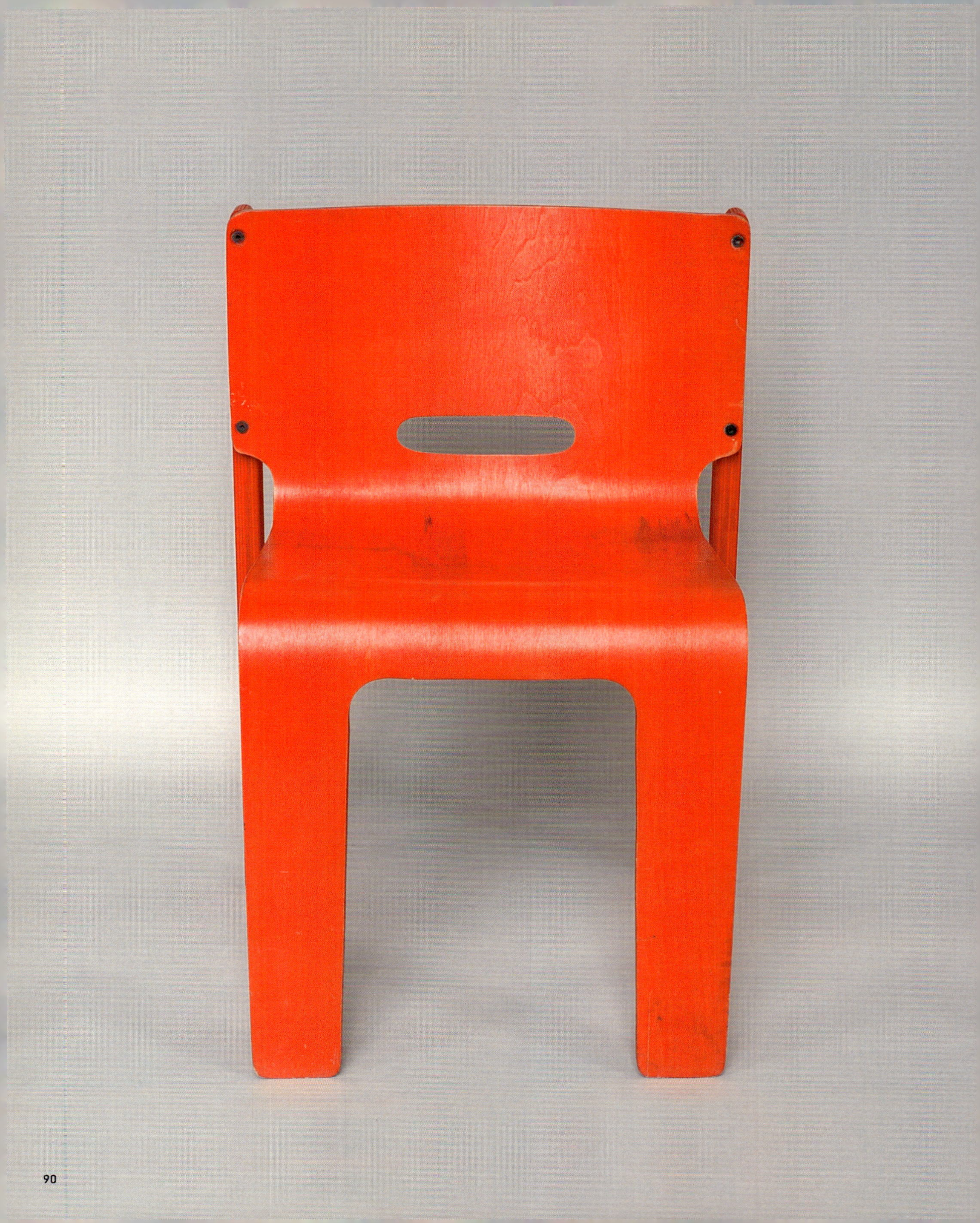

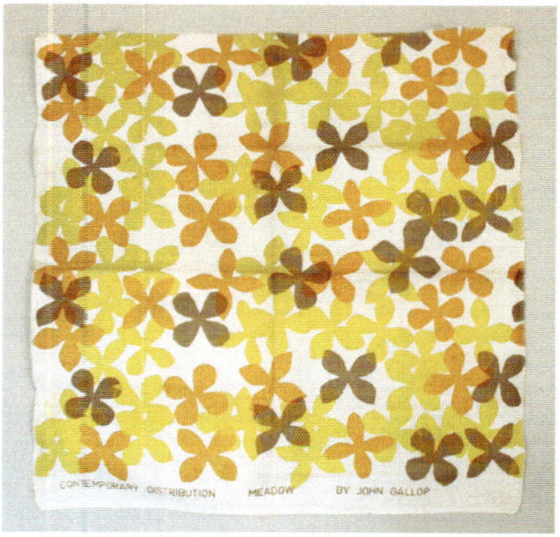

59 | John Gallop, designer
J & J Brook, Contemporary Distribution, Toronto, ON, manufacturer. *Meadow*, c. 1967. Block print on hand-blocked Peru linen, 60 x 60 cm. Design Exchange Permanent Collection, 2001.7.1, gift of Joanne Brook
Image courtesy of the Design Exchange

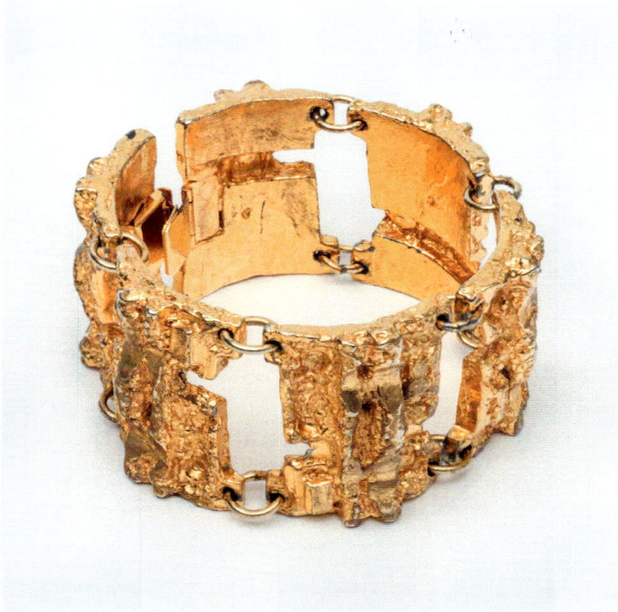

60 | Robert Larin
Bracelet, 1968–1977. Gold-plated metal, 17.8 cm
Private collection. Photography by Toni Hafkenscheid

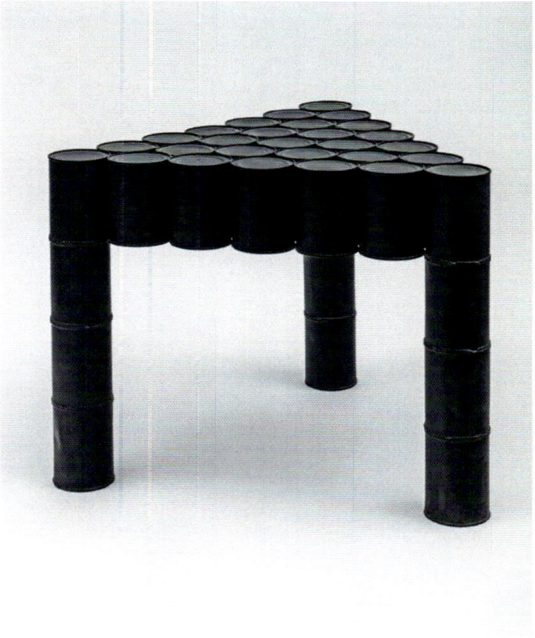

58 | Keith Muller (1938–2003)
Michael Stewart (b. 1940), designers
Ambiant Systems, Toronto, ON, manufacturer
***MS-SC Stacking Chair*, 1968.** Moulded plywood, exposed bolts, 73 x 49.5 x 47 cm. Design Exchange Permanent Collection, 996.6, gift of Keith Muller
Image courtesy of the Design Exchange

61 | Donald Lloyd McKinley (1932–1998)
***Soup Can Table*, c. 1963.** Metal, 40.6 x 45.7 x 40.6 cm. Courtesy of Stephen Hogbin
Photography by Toni Hafkenscheid

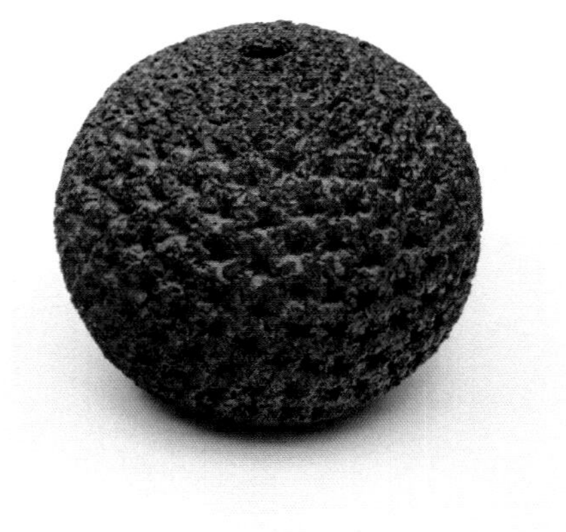

62 | **Roman Bartkiw (1935–2010)**
Untitled, c. 1970. Porcelain, 10 x 11.5 cm
Collection of Lorna Marsden
Photography by Toni Hafkenscheid

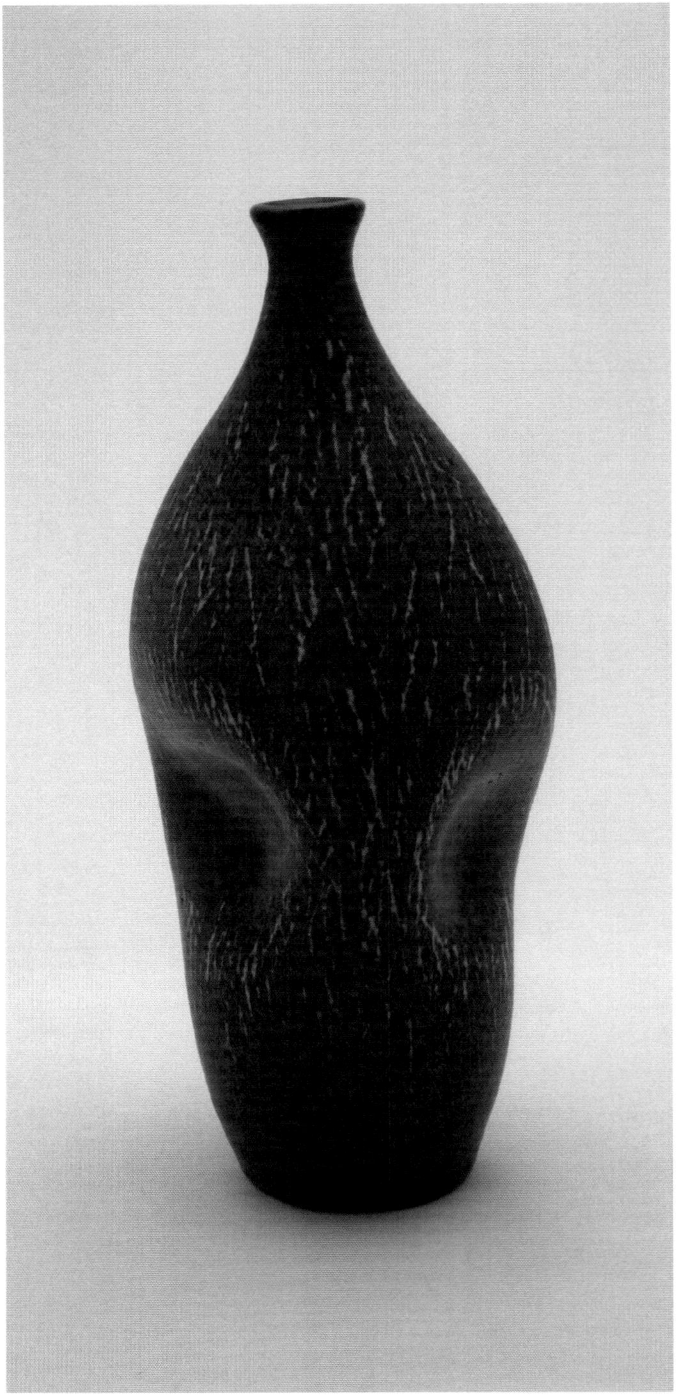

63 | **Ernst Lorenzen (1911–1990)**
Alma Lorenzen (1916–1998)
Vase, c. 1969. Ceramic, 23.5 x 10 x 9 cm. Courtesy of Allan Collier. Photography by Allan Collier

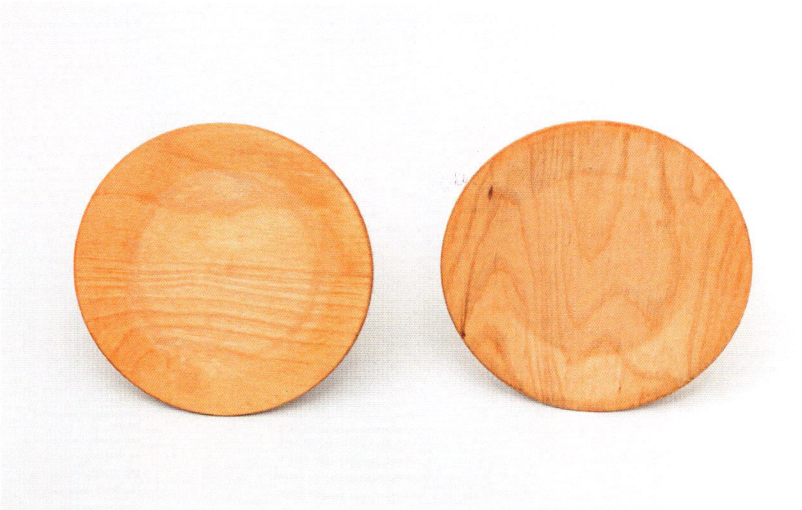

64 | Unattributed
Plate, c. 1970. Wood (fir), 22 cm each. Private collection Photography by Toni Hafkenscheid

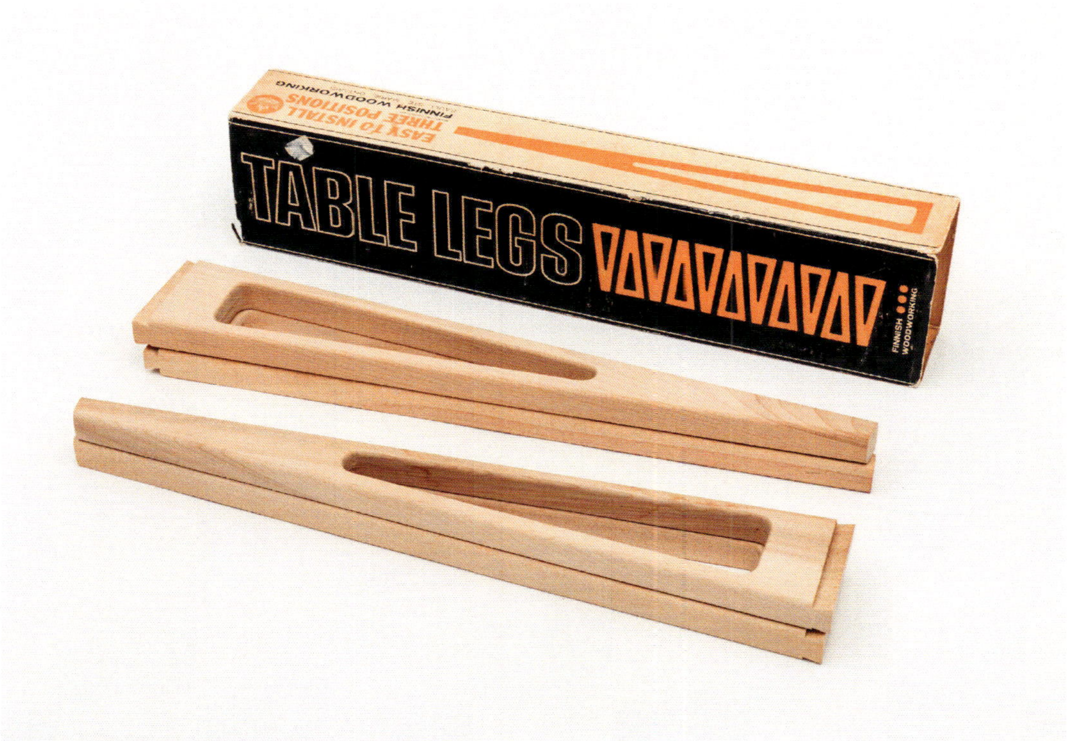

65 | Finnish Woodworking, Sault Ste. Marie, ON, manufacturer
Table leg kit, c. 1970. Wood, (maple). Cardboard box: 8.9 x 5.7 x 40.6 cm, legs: 7 x 39.4 cm. Private collection
Photography by Toni Hafkenscheid

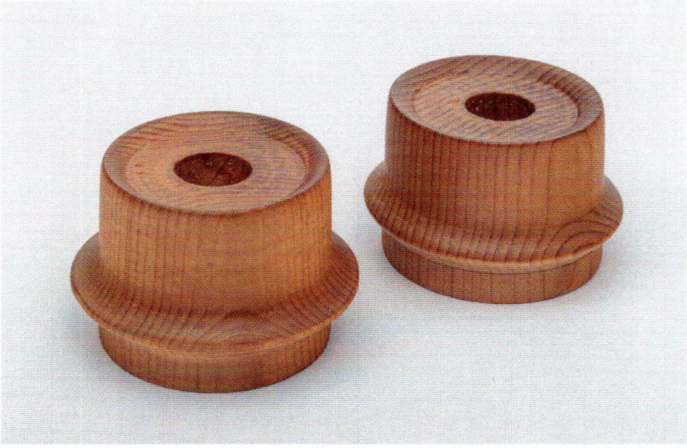

66 | Taipale Woodworkers, Toronto, ON, manufacturer. Candlesticks, c. 1975
Wood (pine), 7 x 8.9 cm. Private collection
Photography by Toni Hafkenscheid

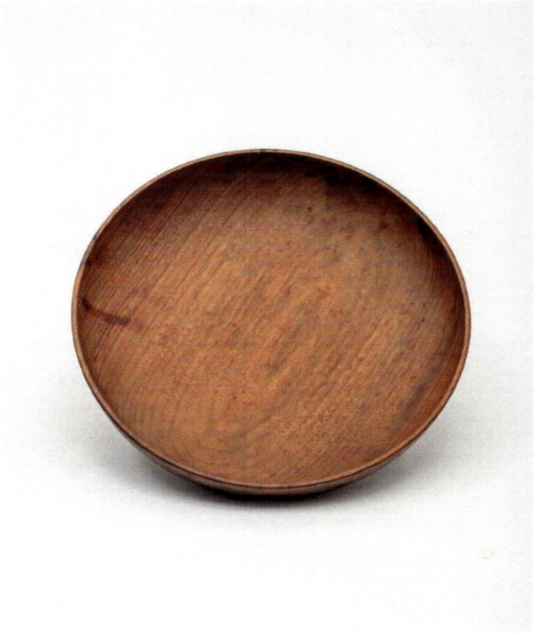

67 | Donald Lloyd McKinley (1932–1998)
Turned bowl, c. 1975. Wood, 5.1 x 25.4 cm
Courtesy of Lauren McKinley Renzetti
Photography by Toni Hafkenscheid

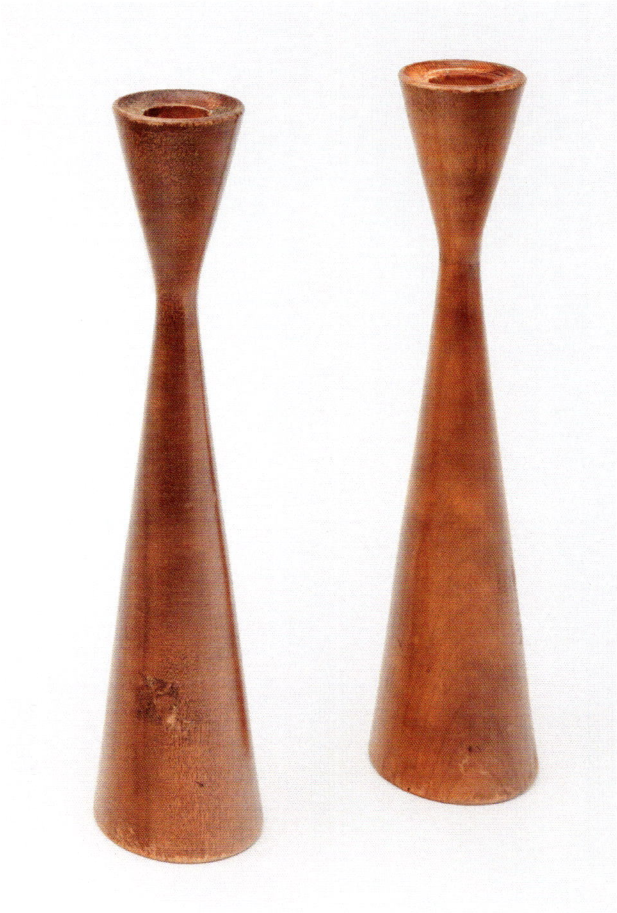

68 | Baribocraft, Lévis, QC, manufacturer
Candlesticks, c. 1972. Wood (maple), 27.9 x 5.1 cm
Private collection. Photography by Toni Hafkenscheid

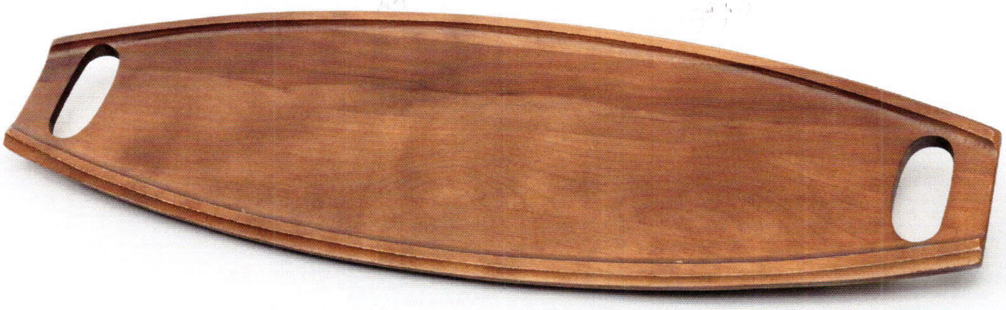

69 | **Baribocraft, Lévis, QC, manufacturer**
Serving tray, c. 1972. Wood (maple), 2.5 x 19.1 x 61 cm
Private collection. Photography by Toni Hafkenscheid

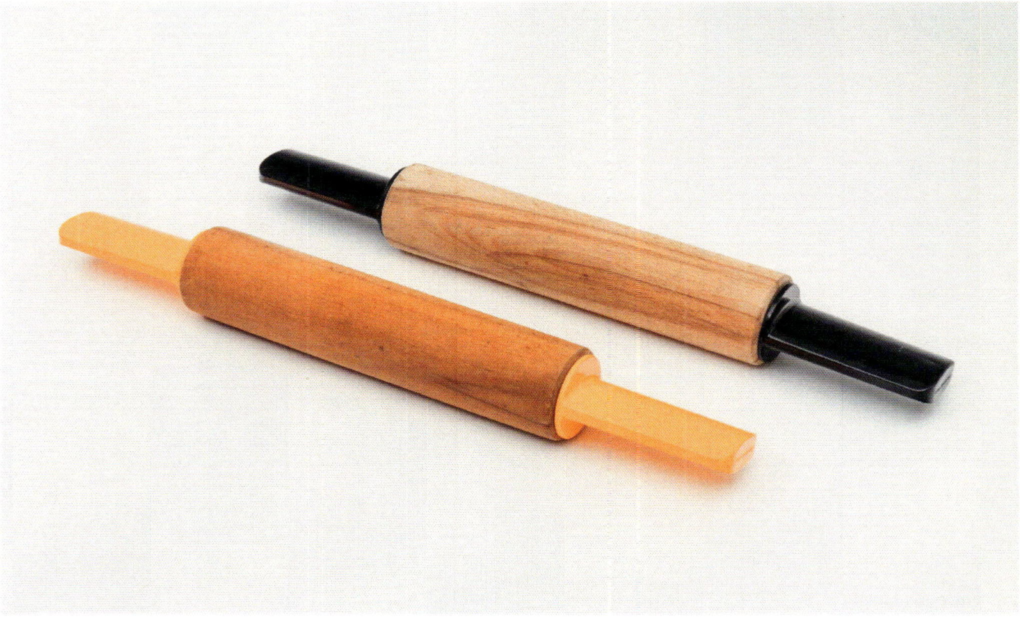

70 | **Koen de Winter (b. 1943), designer**
Danesco, Montreal, QC, manufacturer. Rolling pins, 1972. Wood (maple), plastic, 45.7 cm. Private collection
Photography by Toni Hafkenscheid

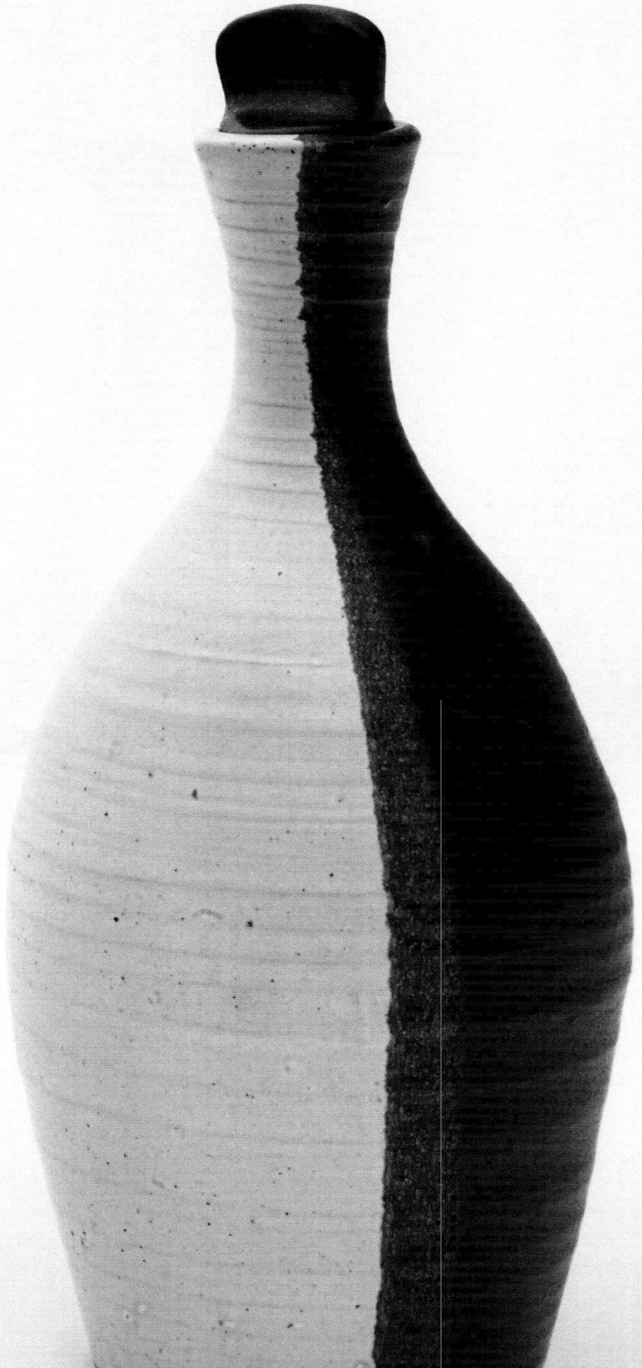

71 | **Luke Lindoe**, Ceramic Arts, Calgary, AB
Two-toned bottle, c. 1974. Ceramic, 26 x 11 cm
Private Collection. Photography by Toni Hafkenscheid

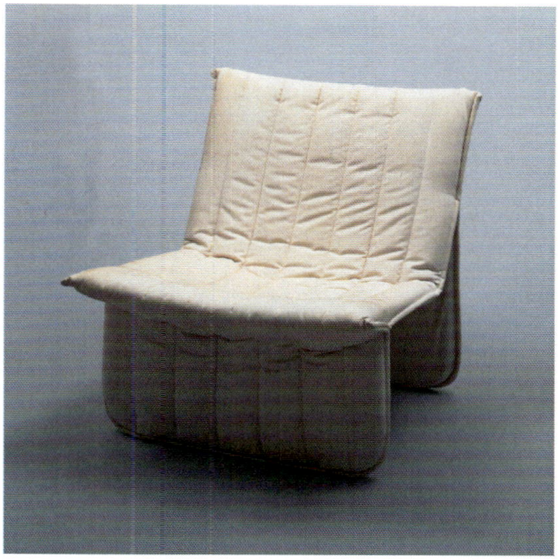

72 | **Niels Sylvester Bendtsen (b. 1943), designer**
Kebe Møbler ApS, Copenhagen, DK, manufacturer
***Ribbon Chair*, 1975.** Tubular steel, cotton canvas, polyester fill, 69.9 x 71 x 71 cm. Digital Image © The Museum of Modern Art/Licensed by SCALA/Art Resource, NY

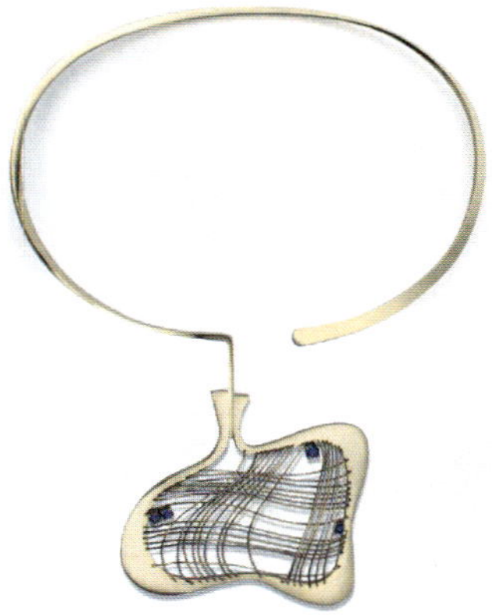

73 | **Martha Glenny (b. 1953)**
Neck ring and pendant, 1974. 14-carat yellow and white gold, sapphires, neck ring: 13 cm diameter; pendant: 6 x 6 cm. Courtesy of Martha Glenny. Image courtesy of Digital by Design

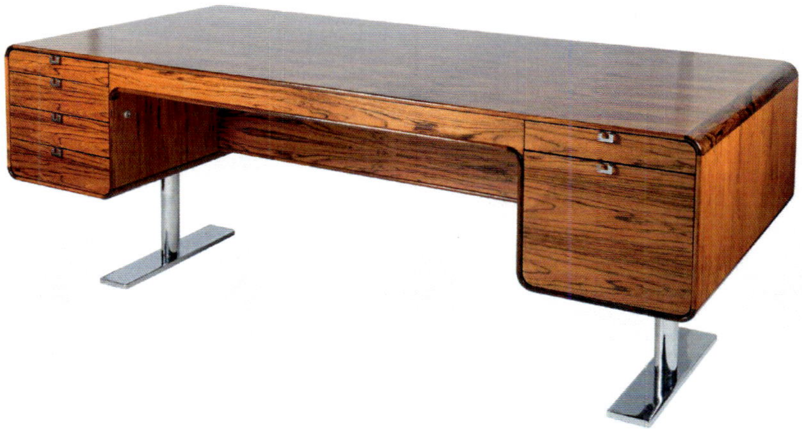

74 | **Leif Jacobsen**
Svend Nielsen (b. 1930), designers
Leif Jacobsen Ltd., Willowdale, ON, manufacturer
***701 Desk*, c. 1974**. Wood (rosewood), chrome-plated steel, 73.7 x 198.1 x 91.4 cm. Collection of Irena and Gord Germann. Image courtesy 507 Antiques

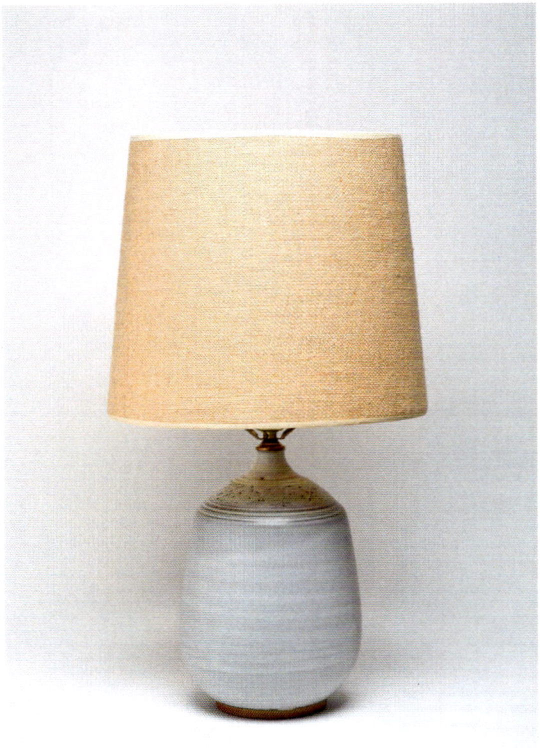

75 | Folmer Hansen (1930–2014)
David Ross (1925–1974)
Hansen-Ross Pottery, Fort Qu'Appelle, SK, manufacturer. Lamp, 1975. Stoneware, 29.1 x 19.1 cm. Saskatchewan Arts Board Permanent Collection. Photography by Gary Robins

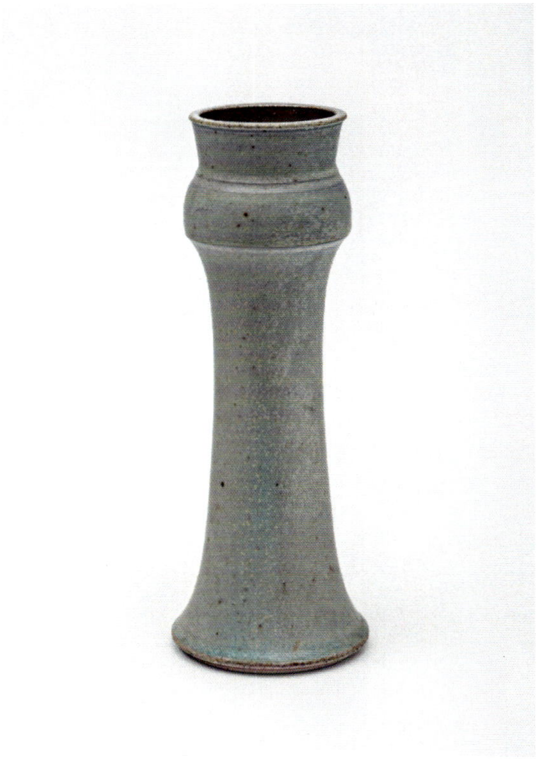

76 | Ruth Gowdy McKinley (1931–1981)
Vase, 1975. Ceramic, 22 x 8 cm. Courtesy of Lauren McKinley Renzetti. Photography by Toni Hafkenscheid

77 | Waldec of Canada Ltd., Rexdale, ON, manufacturer. *Viborg*, fabric sample, c. 1975
Cotton, 132 x 172 cm. Private collection
Photography by Toni Hafkenscheid

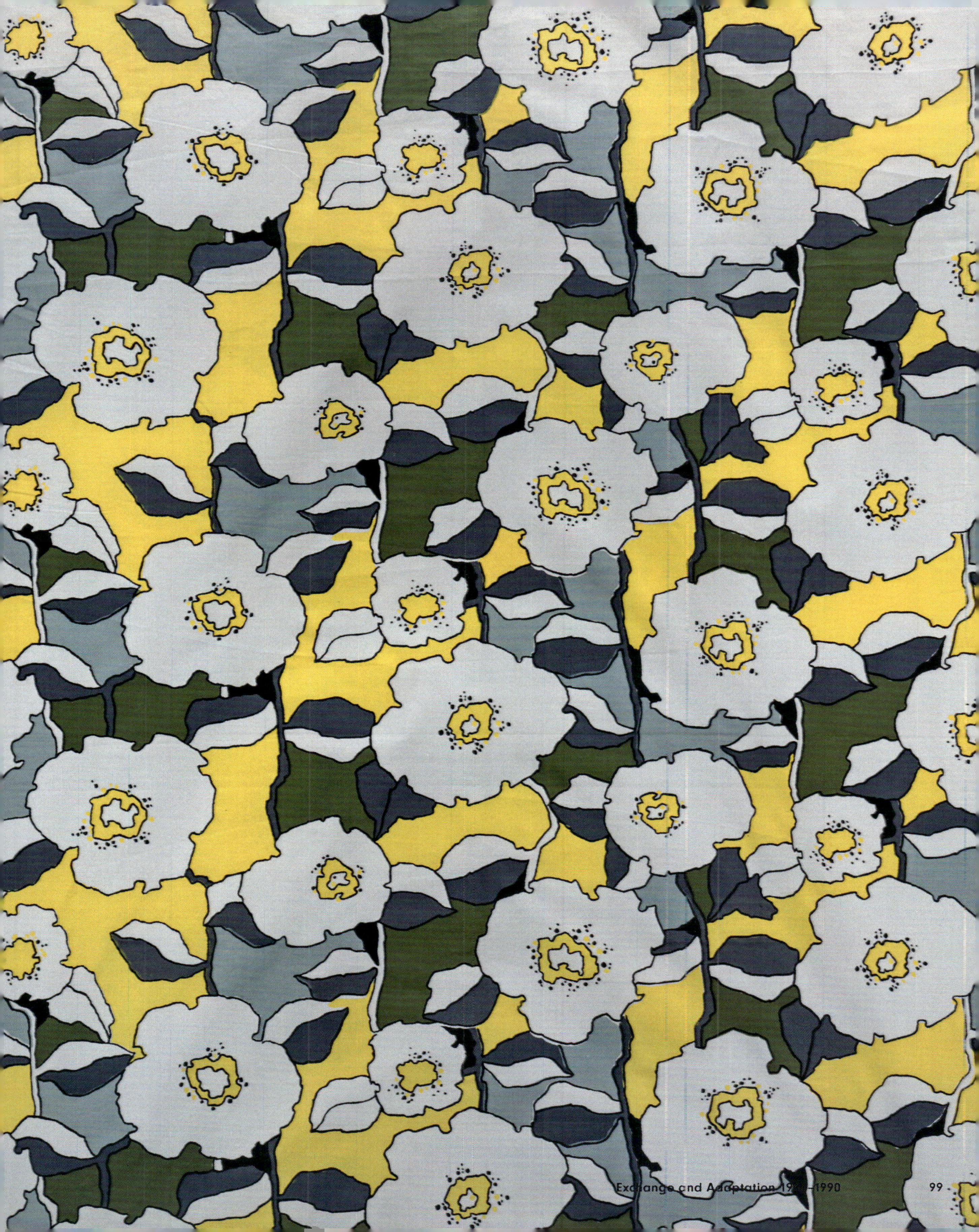

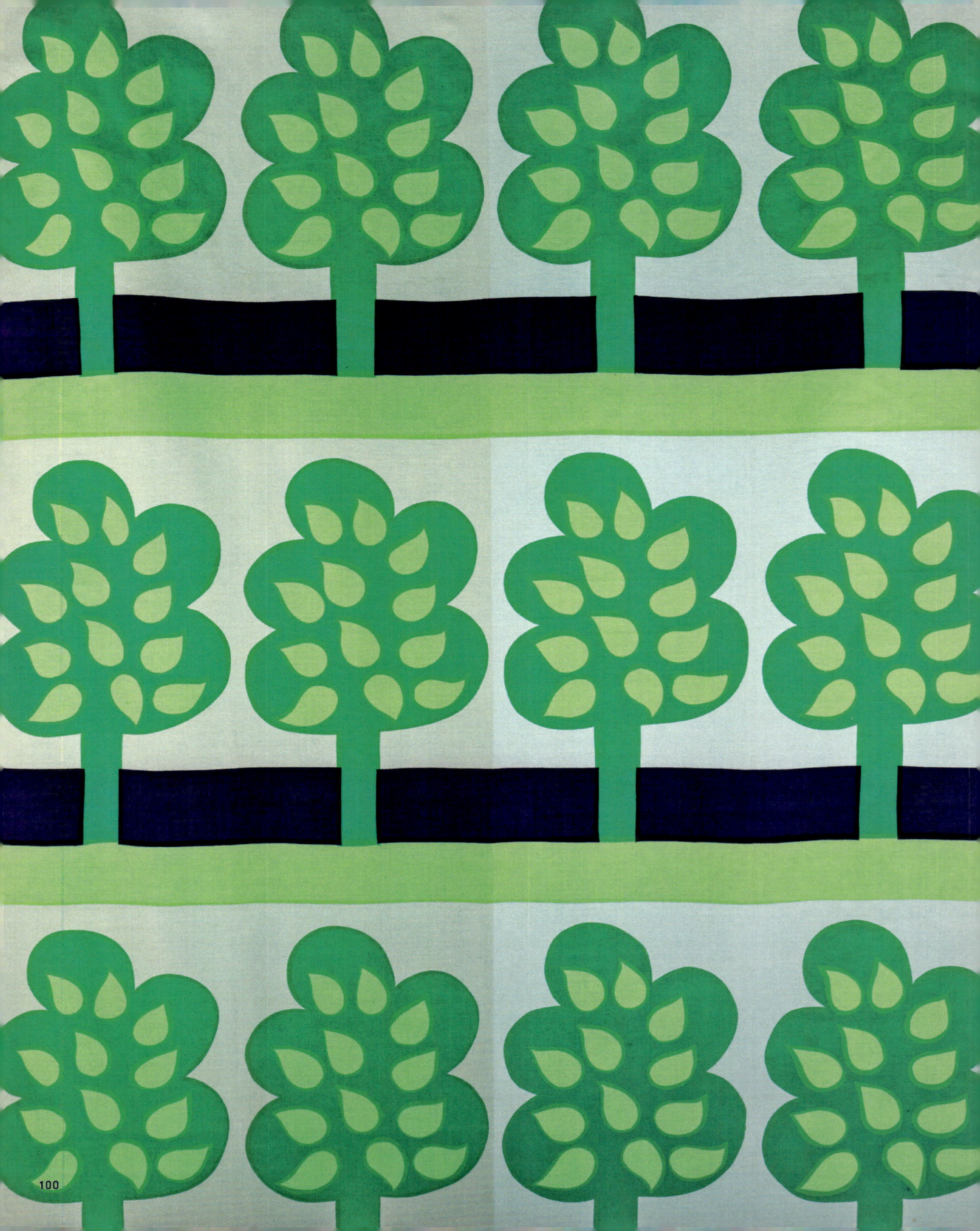

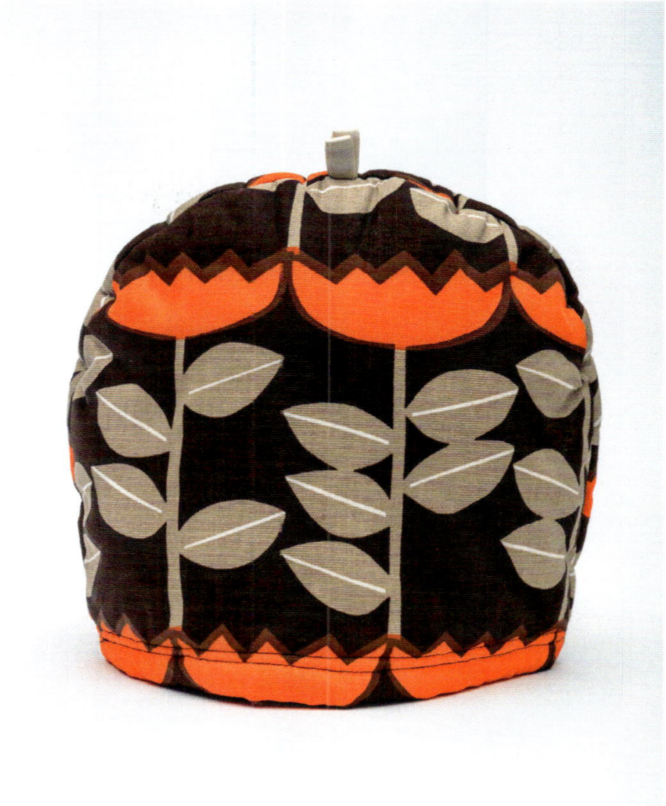

79 | **Esa Niemi Design, Etobicoke, ON**
Tea cozy, c. 1975. Cotton, polyester, 24.8 x 29.2 cm
Private collection. Photography by Toni Hafkenscheid

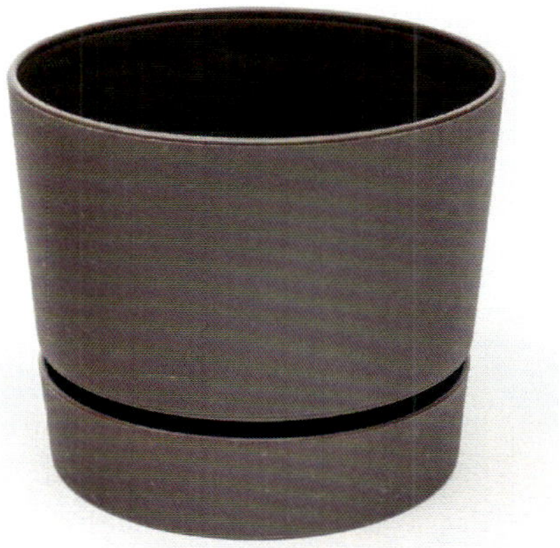

80 | **Jakobsen Industries, Burnaby, BC, manufacturer. Flowerpot, c. 1975**. Plastic, 14.6 x 16.5 cm. Private collection. Photography by Toni Hafkenscheid

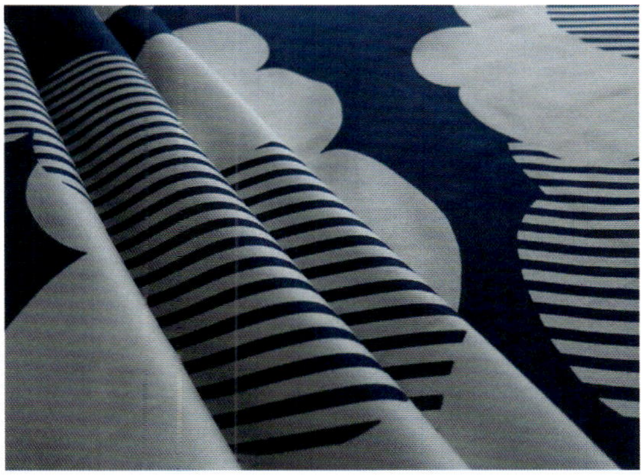

81 | **Monique Beauregard (b. 1945), designer SÉRI+, Montreal, QC, manufacturer. *Nuages*, fabric sample, 1979 (first ed. 1976).** Cotton, 130 x 235 cm. Courtesy of Monique Beauregard
Photography by Danny Gauthier

78 | **Esa Niemi Design, Etobicoke, ON**
Printed textile, c. 1975. Cotton, polyester, 132.1 x 172.7 cm
Private collection. Photography by Toni Hafkenscheid

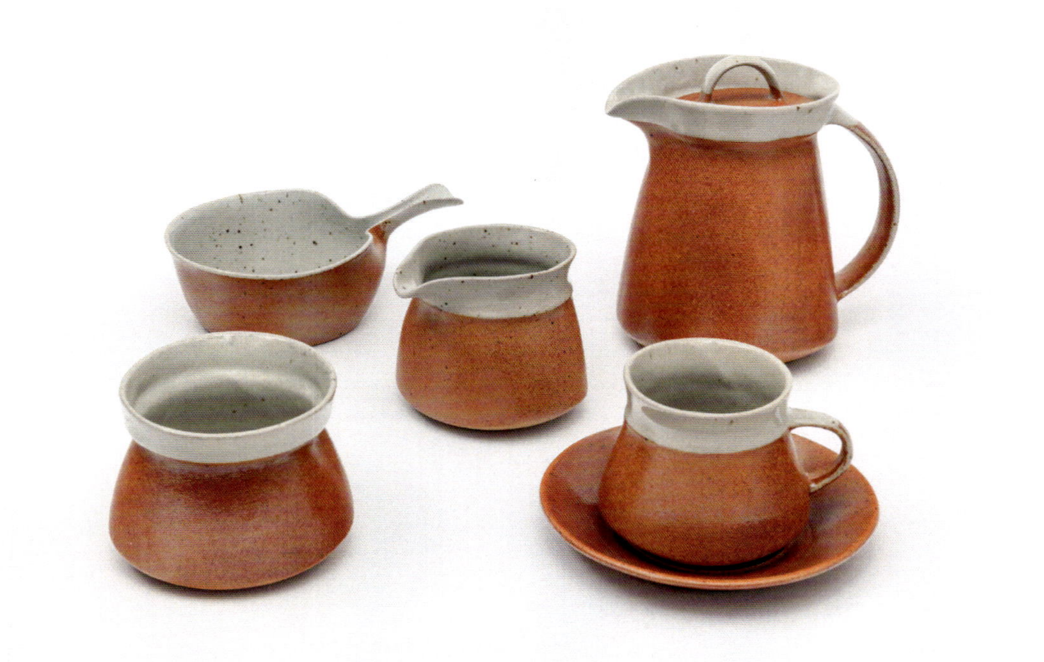

82 | **Gaétan Beaudin (1924–2002), designer**
SIAL 2, Laval, QC, manufacturer. Place setting, 1978
Porcelain and stoneware, coffee pot: 16 x 14 cm; creamer: 8.5 x 10 cm; sugar bowl: 8 x 10 cm; oatmeal bowl: 7 x ´3 x 16.5 cm; cup: 8 x 10 cm; saucer: 2 x 15 cm
Private collection. Photography by Toni Hafkenscheid

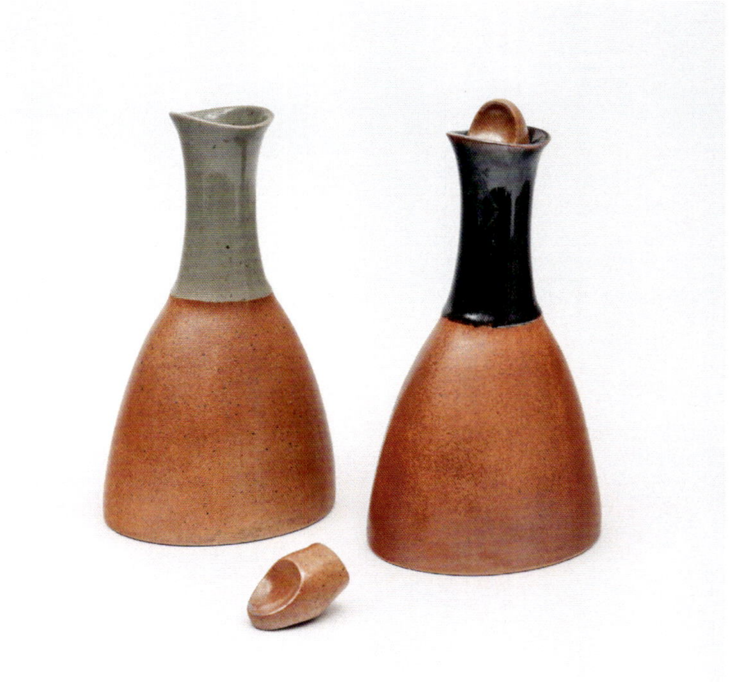

83 | **Gaétan Beaudin (1924–2002), designer**
SIAL 2, Laval, QC, manufacturer. Two carafes, 1978
Porcelain and stoneware ceramic, 25.5 x 14.5 x 11.5 cm each. Collection of the Gardiner Museum, anonymous gift, G12.12.1-2. Photography by Toni Hafkenscheid

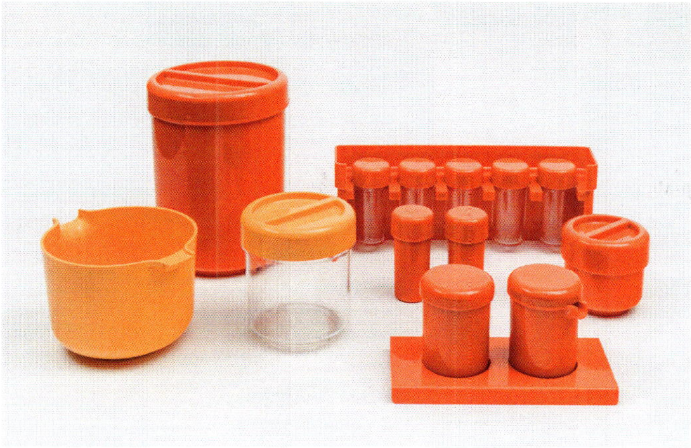

84 | André Morin (b. 1941), designer
IPL Plastics, QC, manufacturer. Moulded plastic kitchenware, 1979. Plastic (acrylic). Private collection. Photography by Toni Hafkenscheid

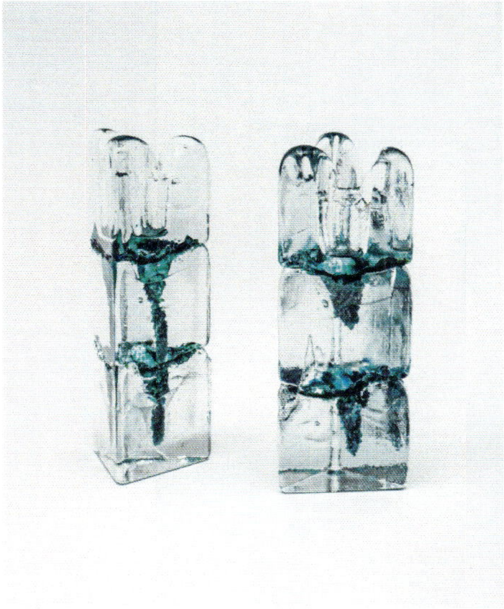

85 | John Kepkiewicz (b. 1955), designer
Thorn Glass Studio, St. Jacobs, ON, manufacturer
***Ice candlesticks*, c. 1985.** Glass, 14 x 5.1 cm each. Private collection. Photography by Toni Hafkenscheid

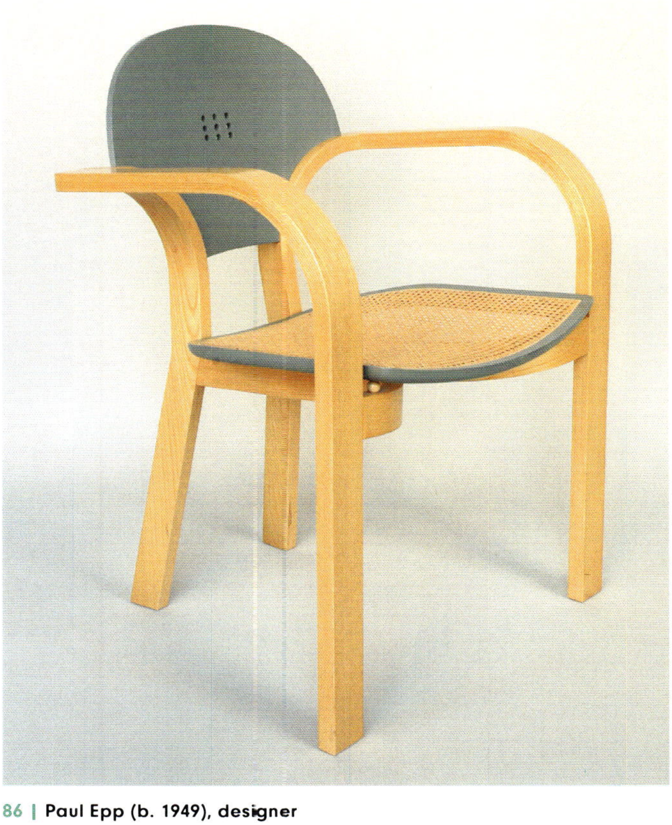

86 | Paul Epp (b. 1949), designer
Ambiant Systems, Toronto, ON, manufacturer
***Nexus Chair*, 1983.** Moulded bleached ash plywood, lacquered wood, cane, 81.5 x 62.4 x 49.5 cm
Design Exchange Permanent Collection, 2000.2, gift of Paul Epp. Image courtesy of the Design Exchange

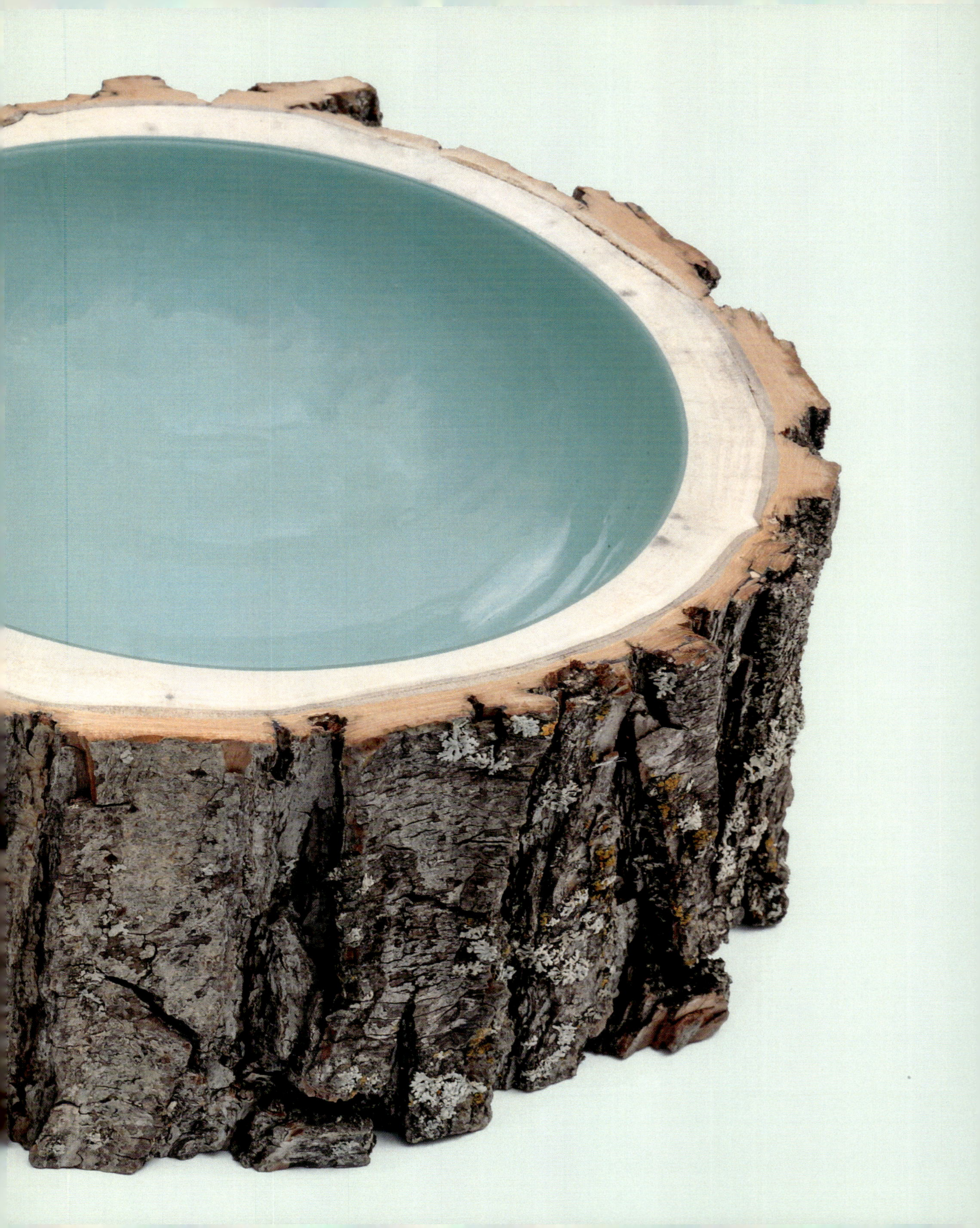

Persistent Variations
1990–present

By the 1990s, the realities of pluralistic taste in North American design culture were firmly established. However, many designers in their journey of discovery sought to determine a personal visual language appropriate to time and place. Geography, climate, and social and political culture remained important considerations.

Not surprisingly, any number of Canadian designers continue to work within the aesthetic traditions of Scandinavia because of its depth of meaning, its enduring appeal, and what is seen to be as its effective message in the context of Canadian experience. Some contemporary designers have purposefully sought to reference "classic" designs from Denmark and Sweden. Some look specifically to the realities of climate and topography. Others draw inspiration from the flora and fauna of the country. In all cases, the contemporary makers for whom Scandinavian aesthetics and design hold meaning seek to create objects that both satisfy their personal and professional aspirations that will be critically well received and commercially successful. The result is a rich and varied contemporary design landscape in Canada where the principles of Scandinavian design—materials, use, scale, and appearance—inform current practice. Moreover, as a result of the nation's diminishing manufacturing industries, expanding digital and global marketplace, and heightened awareness of climate change, there is for many designers the active desire to make work that reflects and affirms such concerns. Perhaps more than ever, Canadian artisans, craftspeople, and designers seek to have their work represent the place and the society in which they live. It is as if what can be called aesthetic nationalism has matured to a point where imagery drawn from nature and forms of objects that reference history no longer necessarily function as stereotypes but exemplify the genuine character and culture of the country at a point in time. And that the tradition and legacy of the cultural exchange between Canada and Scandinavia thrives is significant: Canadian designers study, teach, and work all over Scandinavia; Canadian designers produce Nordic-inspired goods that are distributed outside of Canada; Canadian manufacturers commission Scandinavian designers; and Canadian designers create objects for Scandinavian companies. All of this is to say that in the first quarter of the new millennium the shared cultural and visual sensibilities between Canada and Scandinavian are as meaningful and relevant as ever.

We have always been drawn to the natural material palette and sacred quality of light in Nordic architecture and design, perhaps because we share the inspiration of northern nature.

White is an important colour, the love of it might come from seeing the landscape covered in freshly fallen snow and all the changing colours of sunlight across it.

As students of design we admire the Nordic countries for design that is connected to everyday life and culture in a very grounded, meaningful way, such as the simple beauty of practical tools and the ritual of sauna in Finland.

Stephanie Forsythe and Todd MacAllen, 2016

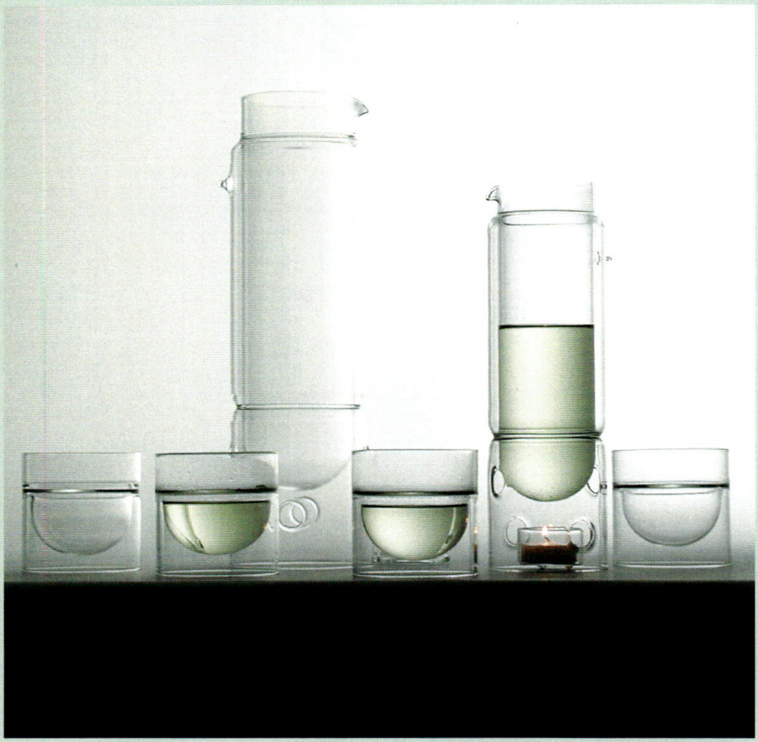

87 | **Stephanie Forsythe (b. 1970)**
Todd MacAllen (b. 1966), designers
molo, Vancouver, BC, manufacturer. *Float Tea Lantern*, 2002. Borosilicate glass hand-blown in the Czech Republic, canister: 33 cm; glass: 9.7 cm; creamer: 7.9 cm. Courtesy of molo. Image courtesy of molo

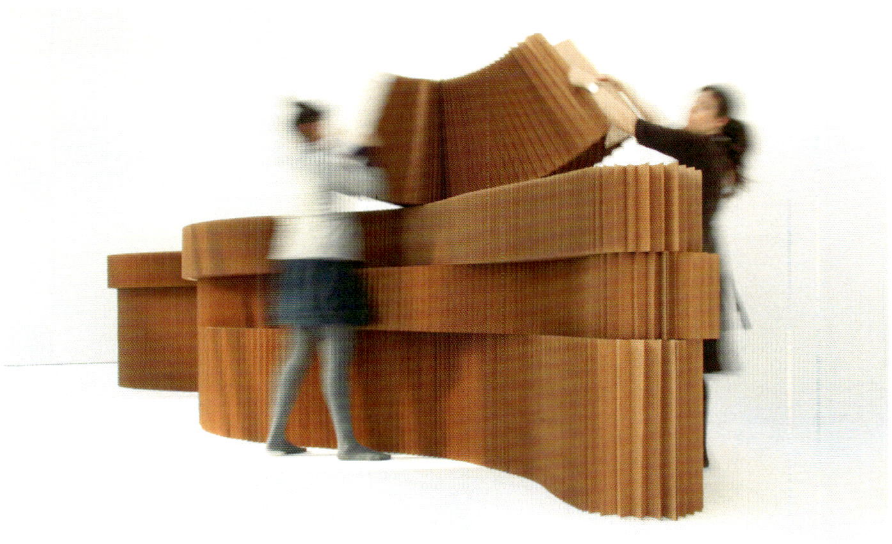

88 | **Stephanie Forsythe (b. 1970)**
Todd MacAllen (b. 1966), designers
molo, Vancouver, BC, manufacturer. *softwall*, 2003
Brown kraft paper with magnetic connectors, various sizes. Courtesy of molo. Image courtesy of molo

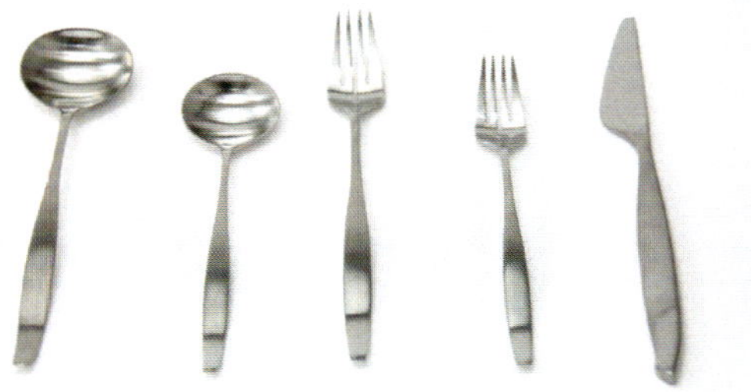

89 | **Helen Kerr (b. 1959), designer**
Gourmet Settings Inc., Toronto, ON, manufacturer
***Balance*, 2001.** Stainless steel, soup spoon: 21 x 5.5 cm; dessert spoon: 18 x 5 cm; dinner fork: 21.5 x 3 cm; salad fork: 18 x 2.5 cm; knife: 24.5 x 2.5 cm
Collection of Helen Kerr. Photography by Jae Yang

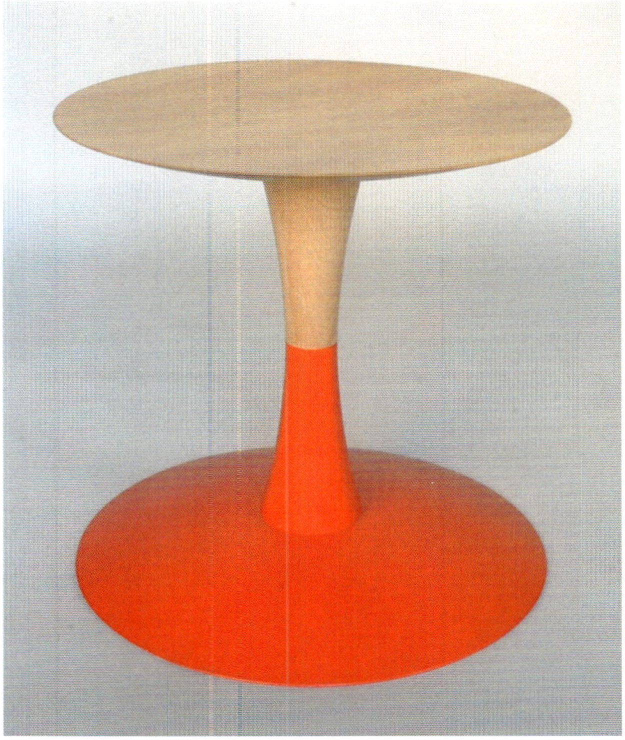

90 | **Patty Johnson (b. 1957), designer**
Keilhauer, Toronto, ON, manufacturer. Stool/ table, 1999. Wood (maple), paint, 35.5. x 35.5 cm
Design Exchange Permanent Collection, 2001.4
Image courtesy of the Design Exchange

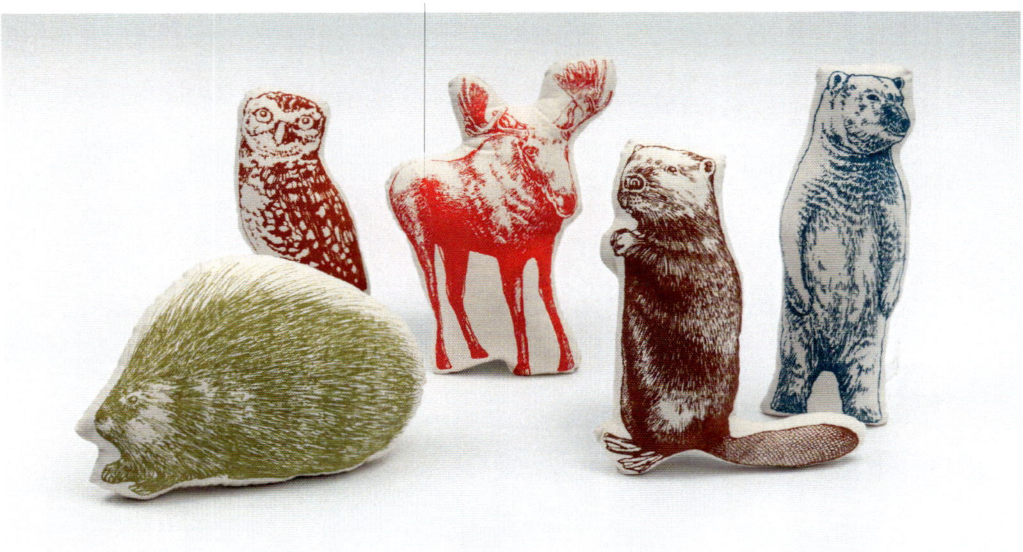

91 | Arounna Khounnoraj (b. 1973), designer bookhou, Toronto, ON, manufacturer. Animal pillows, 2016. Cotton, polyester filling, varied dimensions. Courtesy of bookhou. Photography by Toni Hafkenscheid

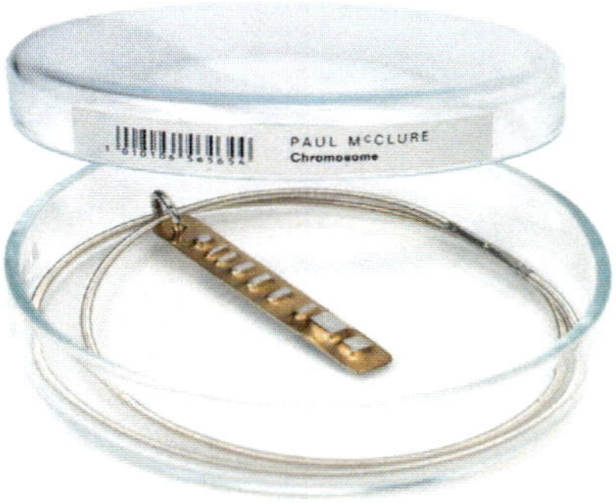

92 | Paul McClure (b. 1967)
***Chromosome X*, necklace, 2003**. Sterling silver and 22-carat gold, oxidized sterling silver cable, 17.8 cm Courtesy of Galerie Noel Guyomarc'h, Montreal Photography by Digital By Design

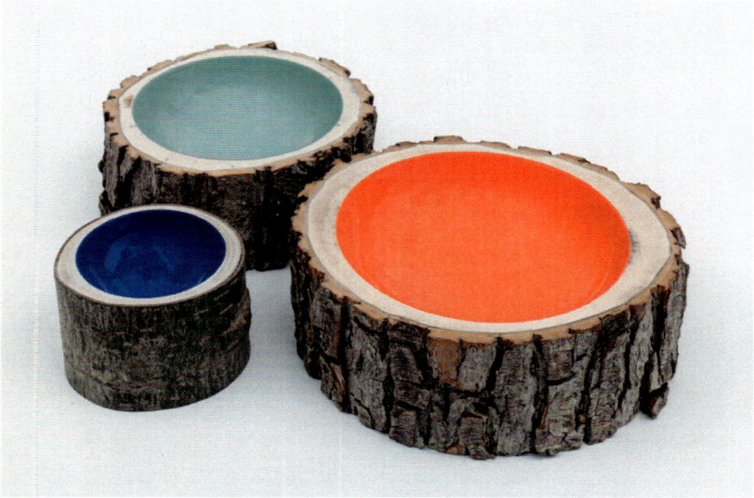

93 | Doha Chebib Lindskoog (b. 1981), designer. Loyal Loot Collective, Calgary, AB, manufacturer Untitled (log bowls), 2004 Reclaimed logs, acrylic paint, water-based glass finish, diameter of cluster of three: 38.1 cm. Courtesy of MADE Design. Photography by Toni Hafkenscheid

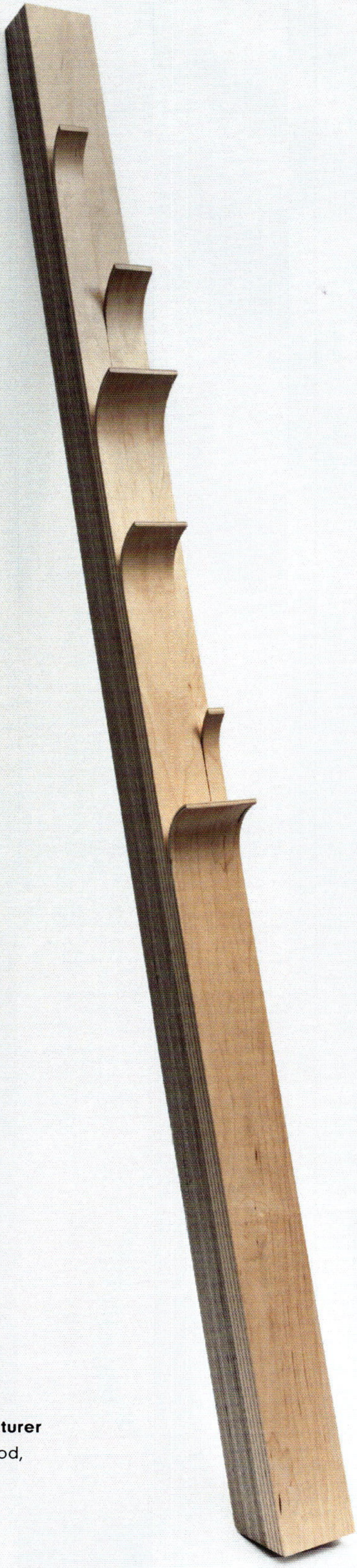

94 | **Dara Humniski (b. 1982), designer**
Loyal Loot Collective, Calgary, AB, manufacturer
Untitled (coat rack), 2004. Baltic birch plywood, maple veneer, 210.8 x 10.2 x 7.6 cm. Private collection. Photography by Toni Hafkenscheid

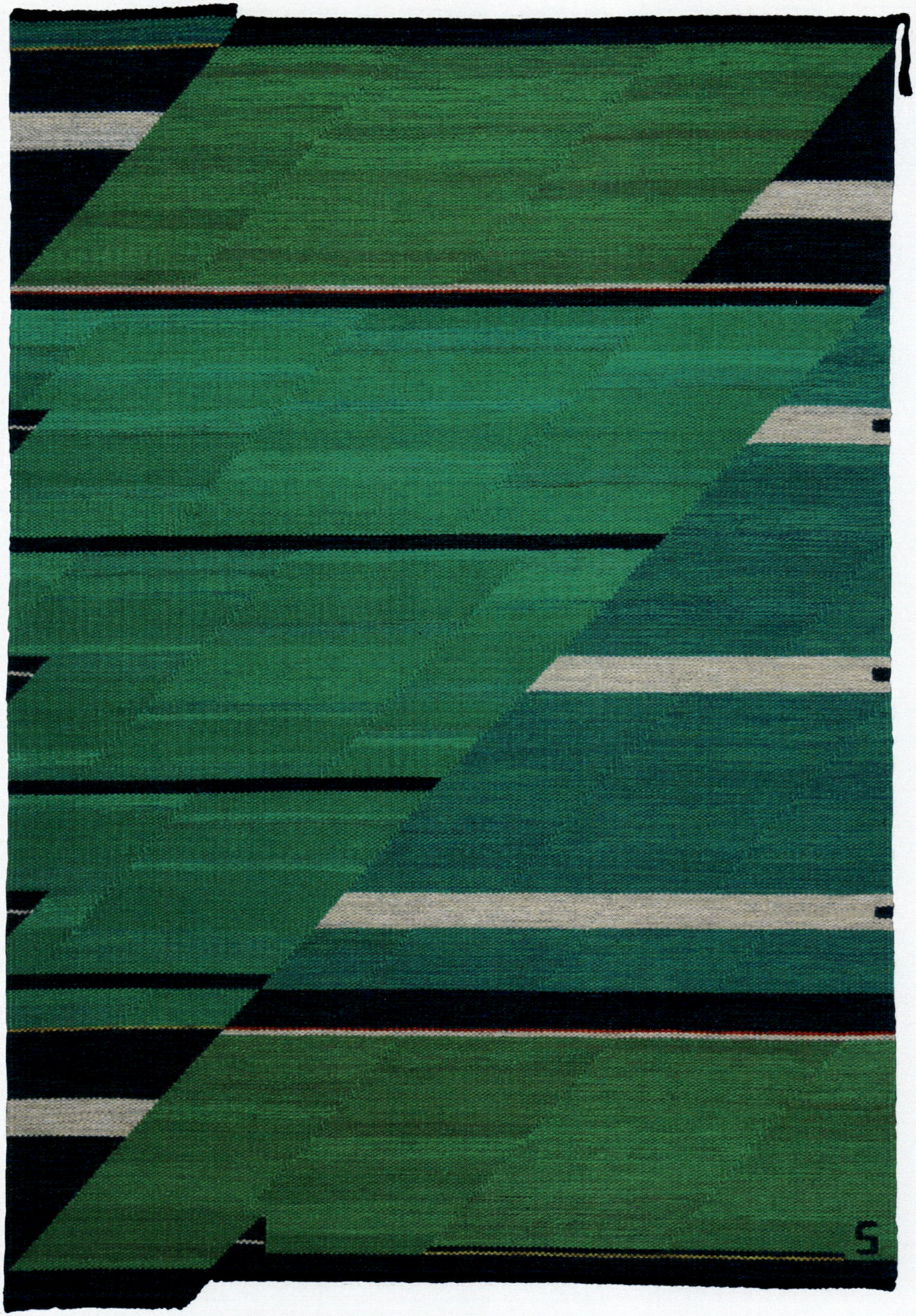

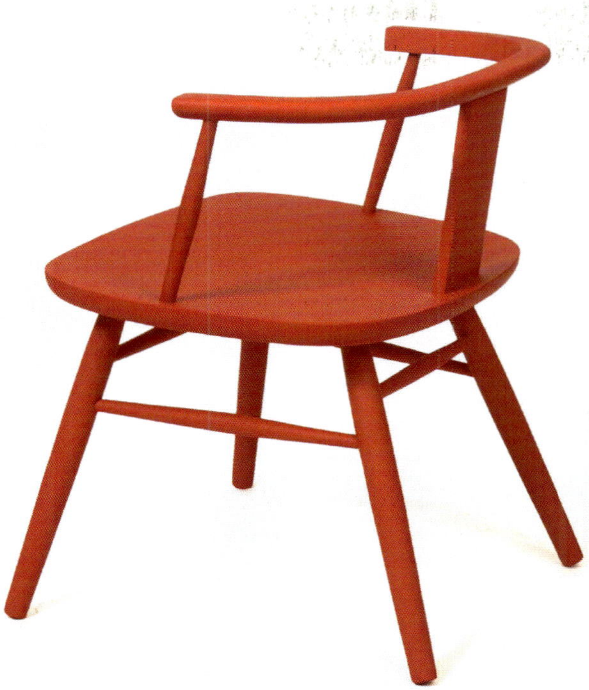

96 | **Patty Johnson (b. 1957), designer Mabeo Furniture, Gaborone, Botswana, manufacturer. *Maun Windsor Chair*, 2004**
Birch ply, 124 x 72 x 100 cm. Courtesy of Patty Johnson. Photography by Peter Mabeo

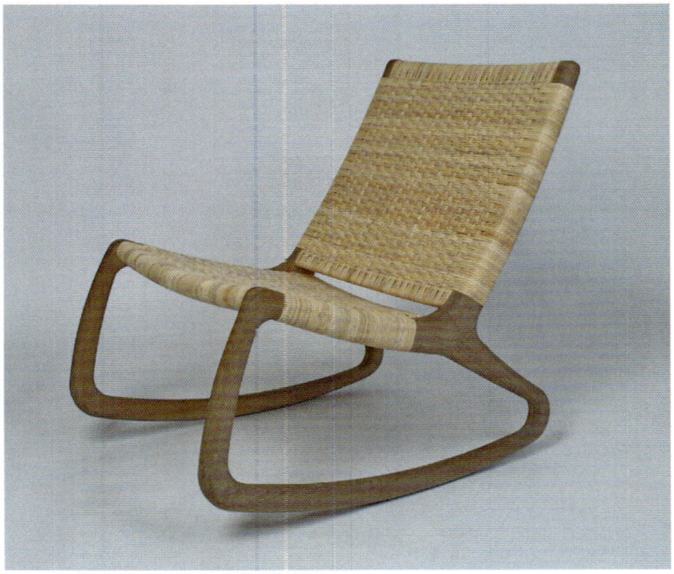

95 | **Suzanne Swannie (b. 1942)**
***Brud II*, 2004.** Hand-dyed Spelsau wool, linen warp, dye, 119.5 cm x 181.5 cm. Art Gallery of Nova Scotia, purchased with funds provided by the Marshall Endowment Fund, 2010, 2010.14. Photography by Raw Photography

97 | **Shawn Place (b. 1967), designer Shawn Place Designs, Prince George, BC, manufacturer *SP210 Rocking Chair*, c. 2004**
Birch ply, stainless steel, zinc, vinyl, 86.5 x 79 x 58.5 cm. Courtesy of Shawn Place. Photography by Shawn Place

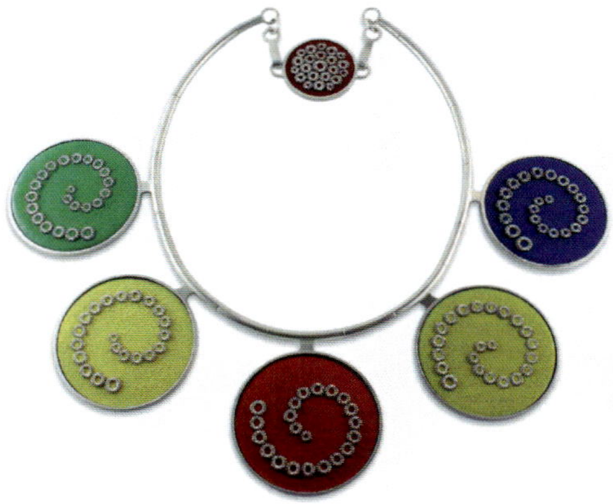

98 | **Pamela Ritchie (b. 1952)**
***Beyond*, 2012**. Sterling silver, enamel on copper with silver inlay, 23 x 25 x 1 cm. Courtesy of Pamela Ritchie. Photography by Pamela Ritchie

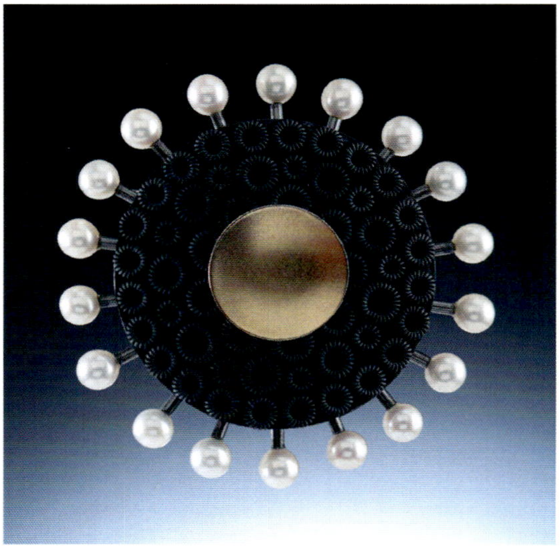

99 | **Pamela Ritchie (b. 1952)**
***Norwegian Soul*, 2007**. Sterling silver, 18-carat gold, pearls, 4.8 cm diameter. Courtesy of Pamela Ritchie. Photography by Pamela Ritchie

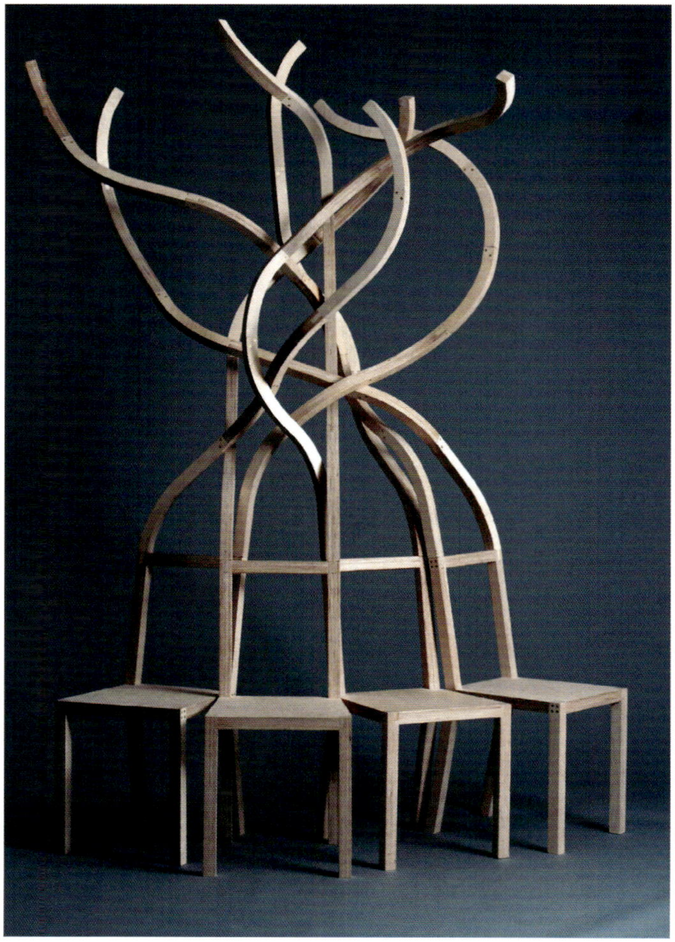

100 | **Robert Southcott (b. 1977)**
***United We Stand*, 2007**. Birch plywood with brass hardware, 243.8 x 152.4 x 121.8 cm Courtesy of Robert Southcott. Photography by Robert Southcott

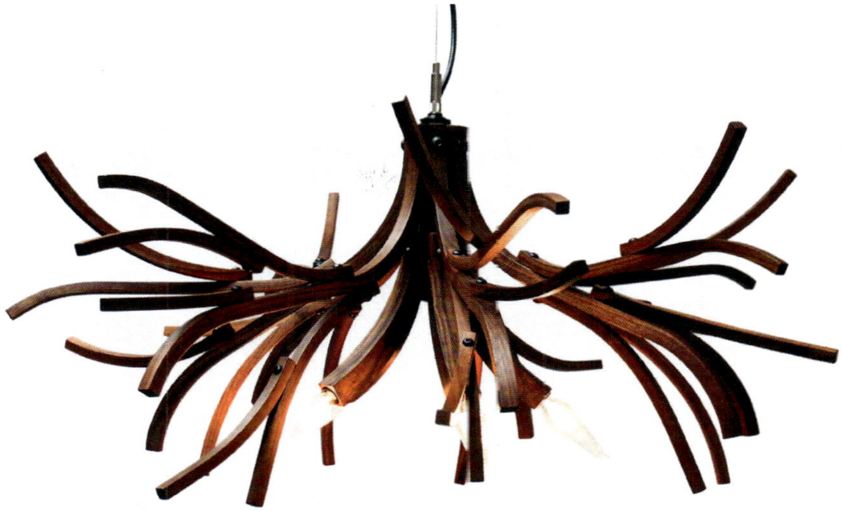

101 | **Lars Dressler (b. 1974)**
Jason Dressler (b. 1974), designers
Brothers Dressler, Toronto, ON, manufacturer
***Branches Chandelier*, 2009.** Wood (white oak),
120 cm diameter. Courtesy of Brothers Dressler
Photography by Brothers Dressler

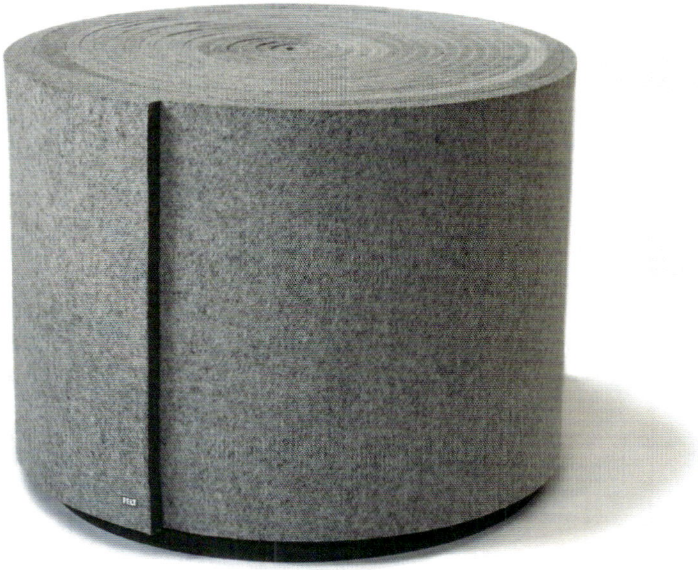

102 | **Kathryn Walter (b. 1963), designer**
FELT Studio, Toronto, ON, manufacturer
***FELT spool stool*, 2009.** Felt and foam rubber,
43.2 x 50.8 cm. Courtesy of Kathryn Walter
Photography by Greg Woodbury

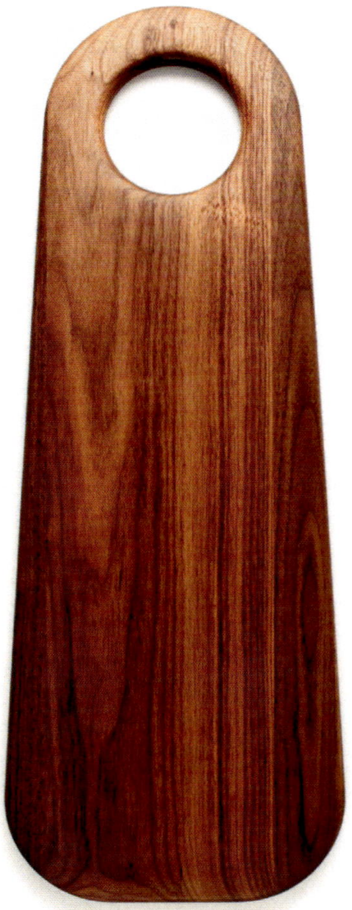

103 | Geoffrey Lilge (b. 1967), designer
On Our Table, Edmonton, AB, manufacturer
***Hole Slab Long*, 2009.** Wood (solid walnut), 61 x 23 x 2 cm. Courtesy of the Gardiner Museum Shop
Photography by Geoffrey Lilge

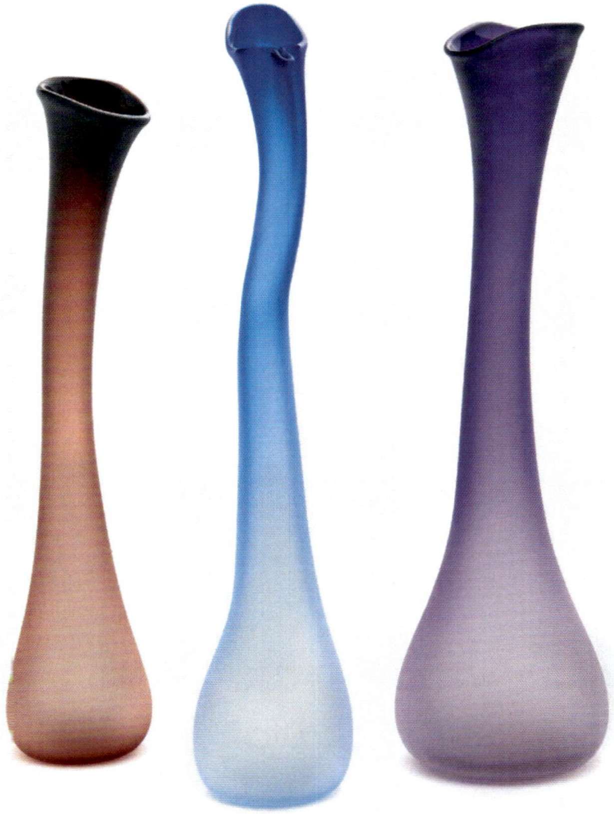

104 | Minna Koistinen (b. 1967)
***Nordic*, 2010**. Blown glass, 50 x 11 cm
Courtesy of Minna Koistinen
Photography by Toni Hafkenscheid

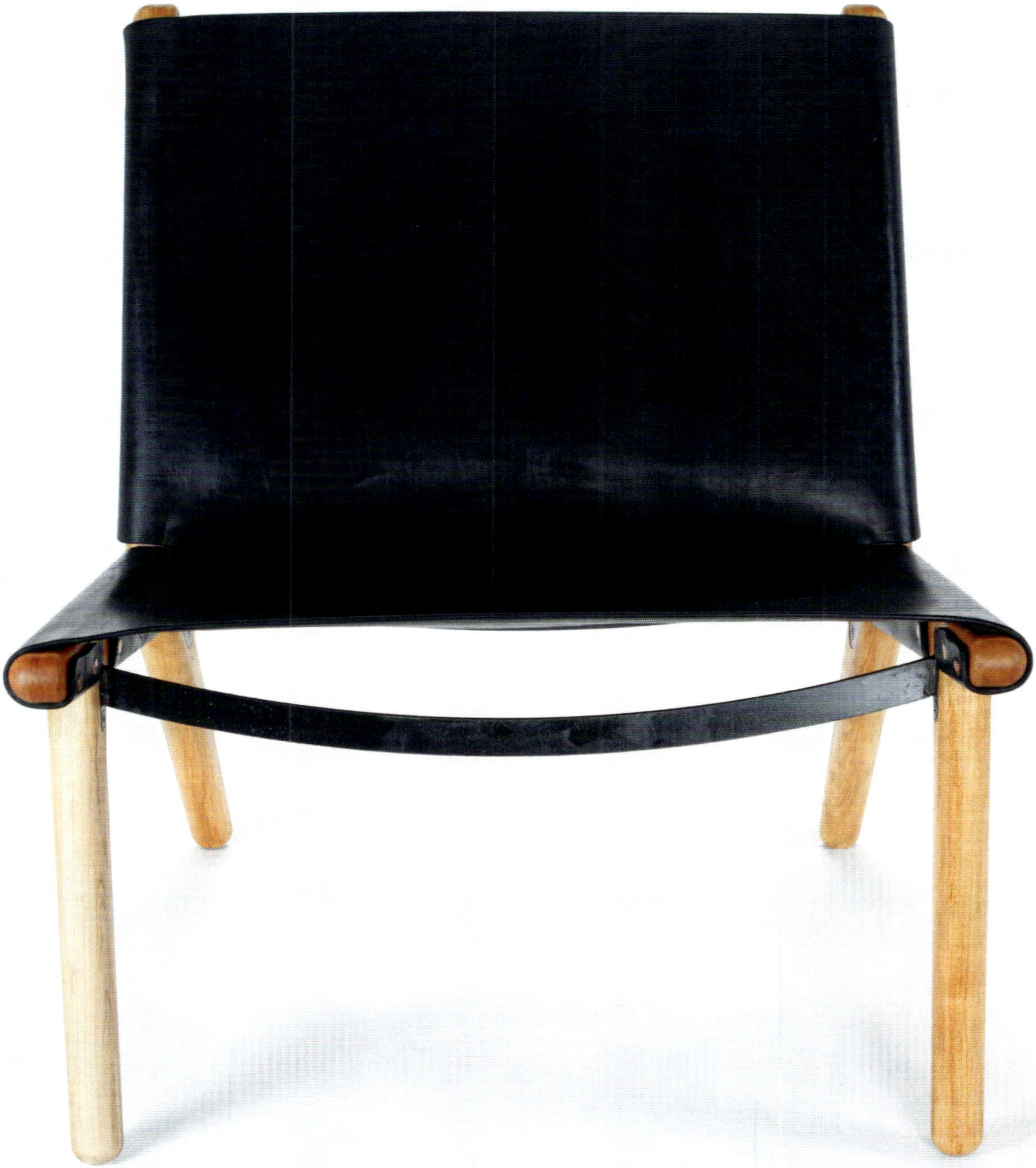

105 | **Derek McLeod (b. 1980), designer**
Derek McLeod Design Inc., Toronto, ON, manufacturer
***Leather Sling Chair*, 2012.** Leather, wood (maple), steel, copper fasteners, steel fasteners, 71.1 x 66 x 61 cm
Courtesy of Derek McLeod. Photography by Shanghoon

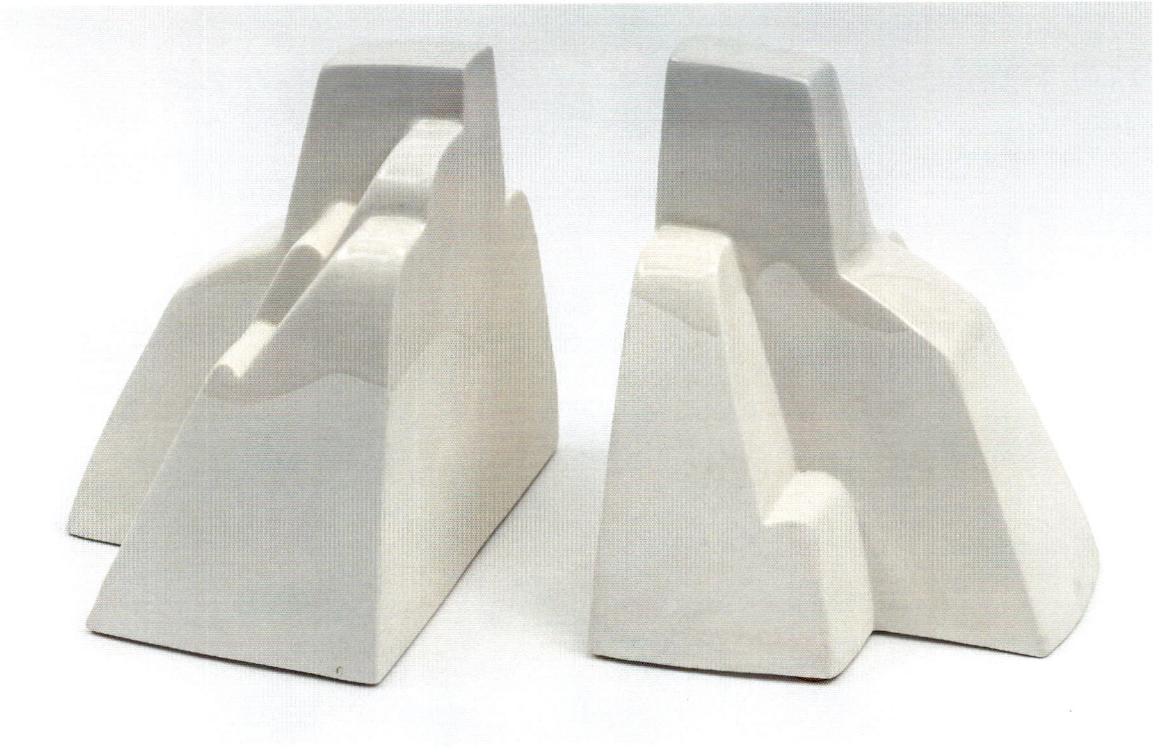

106 | **Katherine Morley (b. 1973)**
***Arctic Bookends*, 2013**. Slip-cast porcelain,
17.8 x 17.8 x 25.4 cm. Courtesy of Katherine Morley
Photography by Toni Hafkenscheid

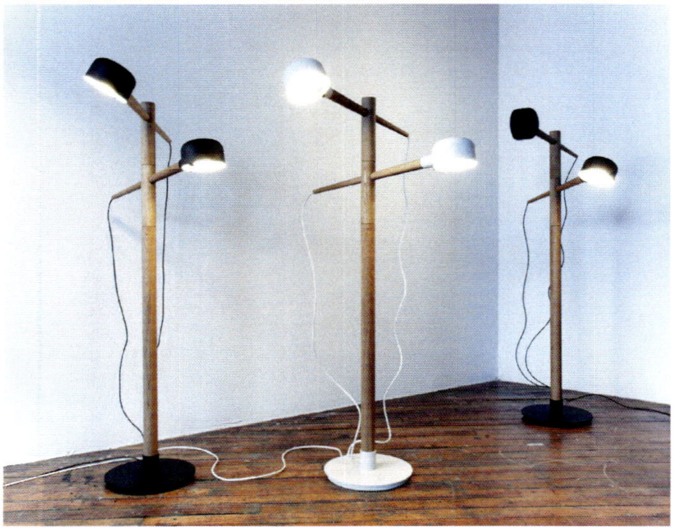

107 | **Brian Richer (b. 1968)**
Kei Ng (b. 1964), designers
Castor Design, Toronto, ON, manufacturer
***Deadstock Floor Lamp*, 2012.** Steel, wood
(oak), 160 x 77.5 cm. Courtesy of Castor Design
Photography by Derek Shapton

There's a very Scandinavian directness in my work that appeals to people. We've come through a period where everything was overdone. Simplicity is timeless.

My design sense comes from many places, Canada, Scandinavia. My dad was a cabinetmaker so the precision I learned from him is part of my work too.

I have this line I like to use: "Less is Never a Bore". It's my own riff on Less is More, and it's true. The best things are simple and timeless and last forever. Maybe that's a Scandinavian thing, and maybe it isn't. I just know that it works for me.

Niels Bendtsen, 2016

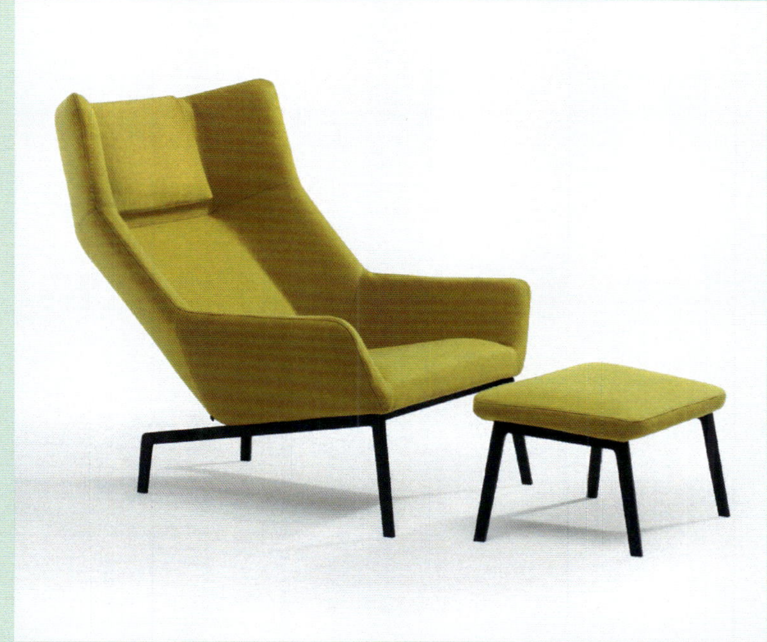

108 | **Niels Bendtsen (b. 1943)**
Bensen, Vancouver, BC, manufacturer
***Park Lounge and Ottoman*, 2011**. Moulded foam, steel, upholstery, chair: 88 x 96 cm; ottoman: 39 x 34 cm. Courtesy of Nancy and Niels Bendtsen
Photography by Eydís Einarsdóttir

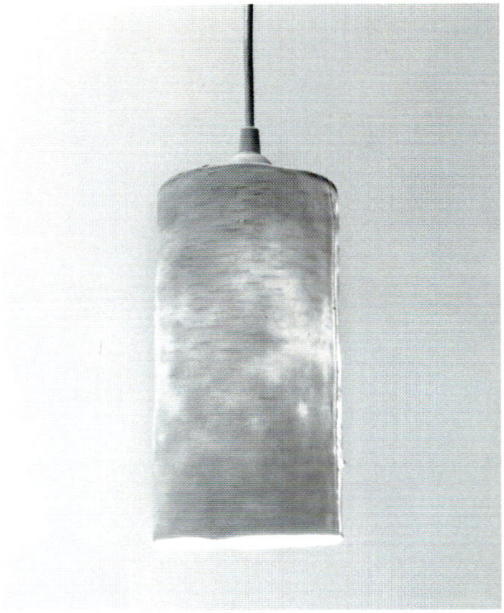

109 | Chari Cohen (b. 1952)
***Birch Pendant Lamp*, 2013–2016**. Slip-cast ceramic, 22.9 x 12.7 cm. Courtesy of MADE Design
Photography by Toni Hafkenscheid

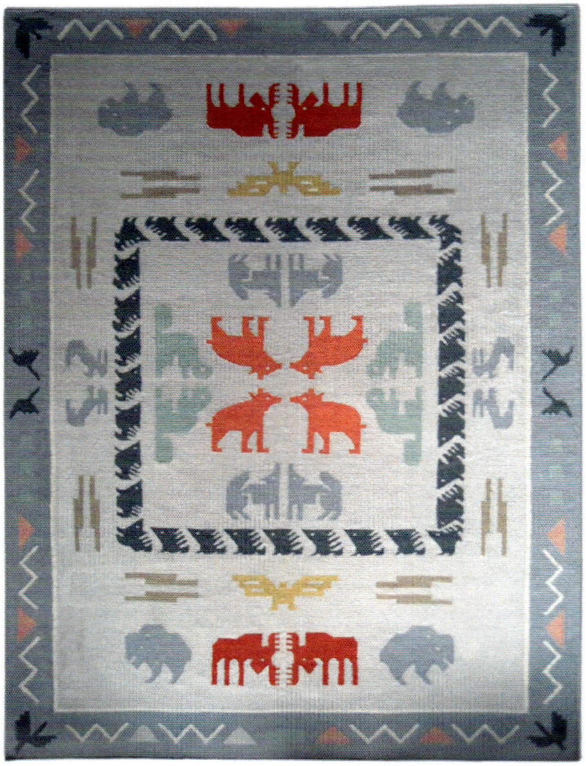

110 | Liz Eeuwes (b. 1983), designer
Studio Eeuwes, Toronto, ON, manufacturer
***Land Rug*, 2014.** Pure hand-woven New Zealand wool, 198.1 x 152.4 cm. Courtesy of MADE Design
Image courtesy of MADE Design

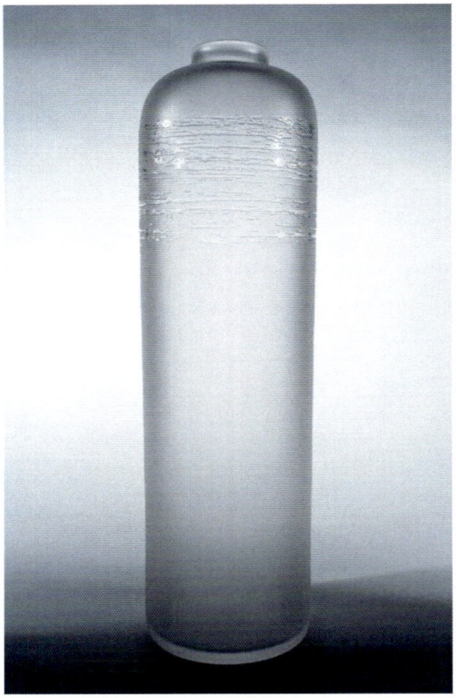

111 | Nick Chase (b. 1978), designer
Jeff Goodman Studio, Toronto, ON, manufacturer
***Bio Glass*, 2014.** Hand-blown glass, 38 x 9 cm
Designed by Nick Chase for Jeff Goodman Studio
Photography by Nick Chase

The most cherished designs in my home are of Scandinavian origin. I use many of them every day and they are always trustworthy, a pleasure to use, and well worth the extra expense. By living with Scandinavian design, I am able to connect with a culture which respects materials and honours the accumulated knowledge [of] how to make things well. Scandinavian design is seldom frivolous, but often possesses a modest charm. Scandinavian designs add beauty to everyday simple tasks and are the humble pillars of good design that I aspire to as a designer.

Andrew Jones, 2016

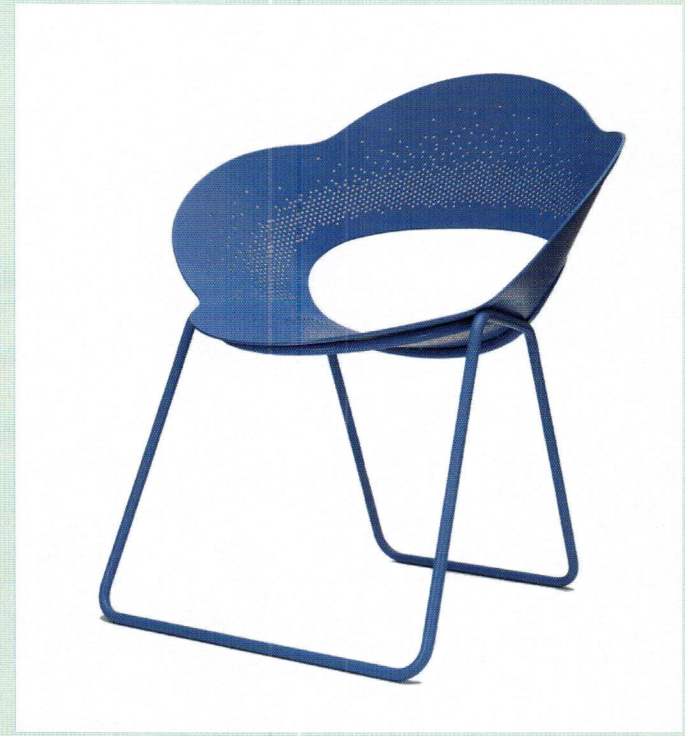

112 | **Andrew Jones (b. 1966), designer Andrew Jones Design, manufacturer.** ***Fleurt Chair,*** **2012–2014.** Steel, 58.4 x 64.8 x 48.3 cm. Courtesy of Andrew Jones. Photography by John Howarth

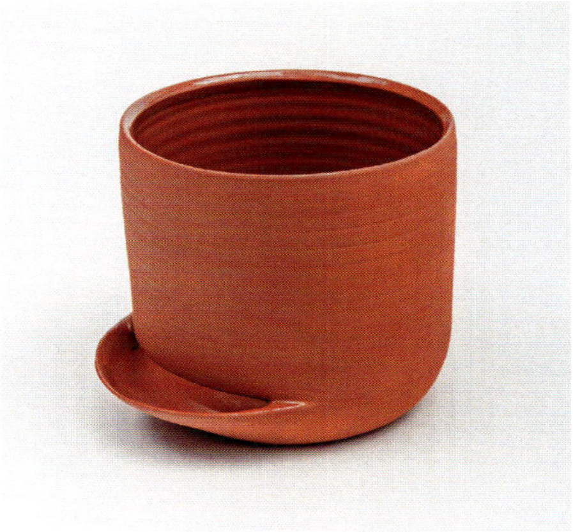

113 | **Torbjørn Anderssen (b. 1976)**
Espen Voll (b. 1965), designers
Herb pot, 2014. Terracotta, 13.3 x 14 cm. Hand-thrown by Filipa Pimental. Courtesy of Mjölk Photography by Toni Hafkenscheid

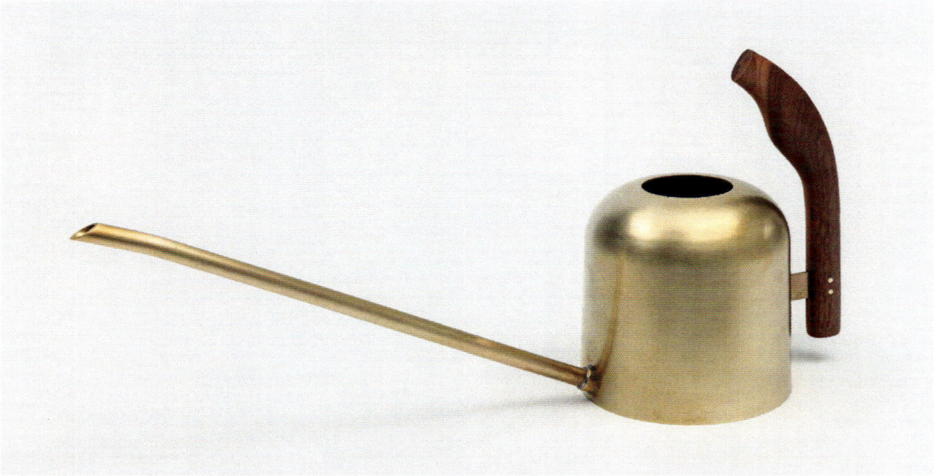

114 | **Torbjørn Anderssen (b. 1976)**
Espen Voll (b. 1965), designers
Harnisch Lamps, Toronto, ON, manufacturer
Watering can, 2014. Hardwood, copper, 24.1 x 14 x 48.3 cm
Courtesy of Mjölk. Photography by Toni Hafkenscheid

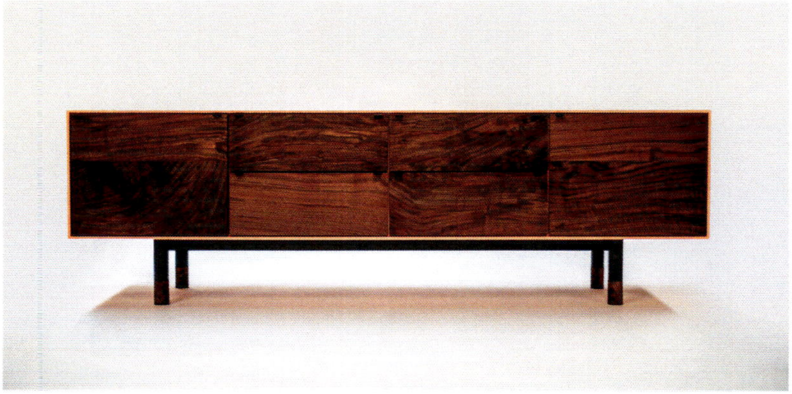

115 | **Jeff Martin (b. 1984), designer**
Jeff Martin Joinery, Vancouver, BC, manufacturer
***Coastal Credenza*, 2014.** Wood (walnut), bronze, 67.3 x 54.6 x 213.4 cm. Courtesy of Jeff Martin
Image courtesy of Jeff Martin

Our goal isn't recreating Scandinavia here in Canada; our aim has always been to create a picture of Canada through utilizing the optimistic and natural design tradition of Scandinavia.

Working with Scandinavian designers we lean on their expertise in translating a warm and tactile craft language into industrialized products.

As craft production slowly disappears in Scandinavia, there is the opportunity to take the rich design language developed by Scandinavian designers and implement them through small-scale production here in Canada.

John Baker and Juli Daoust, Mjölk, 2016

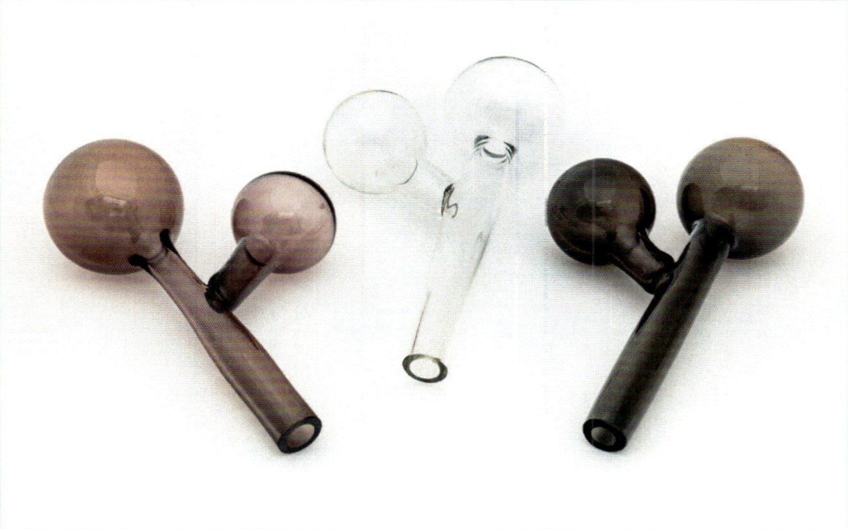

116 | **Torbjørn Anderssen (b. 1976)**
Espen Voll (b. 1965)
***Water Bulb*, 2014**. Glass, mouth-blown by Gregor Herman (b. 1958), 25.4 x 15.2 x 7.6 cm. Courtesy of Mjölk. Photography by Toni Hafkenscheid

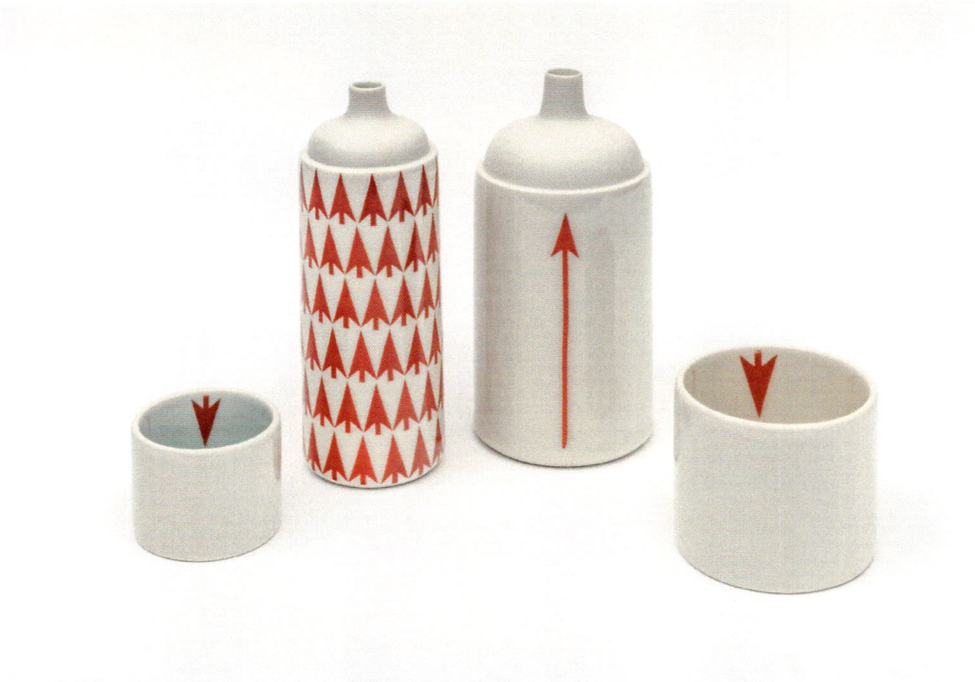

117 | Jenna Stanton (b. 1978)
***Pour me... the self-medicating series*, 2014–2015**
Slip-cast porcelain, with silkscreened enamel decals, underglaze decoration, 21.6 x 7.6 cm. Courtesy of MADE Design. Photography by Toni Hafkenscheid

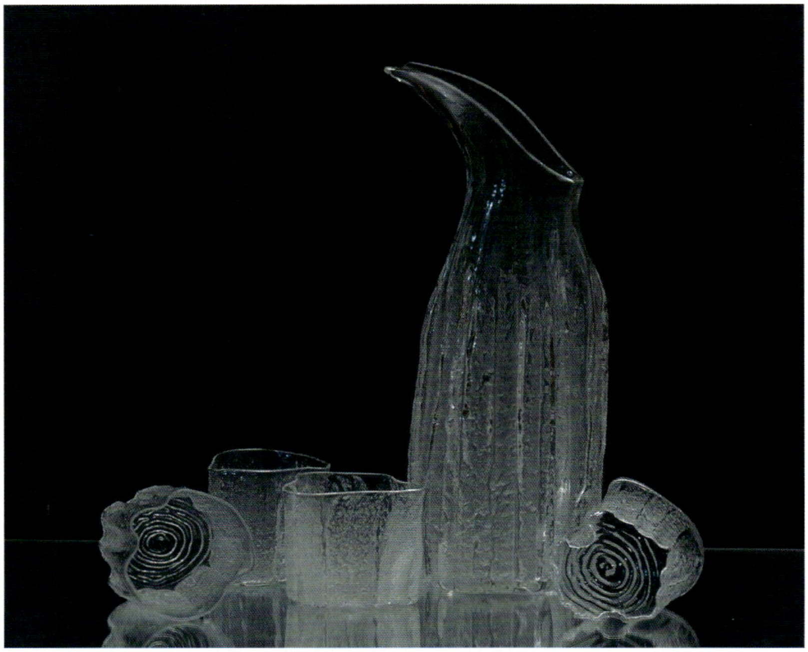

118 | Brad Copping (b. 1964)
***Barkbird* decanter and *Stumpware* cups, 2015**
Unique mould blown glass, decanter: 32.5 x 15 x 11 cm; cups: 5 x 7.5 x 7.5 cm each. Courtesy of Brad Copping. Photography by Brad Copping

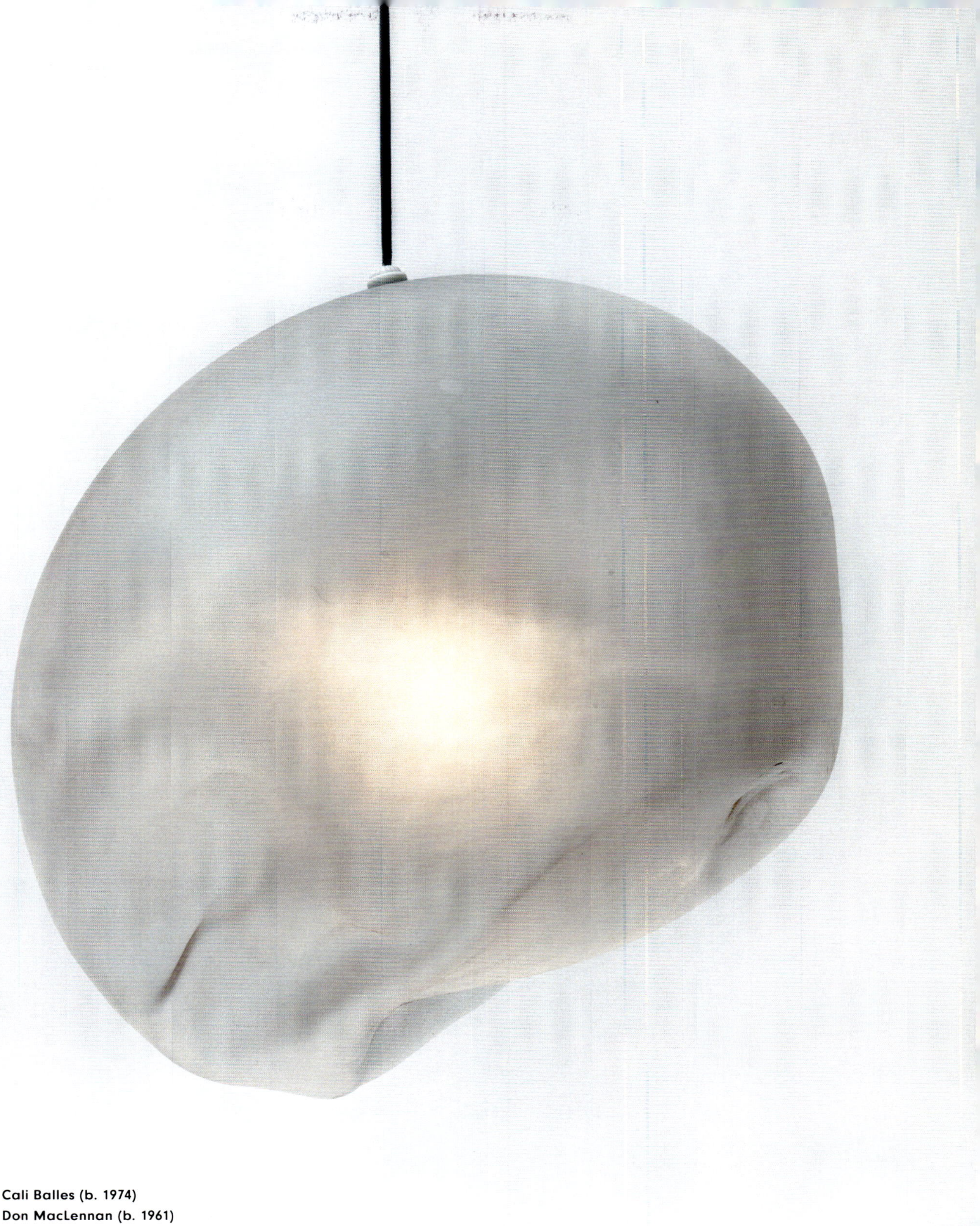

119 | **Cali Balles (b. 1974)**
Don MacLennan (b. 1961)
***Shadow Light*, 2008**. Blown glass, 50.8 x 40.6 cm
Courtesy of MADE Design. Photography by
Toni Hafkenscheid

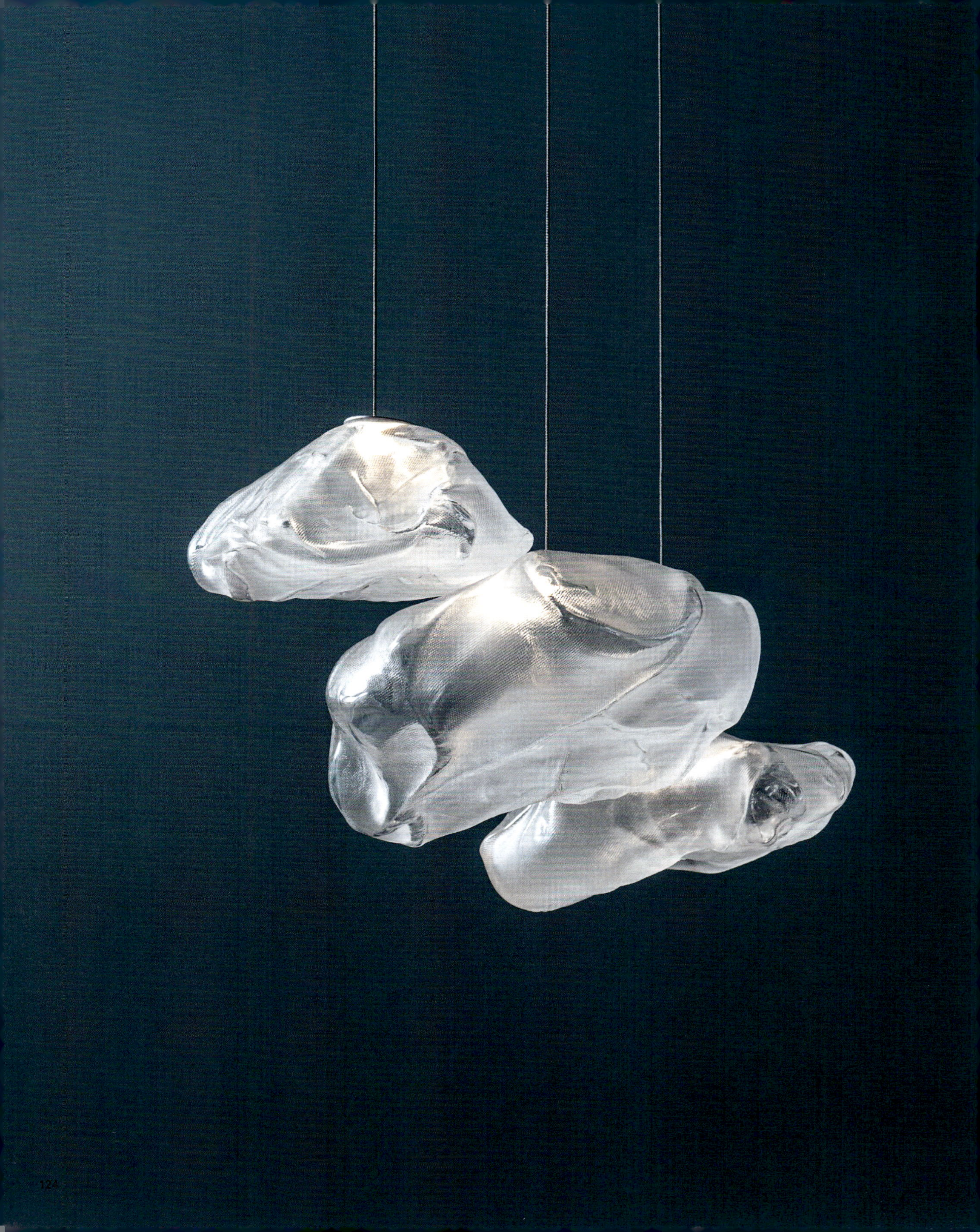

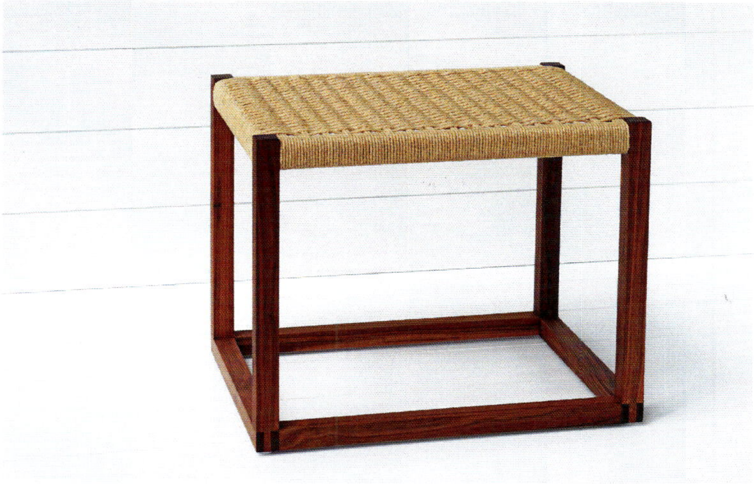

121 | Heidi Earnshaw (b. 1969), designer
Heidi Earnshaw Design, Toronto, ON, manufacturer
***Woven Cube*, 2016.** Wood (oiled walnut), Danish cord, 42 x 35.5 x 48 cm. Courtesy of Heidi Earnshaw Design. Photography by Chris Jackson

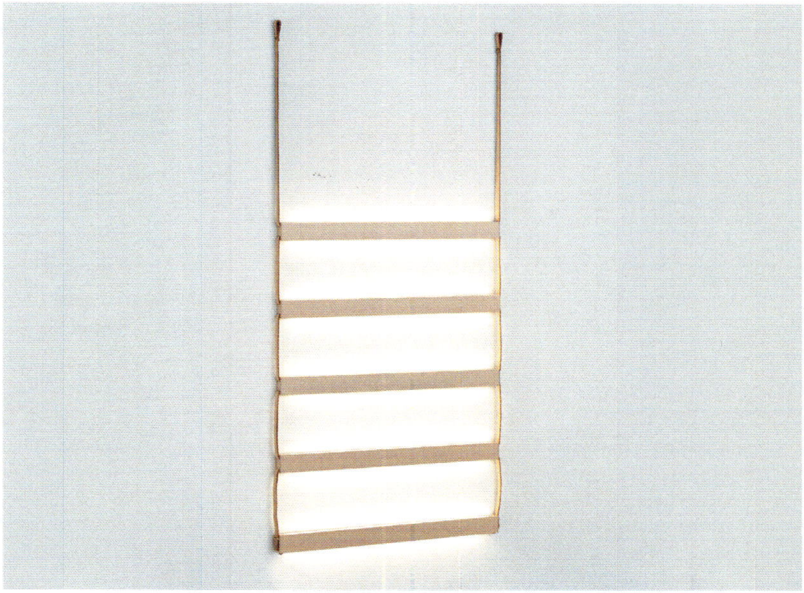

122 | Jonathan Sabine (b. 1976)
Jessica Nakanishi (b. 1981), designers
MSDS Studio, Toronto, ON, for Woud, DK, manufacturer
***Ladder Back Lamp*, 2016.** Copper, leather, LED fixtures, 91.4 x 61 cm. Courtesy of MSDS Studio. Image courtesy of Woud

120 | Omer Arbel (b. 1976), designer
Bocci, Vancouver, BC, manufacturer. *73 Series Pendant Lamps*, 2015. Blown glass, braided metal coaxial cable, electrical components, brushed nickel canopy, varied dimensions. Courtesy of Bocci

List of References

Arrival and Consequences 1925–1956

64 Governor General Vincent Massey quoted in "Scandinavian Design Exhibit Opened by Governor General," *Ottawa Journal*, December 18, 1954, 5.

66 Rudy Renzius, *Hammered Silver Flatware*, ed. Ivan H. Crowell, no. 26, *Macdonald College Handicraft* series (Toronto: Macmillan, 1945).

69 Donald Buchanan, *Design for Use in Canadian Products* (Ottawa: National Gallery of Canada, 1947), 6.

72 Thor Hansen, 1955, Art Quotes presented by the Painter's Keys, accessed April 13, 2016, http://www.art-quotes.com/auth_search.php?authid=2048#.Vw5JEHBFvjM.

75 Sigrun Bülow-Hübe quoted in Bluma Appel, "Gold Medallist from Sweden Liked Canada, and Stayed Here," *The Monitor*, February 14, 1957.

Exchange and Adaptation 1956–1990

79 Mandel Sprachman, "Why Scandinavian 'Traditional' is Perennially Modern," *Canadian Homes and Gardens*, September 1956, 21.

84 Janis Kravis quoted in Shauna McCabe, with contributions from Janis Kravis, "Sharing Is," *Marimekko with Love* (Toronto: Textile Museum of Canada, 2013), 67.

87 Patricia Lamont, Home Decorating Editor, "Scandinavian: Traditional for Today," *Canadian Homes and Gardens*, September 1956, 13.

Persistent Variations 1990–present

106 Stephanie Forsythe and Todd MacAllen, Designers, Vancouver, 2016

117 Niels Bendtsen, Designer, Vancouver, 2016

119 Andrew Jones, Designer, 2016

121 John Baker and Juli Daoust, Mjölk, Toronto, 2016

Image Credits

5 catalogue 31 (detail)

8 catalogue 43 (detail)

23 catalogue 117 (detail)

24 catalogue 114 (detail)

38 catalogue 33 (detail)

46 catalogue 106 (detail)

54 catalogue 110 (detail)

57 catalogue 60 (detail)

58 catalogue 18 (detail)

76 catalogue 73 (detail)

104 catalogue 93 (detail)

Contributor Biographies

Rachel Gotlieb is Adjunct Curator at the Gardiner Museum where she was formerly Chief Curator, and Interim Executive Director. She served as the founding Curator of the Design Exchange, and co-wrote *Design in Canada* (Knopf Canada, 2001). She has curated and co-curated many exhibitions including *On the Table: 100 Years of Functional Ceramics* (Gardiner Museum, 2007), and *Beaver Tales: Canadian Art and Design* (University of Toronto Art Centre, 2008). She is currently a lecturer of Industrial Design History at Sheridan College.

Mark Kingwell is a Professor of Philosophy at the University of Toronto. He is the author of many books and articles about politics and art, most recently the essay collections *Unruly Voices* (2012) and *Measure Yourself Against the Earth* (2015).

George Baird is Emeritus Professor and former Dean of the John H. Daniels Faculty of Architecture, Landscape, and Design at the University of Toronto. As an architecture student there, he visited Finland in the summer of 1959.

Michael J. Prokopow is a historian, curator and critic. His specializations include material culture, design history, and critical theory. He is a faculty member at OCAD University. He holds a Ph. D. from Harvard University.

Black Dog Publishing Limited
10a Acton Street
London WC1X 9NG
United Kingdom

Tel +44 (0)20 7713 5097
Fax +44 (0)20 7713 8682
info@blackdogonline.com
www.blackdogonline.com

British Library Cataloguing-in-Publication Data. A CIP record for this book is available from the British Library.

Printed and bound in Great Britain by
Marston Book Services Ltd, Oxfordshire

ISBN 978-1-910433-63-8

Black Dog Publishing Limited, London, UK, is an environmentally responsible company. *True Nordic: How Scandinavia Influenced Design in Canada* is printed on sustainably sourced paper.

Gardiner Museum

Jack Weinbaum Family Foundation

The McLean Foundation

The Gardiner Museum thanks the following exhibition and catalogue supporters:
Dr. Robert Buckingham
Lee Jacobson
Michael Prokopow (in honour of Wendy Russel and Rosemary Wells)
Diana Reitberger

Canada

RAPHAEL YU CENTRE OF CANADIAN CERAMICS

Ontario

Canada Council for the Arts | Conseil des Arts du Canada

ONTARIO ARTS COUNCIL | CONSEIL DES ARTS DE L'ONTARIO

TORONTO

reuse recycle reduce

art design fashion
history photography
theory and things

black dog publishing london uk

www.blackdogonline.com